Teaching English-Medium Instruction Courses in Higher Education

ALSO AVAILABLE FROM BLOOMSBURY

Language Education in the School Curriculum: Issues of Access and Equity, Ken Cruickshank, Stephen Black, Honglin Chen, Linda Tsung, Jan Wright

Language Learner Strategies: Contexts, Issues and Applications in Second Language Learning and Teaching, Michael James Grenfell and Vee Harris

Language Learning Strategies and Individual Learner Characteristics: Situating Strategy Use in Diverse Contexts, edited by Rebecca L. Oxford and Carmen M. Amerstorfer

Process Drama for Second Language Teaching and Learning: A Toolkit for Developing Language and Life Skills, Patrice Baldwin and Alicja Galazka

Reflective Language Teaching: Practical Applications for TESOL Teachers, Thomas S. C. Farrell

Teaching Listening and Speaking in Second and Foreign Language Contexts, Kathleen M. Bailey

Teaching Pragmatics and Instructed Second Language Learning: Study Abroad and Technology-Enhanced, Nicola Halenko

Using Literature in English Language Education: Challenging Reading for 8–18 Year Olds, Janice Bland

Teaching English-Medium Instruction Courses in Higher Education

A Guide for Non-Native Speakers

RUTH BREEZE AND CARMEN SANCHO GUINDA

BLOOMSBURY ACADEMIC
LONDON · NEW YORK · OXFORD · NEW DELHI · SYDNEY

BLOOMSBURY ACADEMIC
Bloomsbury Publishing Plc
50 Bedford Square, London, WC1B 3DP, UK
1385 Broadway, New York, NY 10018, USA
29 Earlsfort Terrace, Dublin 2, Ireland

BLOOMSBURY, BLOOMSBURY ACADEMIC and the Diana logo are trademarks of
Bloomsbury Publishing Plc

First published in Great Britain 2022

Cover design by Jade Barnett
Cover image © borchee/Getty Images

A catalogue record for this book is available from the British Library.

A catalog record for this book is available from the Library of Congress.

ISBN: HB: 978-1-3501-6976-0
PB: 978-1-3501-8033-8
ePDF: 978-1-3501-6977-7
eBook: 978-1-3501-6978-4

Typeset by Deanta Global Publishing Services, Chennai, India
Printed and bound in Great Britain

To find out more about our authors and books visit www.bloomsbury.com and
sign up for our newsletters.

CONTENTS

ILLUSTRATIONS

Graphs

Figures

Tables

CHAPTER 1

The Rise of EMI

Globalization and the International University Scene

1.1 Introduction

Almost everywhere in the world, university education is now being offered in English, and all the evidence suggests that this trend is gathering momentum. Although this change is not welcomed by everyone, it is becoming broadly accepted as one of the main ways of opening up higher education to international contacts and exchanges, participating in global markets and putting local universities on the world map. At the same time, controversy still surrounds this tendency. A recent British Council report pointed out that many institutions appear to have problems finding enough teaching staff competent to give lectures, lead seminars or conduct tutorials in English. There is uncertainty regarding student language levels on admission to these programmes. There are few pedagogical guidelines concerning the way that English-taught courses differ from courses taught in a shared first language, and there is very little training for teachers who are new to this field (Dearden 2014).

Europe has been one of the leaders in the move to university teaching in English beyond the traditional reaches of English-language influence, and probably the area where the greatest amount of research has been carried out into this process. At the height of the first wave of such programmes in Europe, Wilkinson and Zegers (2007) pointed out that three questionable assumptions underlie this trend. First, they state that it is taken for granted that teaching staff are competent enough in English to give lectures, lead seminars, direct research work and examine students in that language. Second, it is supposed that students have good enough English-language competences to participate in specialized university-level courses taught in English. Third, it is widely assumed that all of this is positive; that is, the students' English level improves as a result, and their content knowledge is not impeded. Ten years later (Dearden 2014; O'Dowd 2018), these assumptions still seem to underlie the thinking behind the implementation of university teaching in English – and there is still no clear consensus on the issues that they raise.

In this chapter we take an in-depth look at the move to teaching in English in higher education, based on previous research and experience. We will show how the situation varies from one context to another, and identify some patterns that can help us to understand what is going on in our own local situation. With a view to supporting teachers who are new to teaching content courses in English, or who are interested in consolidating their experiences in this area, we will address some of the major questions that are being asked, and look at how we can understand our role in the ongoing internationalization process of higher education worldwide.

1.2 The Rise of EMI

In many countries around the world, English plays an important role in education in general, and courses have long been taught in English at university level to students who have a different native language. When we think of this, places like Hong Kong, India or Kenya come to mind as examples of areas where English has a consolidated role in the education system, and is one of the main languages used in higher education. But the last ten years have seen a fast-moving trend towards teaching university courses in English almost everywhere in the world – even in countries with absolutely no historical association with the English language. To give a name to this phenomenon, experts are now using the term 'English Medium Instruction', or 'EMI', meaning the use of the English language to teach academic subjects in countries where English is not the first language of most of the population. So why is this happening? What factors can we identify that make universities in countries as diverse as Italy and China go over to using English to teach university courses?

Thinking of EMI in areas of the world with no historical association with English, we will look specifically at Europe, China and Latin America. If we start by looking at Europe, the trend towards EMI began to be documented there in the late 1990s (Dearden 2014; Wächter & Maiworm 2008, 2014; Wilkinson 2004), where it was interpreted both as an aspect of globalization and competitive forces in higher education markets, and as a correlate of the dominance of the English language in an increasing number of sectors across the globe. Paradoxically, perhaps, another of the driving forces behind university courses in English was the Erasmus scheme, initially set up to foster European integration through cultural, linguistic and educational exchange. As increasing numbers of students applied to take semesters in other EU countries, it quickly became apparent that many countries would be left out of the scheme unless they started to offer courses taught in a language accessible to students from abroad – and the default option was rapidly accepted to be English. Despite initial predictions that this would not work, EMI courses have enjoyed a steady expansion across Europe. For example, the surveys by Wächter and Maiworm (2014) identified a rise from 725 English-taught programmes in Europe in 2001 to 8,089 in 2014. The countries leading this trend were the Scandinavian countries, the Netherlands and Germany, but countries in Southern and particularly Eastern Europe have been catching up rapidly. Interestingly, the original dynamics driving EMI seems to be changing slightly. In the most recent survey, after the need to remove language obstacles for international students, the most commonly mentioned reason given for EMI in Europe was to improve the job prospects for local students (Wächter & Maiworm 2014, 18). Widespread public acceptance of the need for English as the language of international and professional communication is thus still fuelling the move towards EMI, even where the goals of attracting foreign students or taking part in exchanges have largely been met.

Of course, in the global balance we can hardly ignore the importance of English in China. As one of the new internationalization moves ushered in around the time that China joined the World Trade Organization in 2001, it became official policy that children should study English from the age of eight or nine. According to Bolton and Graddol (2012), by 2010 there were around 400 million English learners in China. English is an obligatory subject, alongside only mathematics and Chinese, for students taking the Gaokao, that is, the National University Entrance Exam, taken by around 9 million students every year. But this is not the only thing. For many Chinese people, modernity and prosperity are strongly associated with the English language, and for upwardly mobile Chinese families, schooling with and even in English has become popular, with English taught in kindergartens and in private language schools, as well as throughout the school system. All Chinese university students are required to study English, not only as an admission requirement but also to graduate – those majoring in subjects other than English have to sit the College English Test (CET) before graduation. Educational high achievers are often encouraged to go abroad to take a master's or PhD in the United States, Australia or Europe. In fact, China is the top source country for international students at US universities, and in Europe, too, vast numbers of Chinese students undertake higher education, with around 40 per cent of them choosing the United Kingdom, followed by France and Germany. Unsurprisingly, Chinese universities are now increasingly moving towards EMI programmes, partly in response to local demand, and partly to attract students from elsewhere. In 2012–13 some leading Chinese universities were offering degrees in medicine taught in English, and attracting large numbers of students from India and Pakistan. Currently, there are large numbers of EMI programmes in China across all educational levels from primary school to graduate study, on offer in public and private institutions alike (see Chen et al. 2020).

The third area of the world that we would like to highlight here for special attention is Latin America. We might imagine that at least the Spanish-speaking countries in the Americas would have little need for English, since after all, Spanish itself is a widely spoken language with a massive number of native speakers, a well-developed academic and scientific language, and a buoyant culture. In this particular context, it seems that the initiative to promote EMI comes more from the private sector. Faced with a state sector that is underfunded and overrun, and where higher education is struggling with unmanageable numbers, the middle-class parents increasingly opt for private education, even at university level. The prestigious international schools and private universities favoured by upwardly mobile social groups tend to include English as an integral part of what they offer, thus conforming to global trends and providing added value for their students. Recent surveys suggest that Brazil, too, followed this tendency until the mid-2010s, with EMI programmes widespread in private education at all levels, but with less penetration in the state sector (Dearden 2014). Within Latin America, Argentina and Chile have taken the lead with reinforced English-language education throughout formal schooling, while other countries lag behind, perhaps through lack of resources or an absence of political will in this sense. For example, Mexico recently launched a state initiative to gradually implement English in the state school system, with the aim of having school leavers reach a B1 level by 2037 (Secretaría de Educación Pública 2017), but is currently struggling with a lack of resources and trained teachers, while legislation in Paraguay still only requires students to take two years of English during their schooling, instead giving priority to teaching Spanish and Guaraní. Where EMI is making rapid progress in Latin America is in the competitive private schools and universities favoured by middle-class parents. Throughout the continent EMI is thus becoming associated with an elite education at all levels that makes students upwardly mobile.

This trend in itself may have a knock-on effect on public institutions, and there is evidence from a few countries that some state universities are now opting to launch EMI, despite the enormous investment and reorganization required. For example, in Brazil the short-lived 'Science without borders' programme, and the recent 'Programa Institucional de Internacionalização' (PRINT), have acted as an incentive for many Brazilian state higher education institutions to start implementing EMI, and pilot programmes are now under way in thirty-six universities, with EMI training courses for lecturers, most of whom have intermediate levels of English competence (Martínez & Fernandez 2020). Although such moves are often perceived locally as controversial, or as a waste of scarce resources, one Brazilian seminar participant commented that some universities feel that it is worth persisting, because 'EMI could mean putting an institution on the map as a destination in the international scene' (Madhavan & McDonald 2014, 4).

So universities all over the world are doing EMI – EMI is a truly global phenomenon. But is all EMI the same? Is it safe to make generalizations about EMI? How can we talk meaningfully about EMI in our own context, and think about what it has in common with EMI in contexts that are very different? And how can we understand the special features of our own context that make it different from many of the others? In what follows, we will take a look at the background in more detail. In concrete, we will address some important questions that inevitably arise in any discussion of EMI: Why is English so important? How can we understand the role of English in our own context? Are teachers and students really 'ready' for EMI? What kind of person should the EMI teacher be? Is there any room for language teachers in the new scenario? How can we learn from other institutions' experiences to build a solid basis for developing EMI programmes and courses in our own context?

1.3 Why Is English So Important?

So EMI is a global phenomenon. But why is this the case? In essence, we have to say that this is because English is currently the global language. This is not a political statement, but simply a statement of fact. As David Crystal so eloquently explained in his best-selling book *English as a Global Language* (Crystal 1997, 2003), the rise of English to global status is the end result of a combination of different economic, political and social processes that have taken place over the last two hundred years. As he describes (2003, 3–4), 'a language achieves a genuinely global status when it develops a special role that is recognized in every country' and to achieve this unusual status, this language has to be taken up by other countries around the world, which 'must decide to give it a special place within their communities, even though they may have few (or no) mother-tongue speakers'. This can happen when a country decides to make this language official or co-official, authorized for use in education, the media, law courts and affairs of government. It can also happen when a language that has no official status is made a priority in the education system, as the first or obligatory foreign language to be studied or used as a vehicle of education for large numbers of students.

But why does one particular language achieve this status? As Crystal goes on to explain (2003, 9), 'A language does not become a global language because of its intrinsic structural properties, or because of the size of its vocabulary, or because it has been a vehicle of a great literature in the past, or because it was once associated with a great culture or religion.' Actually, English is not intrinsically easy to learn: its phonetic system is rather complex, its verbal system follows intricate rules, and its spelling is highly irregular, so if English were competing for global status on grounds of simplicity, it would probably lose out. The reason why English is important today has nothing to do with this. In fact, if we want to understand the dominance of English, we have to look to the way that power is shared out in the world. A language achieves global status primarily through the power of its speakers – but there are different kinds of power. Cultural, political, military, technological and economic factors are all important in the race to making a language powerful, and in all of these areas, English has gradually overtaken its closest competitors.

But if this is making speakers of other languages feel somehow worried, this was not our intention. Because when a language 'goes global', in some way it also frees itself from its former identity and associations as the language of the dominant power. As Crystal also points out (2003, 11), there is a sense in which the world actually needs a global language: for trade, diplomacy, knowledge exchange, travel – for so many reasons, it is very useful to agree on one language that everyone can learn for communication with others. The absence of major conflicts and the processes of globalization in business, academia and the media have also played a role in pushing forward the role of English as a useful 'lingua franca' – and one that can be used quite easily (or perhaps most easily) when there is not a single 'native speaker' in the room!

Developing this idea more fully, many people have reached the conclusion that English no longer belongs to the natives. English-language textbooks no longer centre on 'native speakers' and 'native pronunciation', and often contain no references to the culture or history of the core English-speaking countries. This process of decentralization may be facilitated by the fact that English has no 'royal academy' to purify it of foreign elements or codify its grammar. Rightly known as 'the mongrel tongue', English has always been receptive to large numbers of loan words from different languages.

Although, as we said before, English is not a global language because of its intrinsic qualities, its openness to novelty and acceptance of difference mean that it carries its global status with a certain flair.

To understand the way that English operates in the world today, various different models have been devised. Here we will just look at two broad and interrelated approaches: Kachru's circles and the emergence of ELF/EIL.

Indian linguist Braj Kachru came up with an interesting way of understanding the role of English as a native/second/foreign language in the different countries where it is spoken. His influential 'circles' model (Kachru 1992) captures the nature of how English can be seen in three different kinds of situation. First in historical terms, we have the 'core' of English-speaking countries as such, starting with England, but also now including the United States, Australia and other countries where English is not only official but also has a large number of native speakers. As he puts it, this 'inner circle' represents the first diaspora of English speakers who spread across the world in colonial times. It is here that English is most firmly embedded in the system, and enjoys great dominance over other languages that might be present.

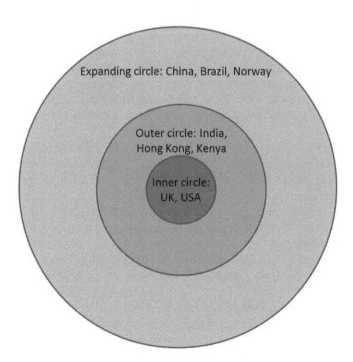

Expanding circle: China, Brazil, Norway

Outer circle: India, Hong Kong, Kenya

Inner circle: UK, USA

FIGURE 1.1 *Kachru's three circles model explaining the situations of English across the world.*

The second phase of colonial expansion explains the 'outer circle'. The role of English in these countries mainly came about as a result of British imperial expansion in Asia and Africa, but also through US influence in areas like the Philippines. The essence of the outer circle is that it contains hundreds of millions of speakers of English, but many of these people would not regard themselves as native speakers. The majority either learn English at school or pick it up as an ambient language that they need for trade, or for their dealings with the authorities. In most of these countries, English is official or co-official, and coexists with a considerable number of different local languages. In some countries, such as India, English actually fulfils the need for a (relatively) neutral lingua franca that can be accepted by members of different language groups and ethnicities.

The last circle is the 'expanding circle', which takes in a vast number of countries where English has traditionally played no special historical or administrative role. These countries – which account for a truly massive proportion of the population of the globe – are adopting English in their education systems because they perceive it as necessary for international trade, participation in international organizations, for knowledge and cultural exchange, for travel and so on.

This way of looking at the situation and roles of English across the world is particularly useful for our present purposes because it opens our eyes to two important things:

1. The majority of the people who use English in their lives are not native speakers – there may still be a majority of mother-tongue English speakers in the inner circle countries, but the citizens of outer circle countries usually learn English during their formal education and speak other languages at home. As for the expanding circle countries, English is basically a language learnt at school, and has no particular role in the internal life of the country (for administration, law, trade etc.). In these countries – which are homes to the majority of today's English users – there is no special 'bond' with English, and the number of native speakers, or people who regard themselves as culturally part of the English-speaking world, is very low. In other words, in many parts of the world English has the role of a lingua franca, a language spoken as a vehicle of communication, an instrumental language that people use to do things with, not an aspect of cultural identity and emotional affiliation. No one is learning English, or using English, because they want to 'be American' or because they 'love Shakespeare/Hollywood/Justin Bieber'. They may, but that is not their main motivation. They are impelled to learn to function in English by the forces of globalization that we have discussed earlier.

2. The vast spread of English as a global and instrumental language inevitably has consequences for the kind of English that people are using (and learning). We have seen that the position of English as a global language means that English is somehow out of the control of the native speakers. English belongs to the world. People all over the world, from all different language backgrounds, need English to do things (trade, science, technology, academia, legal and institutional relations). They are not interested in the details of grammar or the fine nuances of vocabulary. This tends to mean that questions like 'what is the correct form?' and 'what is the best pronunciation?' have little meaning. What matters in reality is the ability to communicate with other people – who are usually not native speakers either, and are only interested in your English skills insofar as they enable you to get things done in the real world.

In fact, when it comes to the question of normativity and 'speaking good English', many of the ideas we have are constantly being challenged by what is going on in the real world. Although we might have been taught that one form of English is somehow 'better', or 'more correct', or 'more authentic' than another, the English language is subject to many variations in terms of pronunciation, vocabulary and even grammar. If we look first at the countries in the inner circle, from the very beginnings of the English language in England there were different dialects spoken in different regions of the country, and some of these still survive. On a larger scale, it is clear that the English spoken in the United States is not the same as the English of England (or Australia, or Canada), which has led some people to talk of the existence of different standard forms. In outer circle countries, local varieties of English have arisen, usually with their own special accent, and with different vocabulary for local things and concepts. The clearest example of this is Indian English. In India, a country with a population of over 1.3 billion, less than 0.1 per cent of the population have English as their first language. However, over 10 per cent of the population are reported in the most recent census (2011) as knowing English. But the English they use is strongly influenced by Indian languages, and particularly by Hindi, which is the other lingua franca. The differences are perhaps most apparent in pronunciation, but they also occur in vocabulary, grammar and even in the system used for counting. As for the expanding circle countries, most of them have not developed a specific, classifiable form of 'local English', although there is generally a perceptible influence from the local language, and informally people do speak of 'Spanglish', 'Japlish' and so on, usually in a derogatory sense. The English spoken in expanding circle countries is often 'school English', that is, it is English that follows the norms of standard British or American English. At the same time, because this English is used as a means of communication between people who are not native speakers of the language, the neutral or formal register of the language tends to prevail; 'difficult' aspects of the language such as phrasal verbs or idioms are used only sparingly, and since most people have some kind of 'foreign' accent, the whole issue of accent loses its importance, with the emphasis being placed on clear pronunciation rather than on the value of specific vowel or consonant sounds.

This trend has been documented far and wide, and has even led to systematic analyses of 'English as a lingua franca' as it really appears in different settings. For example, Jenkins (2000) proposed that the English used for international communication in Europe has lost phonemic distinctions between the different values of 'th' (the difference between 'thing' and 'then', for example), and between the long and short vowel sounds ('ship' and 'sheep'). In one of her more radical assertions, she even stated that since many non-native speakers fail to use 's' in the third-person singular, this morpheme could be discarded in a new 'international' version of English. However, as Maley argues in his introduction to a useful edited volume on this topic (Maley 2011), although these trends towards lingua franca English undoubtedly exist, and may be gathering momentum, the notion of 'English as a lingua franca' or 'English as an international language' is unworkable in the classroom, because teachers and learners both have a vested interest in promoting standard forms of the language. For our present purposes, we would like to emphasize just two aspects of all this, which may seem contradictory, but which all English users have been learning to live with over the last few years.

First, it is clear that schools and universities will go on teaching students the standard forms of English that we ourselves have learnt and taught: school textbooks and certification exams need to teach a concrete, specific form of English, and they usually opt for one of the most socially recognized standard forms, namely British English or American English. When we are looking at written English, these standard forms still apply, and although there is some evidence that things are changing, most international publishers, media, academic journals and so on insist that written texts should comply with the standard rules. But second, in seeming contradiction to this, in the real world many people learn to manage on a day-to-day level with a good functional level of English without aspiring to native-like competence. This applies particularly to spoken English, and especially the area of pronunciation, where different accents are widely accepted as a fact of life (and indeed, if we are talking about practical comprehension, 'foreign' accents may be much easier to understand than many 'native' accents). When it comes to spoken English, there is a consensus that what matters most is comprehensibility and good communication skills, and that pronunciation should be clear – but the issue of accent is now regarded as having only secondary importance (but see Appendix 2 for some ideas if you are concerned about this).

1.4 The Ecosystems of EMI

To understand fully the ecosystems within which EMI is being established, we can start by looking at the situation of the country and/or region in which we are working. The 'circle' we are in will have a major impact on the patterns of EMI that are established. But, of course, the different roles of English outlined in the previous section must also be considered in the light of the different situations in universities around the world. Are you working in a huge public university with massive student numbers, or are you part of a smaller, private university where people pay for a more personalized style of teaching? Do your students' families have the resources to pay for private international schools, finance overseas travel and so on, or are they finding it difficult to scrape together enough money to allow their children to study at all? Do your students regard learning the English language as an important investment for their professional future, or as a threat to their own language, culture or religion? Economic, social and cultural factors will all have a bearing on the way that students respond to EMI, and these different factors together will contribute to the ecosystem in which your EMI classes take place.

One of the most important aspects of our local situation is the coexistence of different languages and the place of English within the linguistic ecosystem. In many countries this is very complex. For example, in Algeria some students are taking EMI courses at university, but the languages of the university are French and Modern Standard Arabic, while the students feel more at home using the Algerian variety of Arabic, although many of them may speak Berber at home. Some of these students may welcome EMI, and English in general, seeing it as a way of freeing the country and its people from the French colonial past. Others may resent English, regarding it as a threat to their Islamic values and traditional way of life. In many multilingual areas, the balance between different languages is already complex, and English just adds further complications. However, these very multilingual areas have also been found to be a receptive setting for EMI. Costa (2016) provides an overview of bi- and multilingual education in various European countries, showing that the historical and political background determines the way that teaching in English is conceptualized. In areas where bilingualism is the norm (South Tyrol, Catalonia) there is greater acceptance of multilingual practices, code-switching and so on, and less difficulty with the idea that a university might be able to function well in several languages.

Aside from attitudes, which are enormously complex, one of the most important aspects of the local language ecosystem is whether or not students are getting any input from English outside your classroom. The amount of exposure they have will probably influence their general coping skills in English, and will have an impact on the kind of support you need to provide.

For example, students who go to study in Australia or the UK will probably be in a situation of total immersion, and will need to use English to get around, solve their everyday problems and make friends. By contrast, local students who are taking EMI courses at an Italian university will probably use no English outside the classroom, unless they belong to that rare group of students who actually talk to the international exchange students!

In general, we can put together a few pros and cons concerning the way EMI is working in the 'expanding circle':

- On the positive side, the situation is easier for students, since there is no need for students to use English outside the classroom, unless the teacher or the university creates situations or opportunities for this.

- But, precisely because there is no input or interaction outside the classroom, students' English does not receive an extra boost owing to the 'immersion effect'.

- Since (nearly) all students are in the same situation, the lecturers will tend to accommodate more, both linguistically and culturally, which will make matters easier for both parties.

- The style of teaching conforms to local educational expectations, and may often be top-down and lecture-heavy, with less pressure to read, less pressure to participate, write and so on than in countries with an educational tradition inherited from the UK or US universities.

- On the down side, this means that students will not benefit from the stimulus of being exposed to different educational approaches and contact with people from very different cultures.

- On the plus side, fewer cultural issues will arise: lecturers understand students' culture and operate within it.

- At the same time as EMI is being implemented in these contexts, students may be receiving support in the form of English language classes, English for Academic Purposes classes or English for Specific Purposes classes. These have an important role in helping students reach the level of competence they need to benefit from EMI classes, and also in filling the gaps often left by EMI courses in terms of the acquisition of productive language skills like academic writing or oral competences (see Chapter 6 for more details on this important aspect, and on other forms of institutional backup for EMI).

So how do you see the ecosystem of your own situation? How does English fit into the linguistic landscape? How do economic, social and cultural factors impinge on your EMI teaching (and the students' EMI learning)? Worksheet 1.1 will help you to reflect on your local situation and relate it to other situations that we have described here.

> ## WORKSHEET 1.1: WHAT IS THE ROLE OF ENGLISH IN YOUR INSTITUTION?

Think about these questions, or discuss them with a colleague:

1. Which 'circle' is your country in?
2. What is the role of English in your country, and how does it coexist with other languages?
3. In particular, how important is English in the education system in your country? At what age do children start learning English? What kind of level do they reach in their school years? In schools, are content courses taught in English?
4. What is the role of English in your university? Think about:
   a. Website and information for prospective students
   b. Information and administrative procedures for current students
   c. Programmes and courses offered in English
   d. Other activities organized in English
   e. Language learning provision: what languages can students study?
   f. Ambient languages (what do people really speak in the cafeteria, the halls, etc.?)
5. Attitudes to English (e.g. are staff and students eager to use English in the classroom, in tutorials and in their everyday activities?)
6. How do other stakeholders see the importance of English in your university? Think about:
   a. University and faculty authorities
   b. Local authorities and people responsible for the education system
   c. Parents
   d. Employers

1.5 Are the Teachers Ready for EMI?

The first questionable assumption mentioned by Wilkinson and Zegers (2007) centres on the university teaching staff: it is taken for granted that lecturers, professors and so on are competent enough in English to give lectures, lead seminars, direct research work and examine students in that language. We might expect that universities would take great care to make sure that the people responsible for teaching subjects in English would actually have a high level of competence and plenty of confidence in using that language. In fact, without wanting to offend anyone, we know that there are many issues with this subject, and that many institutions are concerned about the level of English among the people who actually teach.

Back in the 1990s when the first reports were published on EMI in Europe, there was a widely voiced concern that classes were being given by 'teachers who could not properly express themselves in English' to 'students who were unable to fully understand' (Wächter & Maiworm 2014, 98). However, broad surveys carried out in 2001 and 2007 showed that this was not really the case, or at least, that the problem was not as grave as some people had thought. By the time the 2014 survey was conducted, 95 per cent of the programme directors questioned at European universities rated the English proficiency of their academic staff as 'good' or 'very good', although there were notable differences between countries: in Austria, Belgium and Norway, 100 per cent of the directors placed their teachers in these categories, while in Spain only 88 per cent did so (Wächter & Maiworm 2014, 100). Nevertheless, as these authors themselves note, these findings seem to paint an unrealistically optimistic picture, as they seem to clash with the criticisms often heard from students and from the teachers themselves. As they themselves suggest, this apparent contradiction may well have arisen as a result of differences in expectations: what programme directors consider to be 'good' may not necessarily be the same as what students (who actually sit in the classroom for many hours) regard as satisfactory. The massive generational difference in English proficiency in many countries means that students and younger lecturers may feel much more comfortable in English than the older, more senior teaching staff, many of whom are currently senior professors or programme directors. Vague terms such as 'very good' are, in any case, unhelpful when it comes to assessing language competences. Evidence from other sources, including survey research (Costa 2016; Dearden 2014; O'Dowd 2018), suggests that there are still problems – either with the English skills of the teaching staff, or with the way they actually use those skills to teach international student groups. As Wächter and Maiworm put it (2014, 106), the 'English proficiency of the teaching staff does not imply that they can readily handle the heterogeneous command of English, academic and cultural differences of the students in the classroom. As a result, the need to train the teachers, including native English speakers, to handle linguistic and cultural diversity was mentioned by quite a few of the respondents'.

Focusing just on the language component, we can say that the concern with lecturers' language levels is still an important issue, and has recently been documented in various ways. In a study carried out by O'Dowd (2018) covering seventy different universities in Europe, one of the most commonly cited problems was the low level of communicative competence among the university teachers (referred to twenty-two times). Of the seventy institutions he questioned, 43 per cent required their teachers to demonstrate a B2 level in English, 44 per cent required a C1 level and 13 per cent required a C2. A different perspective comes from Costa (2016), who surveyed thirty-eight universities in Italy, and found that 59 per cent of institutions said that they chose teachers for EMI according to specific competences (among which English figured, but was not the only factor), while only 26 per cent stated that they simply asked for volunteers. In a study focusing only on Spanish universities carried out by Halbach and Lázaro (2015), over half of the Spanish universities questioned required a B2 or less of their teachers in order to teach class in English. The notion that a B2 level would be sufficient to teach a university-level course in English is surely highly questionable, even given the obvious subject bias in people's language skills, which means that a B2-level speaker with professional knowledge and skills is likely to be able to perform better in his/her area of specialization than in a context requiring general English knowledge. As we shall see in the context of students (see below), it is obvious that the C1 level reflects better the kind of full academic and professional language competence or 'effective operational proficiency' that a lecturer needs to handle the requirements of teaching a university course. However, we also know that other constraints exist which may make it difficult for universities to find, or employ, lecturers who bring together all the desirable skills, and that universities have had to reach out for other solutions in order to meet the massive need for EMI teachers.

In the context of readiness for EMI among the university teaching staff, although language competences tend to dominate the discussion, some other issues are also raised with a certain frequency. For example, O'Dowd (2018) also reports that concerns about language proficiency were followed by a variety of other issues and problems including the lack of training and support for teachers wishing to engage in EMI (mentioned ten times in his survey of seventy institutions), and the perceived drop in standards of teaching when carried out in a second language (also mentioned by six out of seventy institutions). Other selection criteria for EMI teachers were also mentioned in this context: according to O'Dowd (2018, 561), before appointing lecturers to give classes in English, some universities also considered: previous teaching experience; teaching methodology assessed by observation or by student questionnaires; participation in methodology courses and evaluation of previous experience (e.g. international research stays or teaching experience abroad).

So the question remains. Our own experience suggests that in Southern Europe, lecturers' language competences are still a problematic issue that affects the way EMI is being implemented. In other parts of the world, such as Asia and the Middle East, the issues have so far not been researched in depth, but since some major countries such as China are now introducing EMI on a large scale, it is likely that the same kind of problems and uncertainties are arising there as we experienced in Europe at the start of the EMI adventure – which to some extent still persist. However, it is very important to note that the lecturers' actual language competences, measurable as a TOEFL result or on the CEFR scale, are probably not the main criterion. Language skills matter – but what matters most is the use that you make of them.

The good news, perhaps, is that the problem – if it is one – tends to be self-limiting. The people who can do EMI and want to do it are generally the people who end up doing it. The people who can't do it, or don't want to, will end up not doing it. The more difficult news is that if you are a young lecturer applying for a position, your ability to teach effectively in English will probably have a strong influence on your career prospects. The purpose of this book is to help EMI teachers and potential EMI teachers, and all people who feel that they would like to rise to this challenge, by sharing some good practices and helping them to build a solid conceptual basis for what they do. It is our aim to provide ideas about the language you will need to use – but also about the way you need to approach the task of teaching in English in order to make the best of the language you have. (See Chapter 2 for more about what EMI teachers feel, and Chapter 6 on training programmes for EMI teachers.)

1.6 Are the Students Ready for EMI?

The second questionable assumption mentioned by Wilkinson and Zegers (2007) is that students have good enough English-language competences to participate in specialized university-level courses taught in English. It seems obvious that students who enrol on university-level EMI courses should have a 'good enough' level of English to take advantage of those courses. But what is 'good enough'?

In many countries there is a widespread assumption that (1) incoming students have sufficient language proficiency to study in English and (2) English school-leaving examinations provide relevant proficiency evidence (Wilkinson & Zegers 2007, 28). However, there is also very good evidence to suggest that this is not the case. In Southern Europe, for example, many students leave school with an intermediate (B1/B2) level of English. Yet they are being encouraged to take university degrees with an EMI component. For example, in Italy, in Costa's survey of thirty-eight universities, 46 per cent asked that students should provide English language certification for admission to EMI programmes, while 43 per cent did not. However, we do not know what level of English this certification was supposed to indicate. O'Dowd (2018) covered seventy different universities in Europe, and found that one of the most commonly cited problems was the low level of communicative competence among students (referred to explicitly sixteen times in his survey).

There are several reasons for this laissez-faire attitude to student admissions. One is that many universities have acted reactively, responding to heavy external pressures to offer their courses in English, and that their impulse to compete has led them to sideline other considerations, such as real student language levels. Another is that some universities are constrained by laws that do not allow them to select students in terms of their English language level, but only in terms of their school-leaving grade or national university entrance examination score. Yet another reason is that many students with lower levels of English actually elect to take EMI courses, motivated by the idea that this will actually help them raise their level of English at the same time as they learn the contents of their degree. All of these reasons are very valid in their context, and need to be taken seriously. Unfortunately, the obvious correlate of this situation – that is, that more language courses should be provided to help students reach the appropriate level – is often simply ignored, either on grounds of expense or because the people responsible assume that by taking courses taught in English, students will somehow automatically come up to the required language level within a year or so.

The Ideal World: Students Start EMI with C1-Level Competence

Over the years, various ideas have been put forward concerning the level of English that students need in order to be able to take advantage of EMI courses. What we might term 'the classic theory', the one that has the best theoretical underpinning, is the idea that students need a C1 level. The very construct of the C1 level on the Common European Framework of Reference for Languages (CEFR 2018), encapsulated in the definition 'Effective operational proficiency', is that users at this level are fully equipped for work and study in the target language. According to the CEFR Companion Volume (CEFR 2018, 164), this level is characterized by 'good access to a broad range of language, which allows fluent, spontaneous communication'. The C1 level is widely held to be the desirable level for people who need to study and work using a foreign language. The British Council explains that the C1 level 'corresponds to proficient users of the language, i.e. those able to perform complex tasks related to work and study'. In fact, many universities in English-speaking countries stipulate that applicants should certify that they have a C1 level (such as C1 Advanced, from Cambridge English, or Band 7 in IELTS).

Some of the general descriptors for C1-level language competences read as follows:

- Can use language flexibly and effectively for social, academic and professional purposes.

- Can produce clear, well-structured text on complex subjects, showing controlled use of organizational patterns, connectors and cohesive devices.

- Can understand specialized articles and longer technical instructions, even when they do not relate to my field.

- Can understand the intentions and implications of other contributors on complex, abstract issues and can express myself with clarity and precision, adapting my language and register flexibly and effectively.

All of these seem to fit with what we would ideally like students to be able to do, if they are taking a course taught in English at university level.

On the other hand, we know that we do not live in an ideal world and that people's language competences are often constrained by education and circumstances, resulting in uneven competence profiles. For example, in Europe it is usual for students entering university to have better receptive skills (reading, listening) than productive skills (writing, speaking). If we take another look at the situation facing first-year undergraduate EMI students, we might think that for attending lectures in English, what students really need is to have a good ability to understand what we say: in other words, listening comprehension skills. Particularly at the beginning of the degree, university courses in many countries tend to place higher demands on students' listening skills than on, say, their writing or speaking skills, with a heavy lecture load (sometimes up to eight hours a day) and an emphasis on being able to follow and take notes. Again, one of the descriptors for listening comprehension at the C1 level seems to match quite closely with what we ourselves would say that the students should be able to do in our classes:

- Can understand enough to follow extended speech on abstract and complex topics beyond his/her own field, though he/she may need to confirm occasional details, especially if the accent is unfamiliar.

In a further explanation, the latest handbook to the CEFR adds, for C1 level in the category 'listening as a member of a live audience':

- Can follow most lectures, discussions and debate with relative ease.

However, the C1 level for 'understanding conversation between other speakers', which might be relevant for seminars, class discussions and debates, states:

- Can easily follow complex interactions between third parties in group discussion and debate, even on abstract, complex, unfamiliar topics.

- Can identify the attitude of each speaker in an animated discussion characterized by overlapping turns, digressions and colloquialisms that is delivered at a natural speed in accents that are familiar to the listener.

Moreover, in 'listening to audio media and recordings', the C1-level descriptors state:

- Can understand a wide range of recorded and broadcast audio material, including some non-standard usage, and identify finer points of detail, including implicit attitudes and relationships between speakers.

The Real World: EMI Students with B2 Competences

The problem with all this is that the university admissions policy is generally not only shaped by what would be ideal, or by lecturers' ideas about the kind of students they would like to teach. It is quite possible that we will encounter students in our classrooms who do not match up to the descriptions for C1, in listening or in anything else. Difficulties understanding lectures have been reported by studies from as far afield as Norway, South Korea and UEA (Querol-Julián & Crawford Camiciottoli 2019). It is also important to remember that the situation of students in our own (usually expanding circle) contexts differs from that of students in English-speaking countries, where almost constant exposure to the English language may catalyse a process of rapid language development (see aforementioned).

So what do we know about the students who enter university-level EMI with a B2 level of English listening comprehension, or even less? Some years ago we did a study focusing on whether the students' listening comprehension skills, as measured by an IELTS test, had an impact on their course satisfaction and academic achievement in lecture-taught courses (Breeze & Miller 2012). At that time, in the schools where we conducted the study, no specific entrance requirements regarding English had been imposed, and so we were able to look at a broad cross section of the Spanish undergraduate population enrolled on degree courses in law, medicine and humanities. We tested their listening ability using an IELTS listening test at the start of their first EMI course. We also gave the students a questionnaire on self-perceptions of listening ability, with one global question and fourteen items dealing with listening subskills, and we obtained their final grades from their EMI course.

We found that these students' scores on the IELTS listening test tended to show positive correlations with their final grade obtained on the EMI course. In other words, the stronger their English comprehension skills, the better they did on the course. Graphs 1.1 and 1.2 (from Breeze & Miller 2012) illustrate the extent to which the students' scores on the IELTS listening test correlated with their final course grade for the EMI component taught in the schools of law and medicine.

But even more importantly, we found that the correlations between the students' IELTS listening scores and their global and analytical self-

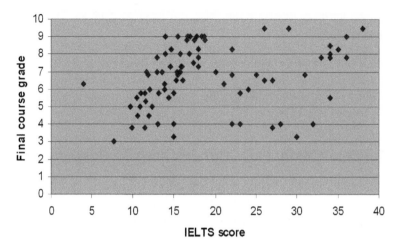

GRAPH 1.1 *Scatterplot showing small correlations between IELTS listening score and final course grade: Law (from Breeze and Miller 2012).*

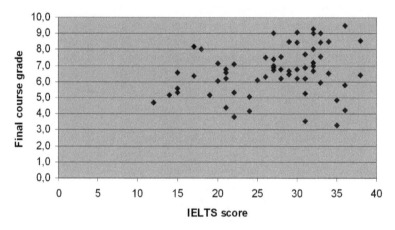

GRAPH 1.2 *Scatterplot showing small correlations between IELTS listening score and final course grade: Medicine (from Breeze & Miller 2012).*

assessment scores were very high. Graphs 1.3 and 1.4 (from Breeze & Miller 2012) show a consistent positive relationship between students' listening scores and their analytical self-assessment scores in EMI, also in law and medicine.

To obtain a more insightful picture of how listening skills affected students' experiences on the EMI course, we also asked students with different levels of competence to comment on their experience.

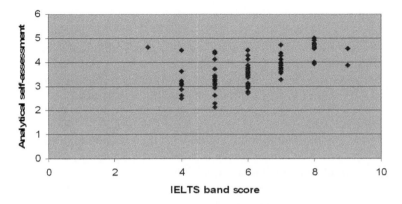

GRAPH 1.3 *Scatterplot showing high correlations between IELTS listening band score and students' analytical self-assessment: Law (from Breeze & Miller 2012).*

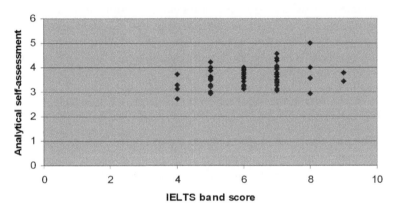

GRAPH 1.4 *Scatterplot showing high correlations between IELTS listening band score and students' analytical self-assessment: Medicine (from Breeze & Miller 2012).*

Among the law students, some representative comments were as follows (comments matched with their level, as measured using their IELTS band scores):

> High C1 level:
> In my case, I don't feel that I need help with the language, but I do think that the course in English requires more work than an equivalent course in Spanish.

Mid-C1 level:
I understand most of what the lecturer says, but I really find it useful to complement the lectures and course notes with information from other sources. The schedule is very intensive and although I understand most things, it is difficult to concentrate for such a long time without losing the thread of a complex argument.

High B2 level:
I think we have a lot of difficulties with the vocabulary. Sometimes we are not even sure what the lecturer is talking about, and we don't feel confident enough to ask questions.
We would definitely benefit from more language support. The course in English was very hard work.

Mid-B2 level:
I don't understand everything the lecturer says. I can manage in this course if I read the book and notes carefully and check all the things I don't understand using a dictionary. In law classes in general, I have to make my own 'picture' in my mind of what the lecturer is saying. That is hard enough in my own language, but in English it is often quite confusing.

So what is the take-home message from all of this? In our view, there are two clear messages:

1. The more competent the students are in English, the more confident they will feel in EMI classes.
2. Students whose English is below the benchmark level for EMI (C1 level, at least in receptive skills) still manage to get by, because success in university courses is not just about understanding lectures. It is a combination of English with other factors, such as motivation, study skills and compensatory skills, that determines their achievement in EMI courses in the longer term.

Against this background, it is obvious that the optimum solution would be to stipulate C1 as the entry level for EMI, and – since EMI has the greatest impact on students' receptive skills – to provide means for students to continue improving their productive language competences in general or specific language courses. But in the real world, setting the entry level at C1 would probably be a major obstacle to many would-be students, so universities need to admit people with lower language competences. Given this situation, universities should seriously consider providing backup courses – English language courses, but particularly more focused English for Academic Purposes or English for Specific Purposes courses (see Section 1.9, and Chapter 6) – in order to ensure that students gain maximum benefit from EMI and graduate from university with excellent professional communication competences in English.

1.7 Do Students Learn English through EMI?

The third 'questionable assumption' mentioned by Wilkinson and Zegers 2007, 28) is the generalized belief that students will learn English by taking EMI courses. If they do not, aside from the basic need to incorporate Erasmus students and fee-paying international students, it all seems rather futile. But things are not quite as straightforward as that.

Sometimes when we hear our colleagues, students and acquaintances talking about courses or degrees taught in English, it all seems very simple. You learn English at school. Then you go to university and take courses that are taught in English. You come out with native-like English competence, because you have taken a degree taught in English. Where is the problem? The problem is that this idea merges together a number of different concepts (comprehension and production, exposure and participation, basic communication skills and academic language proficiency) and assumes they are the same thing. To understand what is really going on in our own EMI classrooms, we need to separate out some of these concepts.

Why Do We Need a Conceptual Approach?
Expectations versus Experience

One of the very real problems that arise is a problem of expectations versus experience. It seems that many stakeholders (students and their parents, university administrators, employers) think that taking EMI courses as part of a 'bilingual degree' will somehow confer a kind of perfect, balanced bilingualism onto all students. The results of empirical research addressing this topic present a confusing picture: some evidence suggests that students' language skills do improve as a result of taking EMI courses (Lasagabaster 2008), while other studies indicate that students' English skills after a year of EMI show no advantage over their non-EMI counterparts (Lei & Wu 2014). As we have seen earlier, the students' level of competence at the outset may well have a strong influence on whether or not they are ready to benefit from EMI. Although many students may feel that their language skills improve when they take a course taught in English, they will also find that their satisfaction with the course and their academic performance are conditioned by the level of English competence that they have at the outset. Yes, of course, they will undergo intensive practice in listening comprehension, and they will get better at understanding lectures. Yes, their note-taking skills will probably improve. Yes, they are very likely to acquire a larger professional vocabulary related to the subjects that they study in their degree. If their EMI courses also have international students, or they themselves are able to take part in exchange programmes, then they may well get to learn more about other cultures, and build a network of international contacts. But none of these positive features is automatic. Students need to be shown how to take advantage of their EMI courses, and given the support needed to overcome any difficulties that come up.

Conceptual Approaches: EMI, CLIL, Immersion, CBI

So how can we start to disentangle the web of discourses and expectations that surround EMI? First, let's start with some of the common terms that are used to describe the courses we teach in English, and think of what they mean – and what they don't mean.

EMI – English Medium Instruction – is the term we are using in this book, because we think it reflects most accurately what is actually happening in most universities. It means that the classes are taught in English, and that some other aspects of university life (tutorials, administrative procedures etc.) may be conducted in English, but it is basically left up to the student to see how he or she is going to manage in all of that. Recently, the more accurate terms EME (English Medium Education) and EMEMUS (English Medium Education in Multilingual University Settings) have been popularized by Dafouz and Smit (2020) to describe what is happening in universities across the world, but since EMI still appears to be the default option that is best understood, we have opted to use this term here.

EMI is sometimes contrasted with *CLIL* – Content and Language Integrated Learning – which is a methodology that was devised with school education in mind. The underlying construct of CLIL is that content teachers using English should consciously teach language at the same time as they teach content, so that students learn new content and new language in an integrated or holistic way. This approach has been very successful in primary school, but perhaps less so in secondary school, and the extent to which it can be implemented in higher education is dubious, not least because lecturers' identities and professional prestige are at stake. One clear message emerging from volumes of research on the perceptions of university EMI teachers is that 'we are not language teachers'. We do not want to be completely categorical on this point. Some universities have implemented training programmes for content teachers in which they have used a CLIL framework to propose ways of making the content courses a richer language learning experience for students. These experiences are valuable, but we cannot help feeling that they will always be the exception. For one thing, the combined weight of institutional tradition, individual experience and stakeholder expectation is stacked against this idea – people go to an anatomy class, or a physiology class, or a corporate law class, to study anatomy, or physiology, or corporate law. They would be surprised, not to say disappointed, if they found that they were getting a language class instead. Another important reason is that content lecturers understand their role as just that – content lecturers. They do not feel qualified to teach language, or even to go part of the way as the

CLIL paradigm might suggest, generally giving more emphasis to language at the same time as they teach content. Even if they were in agreement with this general idea (which they usually are not), they would find this very hard to do. For this reason, although we feel that EMI teachers can and should learn some lessons from CLIL, university-level content courses are generally *not* CLIL courses, and it is not accurate to label them in this way.

Other terms that we hear frequently in this context, and which similarly cause confusion, are 'bilingual' and 'immersion'. *Bilingual* courses/programmes/degrees are understood to be courses, programmes or degrees in which teaching takes place in two languages, usually the local language and English. Unfortunately many people seem to understand that if a student takes a bilingual degree, he or she will automatically become bilingual (in the strong sense of having native-like command of the two languages in question) – which is obviously not the case. Personal bilingualism is a completely different issue! Finally, linguistic *immersion* is the well-known effect that happens when someone – usually a child – is plunged into an environment where everyone speaks a different language from him/her, as in the case of international adoptions, or a year-long school exchange programme. This usually results in swift language acquisition, or at least, accelerated learning of basic survival language, because the child is completely surrounded by people who only speak the other language and is under great pressure to learn enough to meet his/her basic needs. We may note that immersion means being submerged in the other language, and having no option other than to learn some in order to survive. This is quite different from an EMI class at university, where (in the worst-case scenario) only the lecturer speaks English, and the students can meet all their other needs in the local language. Our EMI classes do not usually provide an immersion experience for our students.

Finally, *CBI* (Content-Based Instruction), also known as CBLT (Content-Based Language Teaching), is an approach that developed within the Canadian bilingual education programmes of the later twentieth century. Of particular relevance to EMI are the 'sheltered' CBI courses at the University of Ottawa, in which students whose competence in French, say, was still developing were taught university psychology courses in French in a special programme for non-native speakers, which factored in content-specific language support. These courses have been researched to show that students learned language as well as content in such settings (Snow & Brinton 2017), and provide an excellent example of how content courses taught in the students' second language, combined with highly specific language support, can boost students' language competences as well as their subject knowledge. Unfortunately, such examples are rarely taken into consideration when EMI programmes are set up in outer circle countries, perhaps because resources are lacking, or because the implications of changing the language of education have not been fully thought through, or because the university system operates on a sink-or-swim principle whereby students are expected to evolve the relevant survival techniques.

From 'English-Friendly' to Full EMI

Even though it should now be clear what we mean by EMI, there are still some further grey areas that we need to shed light on. That is because many universities have launched themselves into EMI rather precipitately (e.g. because they need to cope with incoming Erasmus exchange students), and have not had enough resources to address the issue of quality control in their EMI programmes. In the course of our own experience in different countries, we have come across various models that are presented as forms of EMI, but which differ from each other in the degree to which they really fit this description:

1. *English-friendly course.* Course taught in L1 (first language), with material in L1, but textbooks and course material made available in English, possibility of English-speaking academic advisor.

2. *Integration of English.* Courses that include English-language material. Most of the course is taught in L1, and the course material is in L1, but elements of English are incorporated where this is relevant or useful (videos or readings in English, visiting speakers may use English). In this middle option, it is also possible for particular sections of the course to be taught in English (e.g. one of the teachers involved uses English, or English is used for preparation of the students' projects). Team teaching with specialized language teachers may be used, to help the students to acquire a stronger command of the language of the specialized area in general, or to help with specific skills such as writing or presenting.

3. *Course is taught fully in English.* No language support is provided within the specific EMI courses (although the university may also provide some additional language-related courses, which may be credit-bearing or not, in order to support student learning in EMI). The general assumption is that students and teachers have strong enough language skills for this to result in successful learning.

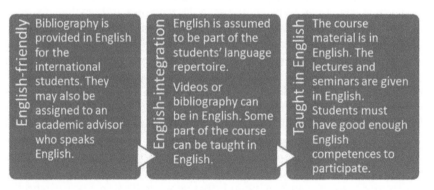

English-friendly
Bibliography is provided in English for the international students. They may also be assigned to an academic advisor who speaks English.

English-integration
English is assumed to be part of the students' language repertoire.

Videos or bibliography can be in English. Some part of the course can be taught in English.

Taught in English
The course material is in English. The lectures and seminars are given in English. Students must have good enough English competences to participate.

FIGURE 1.2 *Continuum from English-Friendly to EMI.*

When we discuss EMI in this book, we are assuming that readers have the third model in mind, but many of the aspects we discuss are also relevant in the case of the second model.

Factors That Influence the Transition to EMI

So now that we have established that our own target model is EMI, how can we understand what is going on as we move towards it? So many factors seem to be involved, which vary according to the cultural, educational and linguistic context. One way of addressing the complexity of EMI has been proposed by Dafouz and Smit (2020), who have devised a framework – called 'ROADMAPPING' – that takes in different dimensions of the EMI phenomenon. Their acronym is made up of the following elements: roles of English (RO), academic disciplines (AD), (language) management (M), agents (A), practices and processes (PP), and internationalization and glocalization (ING).

Using their framework, in any given EMI context, we can inquire into the role of each of these, or the impact that EMI has on it. In the present volume, we have already seen how the roles of English can be conceptualized in different ways depending on the national/regional culture, the historical status of English in that area and the different uses of English inside and outside the classroom. These issues also link to the topic of language management, which refers to the current assumptions about what languages can be used and how, the strategies adopted by teachers and course leaders, and the top-down policies imposed by universities or political authorities. In concrete, practical terms, each academic discipline offers different challenges and opportunities for EMI, and perceives different benefits or threats when EMI is proposed. EMI has to be instantiated within real courses and programmes, and the 'way of doing' EMI will vary according to the academic culture, the norms and conventions of that field. The practices and processes of teaching and assessment within the university, as well as administrative and support systems, also have to readjust to EMI conditions. Changing the language of instructions poses problems for teachers and students alike, and also offers them opportunities to do things differently. Moreover, since in some contexts this change will bring an influx of international students who do not know the local language, other aspects of university life will also have to undergo some adaptations. Of course, in all of this a huge responsibility lies with the agents, especially the teachers, who are the people who will actually put EMI into practice, but also the students themselves, the support staff and the administrators. The final element in this framework addresses the theme of internationalization mentioned earlier as one of the driving forces behind EMI across the world. Interestingly, Dafouz and Smit (2020) suggest that it is important not to think of this only in terms of globalization and homogenization, because local and national forces are also in operation that may tend to counteract or at least complicate EMI, such as the increasing use of regional or minority languages within Europe. They prefer the term 'glocalization' to talk about these tendencies, and insist that universities will always need to remain relevant to the societies in which they are embedded. Although it is far too soon to talk about the inevitable global dominance of English at the expense of all other languages, it is important to consider what the impact of large-scale EMI might be on the other languages in the local ecosystem, thinking particularly of how studying at university in English will affect educated people's knowledge and use of the different languages in their surroundings and attitudes towards them.

1.8 Profile of the EMI teacher

So what kind of content teacher is likely to make progress as an EMI teacher? There is no easy answer to this, because anyone who is a capable and confident lecturer in one language can, with appropriate preparation and language skills, become an excellent lecturer in English. In essence, the same grounding is required for all university teaching: expertise in the subject area, a strong vision of the students' needs and the goals of the particular course in question, an ability to shape the course – and the tasks set for students – in such a way that the specific learning objectives are achieved, and, of course, excellent pedagogical and communicative skills to put all of this into practice. However, in this small section we would also like to suggest some other characteristics or attitudinal factors that would be desirable in an EMI teacher.

Like any other teacher, the content-specialist undertaking EMI must prepare his/her students for life. This apparently fuzzy assertion means that, to foster learner curiosity, and through it self-discovery and autonomous learning, the key to the lifelong-learning mindset demanded today in every society, it is necessary to adopt a student-centred approach. Obvious as this may sound, learner-centred pedagogies are not easy to find in highly specialized teaching contexts (e.g. STEM), outside which disciplinary expertise is difficult to access. Learners, therefore, do not always develop qualities of inquiry, creativity and initiative as might be expected in the humanities, for example. In many STEM settings, teachers usually play the role of expert sources of information rather than facilitators; they do not tend to encourage learning outside the classroom as much as teachers from other disciplines do, and may not start from what students know or integrate knowledge from other fields, literacies and competencies.

Teachers who permanently assume the 'expert role' in their transmission of knowledge and hold the floor during most of the class time or spend it doing calculations on the blackboard understandably fear teaching in another language, as they alone bear the whole discursive weight of the class session. Class dynamics is then normally far from the desirable interactive or Socratic space of dialogue that leads to discussion and critical reflection, as well as from the safe environment where error is merely a learning opportunity. Crammed syllabi and time constraints often favour this kind of absolute class control by lecturers, but in an era when the transmission of knowledge has become more democratic and participative (Stocklmeier 2013), when the agendas of science and technology are jointly set by experts and lay citizens, learners need to be given the opportunity to negotiate meanings and syllabi and perform hands-on task that are as authentic as possible, so as to learn 'by doing'. Student-centred teaching must, in consequence, develop methodologies that are interactive, flexible, practical and collaborative. Recourse to project work, the use of case studies (Dudley-Evans & St. John 1998) and team-teaching with language specialists (Hutchinson & Waters 1987) are steps in that direction.

Higher education teachers, more than ever, should become integrators of knowledge who turn to educate their students into 'knowledge transformers' (English 2011), that is, into professionals able to adapt their expertise to different audiences, goals, disciplinary and national cultures, and communicative situations. To do so, for both outreach and dissemination they will need to shift textual genres competently ('transgenring' in English's terms, 2011) and translate meanings from one mode (aural, visual – pictorial, written, physical) to another, which is known as 'transduction' (Kress 2010). Content specialists are, first and foremost, full-fledged practitioners, members of a 'community of practice' (Wenger 1998) who should show apprentices how to interact in it by extracting and producing meanings across modes, registers and genres and keep track of how they evolve. These three elements form part of what Wenger calls the 'common repertoire' of every professional community (together with tools, concepts, routines and procedures). The other two elements that give professional collectivities a sense of identity are the concepts of 'joint enterprise' (e.g. to troubleshoot and solve technical problems, to explain facts, to preserve health and cure illness, to impart justice) and 'mutual engagement', accomplished through actions such as design, research, calculation, the dissemination of findings or the establishment of relationships with peers. Professionals socialize within their community and outside of it, and need to be equipped with authentic examples of specialist discourse. This equipment concerns not only the control of syntax and lexis (Swales 1988) but also strategies for organizing the information and adjusting it to the circumstances and devices to secure cohesion and coherence.

In light of all the former, content teachers doing EMI should integrate transversal competencies (e.g. communication, critical thinking, creativity, teamwork, intercultural awareness, entrepreneurship, autonomous learning, self-motivation) in the disciplinary topics they teach and not deal with them separately, encourage mutual scaffolding and exchangeable learning roles among students, fostering as many learning styles as possible (e.g. students learning as visualizers, co-thinkers, verbalizers/storytellers, operators). EMI teachers must, in sum, raise curiosity about their community of practice among their students, provide them with the tools necessary to face a changing world in academia and the workplace, help them take on different roles to transform knowledge and keep on learning, and develop a sense of professional identity.

1.9 A New Role for Language Teachers?

Although this book is principally intended for content teachers who are new to EMI, we know that many of them may work alongside language teachers, with whom they may collaborate in different ways and on different levels. Their role has also been called into question by the massive entry of EMI in higher education across the world, and understandably they may sometimes feel threatened by it. However, we take the view that language teachers can actually make a big contribution to ensuring that EMI programmes are successful. However, just like the content teachers, language teachers have to accept that changes are taking place, and that they need to move – and grow – with the times.

On the one hand, since EMI and other factors mean that students are going through university with higher levels of English and better coping skills, English teachers can no longer assume that they will be able to coast through the next ten years teaching intermediate level language classes. In some cases, English teachers need to upgrade their own knowledge and skills, to make sure that they still have something to offer. We see two main fields of action for English teachers on the international university scene:

1. New courses and teaching roles. Qualified and competent English teachers can detect the new needs arising as students come with stronger English skills but also have much more taxing tasks to do in the target language. English teachers should look to the future in terms of providing better, higher-level English for Academic Purposes and English for Specific Purposes courses, which could include tailored modules that will prepare students better for their professional future. The vision of the future should include the aim to become experts in aspects of professional communication.

2. Support for EMI teachers. English teachers are the people who are best equipped in the entire university to fulfil a number of new roles that have emerged with the advent of EMI. Some of these roles are defined by Tatzl (2015, 268): linguistic advisor; provider of materials, resources and reference works; co-creator of learning environments; co-researcher; designer of collaborative teaching and

research; educational innovator; and mediator between different needs and approaches. To this we could add the need for people with good intercultural competences to provide training and support for EMI teachers and for the incoming international students.

In the course of this book, we will examine several of the most prominent roles that English teachers are taking on in the new scenario, and we will see that there is plenty of work for them to do.

1.10 The Baseline: A Practical, Evidence-Based Approach to EMI

Summing up everything we have seen in this chapter, we believe that the way ahead for EMI is to look at what is really happening, and to try to draw conclusions about good practices – always remembering that so many aspects will be context-dependent. In this volume, we will stay away from the controversy about definitions (whether something is CLIL, or immersion, or bilingual), and keep to our knowledge of what teachers actually do in EMI situations. Moreover, our focus is very much on the teaching staff – lecturers, professors, teaching assistants or whatever name we want to give to those people (like us) who are responsible for educating undergraduates and graduate students. Although we know that other players are also important (decision makers, administrative staff, and of course, the students themselves), this book is not specifically directed at them. In this book, then, we aim to draw on a large body of published research, and on our own personal experience of teaching in universities that have undergone processes of internationalization, and of supporting many content teachers along their professional development paths. From this, we intend to pull out the collective experiences of what works – and sometimes the awareness of what does not work. In the next few chapters of this book we will:

- Look at what implementing EMI means in practice for the people who actually teach.

- Take you through a set of good practices for teaching in English.

- Explain techniques for optimizing your interaction with students.

- Address the tricky issue of assignments and assessments in EMI.

- Examine different types of teamwork that can help us develop as EMI teachers.

- Consider strategies for achieving excellence in global settings.

POINTS FOR REFLECTION

1. You have some courses that are not taught wholly in English, but international students are welcome to attend them. The university describes these courses as 'English-friendly' because you are supposed to make some adjustments to facilitate the presence of international students. How English-friendly are the subjects that you teach? You can find out by answering YES or NO in the following questionnaire:

    1. I provide lists of references or bibliographies to those students who want to deepen their knowledge of the topic.

    2. I demand some compulsory readings in English.

    3. I teach in English whenever there are international students in my class.

    4. I teach in the local language but am ready to shift to English whenever my international students ask questions or have difficulties in following the class.

    5. I admit class tasks written or orally presented in either English or the local language.

    6. My 'Teaching/Learning Guidelines' describing my courses and posted online are written both in the local language and in English.

    7. I only teach in the local language because I expect my international students to be proficient enough to follow the course and be participative.

    [1–2 = Not very English-friendly, 3–4 = Sufficiently English-friendly; 5–7 = Very English friendly]

2. In this chapter we have looked at what EMI is – and what it is not. This list of statements hides three 'myths' about EMI. Which are they?

    1. EMI often requires a change of teaching routines.

    2. Fluency in English guarantees good EMI teaching.

    3. Collaborative tasks facilitate EMI.

    4. Content teachers are not linguistic role models.

    5. EMI teaching can be defined as a translation of classroom discourse and learning materials from the first language.

    6. EMI at university has been gradually adopting some elements that have developed in CLIL (Content and Language Integrated Learning) methodologies.

    [Myths: 2, 4, 5]

CHAPTER 2

What Does Implementing EMI Mean in Practice?

2.1 University Teaching in English from the Non-Native-Speaker's Perspective: Personal and Professional Implications

One of the most important points about EMI that many institutions often seem to forget is that EMI – like all teaching – is a very personal question for all of those involved in it. Like all teaching, EMI teaching involves personal dedication, personal development and the acceptance of a personal challenge. It means learning how to take on a number of new roles and play them well. It means undertaking a lengthy preparation, overcoming your nerves, exposing yourself to the risk of misunderstanding, incomprehension, even ridicule. It also means learning from these experiences and developing strategies to do better next time. In short, all teaching is an ongoing personal commitment with major implications for our time, well-being, self-esteem and reputation.

And if all teaching is personal, risky and a huge investment, then EMI teaching is even more personal, even riskier and an even larger investment.

It is *more personal*, because the use of a different language – one that is not our native language or habitual language of professional activity – places significant demands on us. We may feel insecure, vulnerable, even helpless. We become more conscious of our accent. We are frightened of making mistakes. Any insecurity we have about teaching may be compounded by our insecurity as an English user. On top of that, many older people suffer from the sensation that 'younger people speak better English than me', or 'the students know more English than I do'. Although research shows that students do not see things this way, and that accent (for example) rarely has any impact on students' overall evaluation of the course, these self-perceived differences in English skills do sometimes affect teacher confidence and morale (Hellekjaer & Westergaard 2002; Airey 2011).

Teaching in English is therefore *riskier* because, like all new challenges, it makes demands for which we may not be prepared. It puts a strain on our nerves. Some people feel that the confidence and expertise that they have built up over the years as lecturers are suddenly undermined. It is like starting all over again.

All of this means that teaching in English is a huge *investment*. You will have to invest time rethinking and planning your classes, as well as searching for new material (bibliography, resources, videos, case studies). Teachers all over the world have reported that EMI means that they need to invest a much larger amount of time in preparing their courses in the new language (Vinke et al. 1998; Airey 2011; Başıbek et al. 2014). They sometimes offer a larger amount of obligatory reading, or prepare more visual or interactive teaching material (Doiz et al. 2012), and all of this is a lot of work. In some circumstances, universities may reduce the teaching load for people involved in EMI, but in others it is simply not practical to do this.

Many people also feel that they need to dedicate time to studying and practising English, not to mention cultivating their international contacts in order to arrange exchanges, study visits and longer research stays.

It all seems like a huge amount of work! So before we start looking at concrete measures that we can take, it is very important to be clear about *why we are doing this* in the first place. We have seen some of the usual reasons why institutions move to EMI in Chapter 1. But which of those reasons is important in our setting? Once we understand this better, we will start to comprehend our own position in this more deeply.

To get a grip on this situation, it would be a good idea to take a look at **Worksheet 2.1: Understanding Our Own Setting**. This will help us to reflect on what we know about the situation in our own university and country.

It will also help us to get a clear overview of why we are doing this, think about the challenges (not just challenges for *us* but also challenges for our *students*, and for the *institution* as a whole), and also to write a wish list of things we would like to see our institution do to support this change.

Once we have understood our own setting better, we will come to see that it is not all loss, just as it is not all gain. It could be that our own EMI programme is just part of the minor adjustments being made so that our own students can take part in Erasmus exchanges. But perhaps our institution is under enormous pressure to compete in the global market for international students. Or perhaps our institution is highly motivated by the knowledge that its graduates will have a better chance in the job market if they are used to working in English. Or maybe the change to EMI is part of a regional or national language policy. It might help to think that we all play our small part in a large-scale transformation that is under way. We are not personally in the spotlight – we are simply in the same situation as everyone else.

In the rest of this chapter, we will take a look at what we can learn from the experiences of people who have already made the transition to EMI. What changes, and what actually stays the same, when we start teaching our courses in English? How should we go about rethinking our teaching? What support are our students likely to need? And how does all of this fit in the global picture of a world that is transitioning to multilingual higher education?

* * *

WORKSHEET 2.1: UNDERSTANDING OUR OWN SETTING

1. Why are we doing EMI?

Write down four reasons why your university started to give some courses in English. Then compare what you have written with a partner.

2. What are the main challenges of EMI?

For the teachers?
For the students?
For the institution (university, faculty, department)?

3. In an ideal world, how should your institution support the change to EMI?

Training
Resources
Recognition of extra work
Other

4. Does the change to EMI mean any advantages for you personally?

Developing as a teacher
Developing as an academic on the international stage
Making international contacts
Broadening your horizons as a person
Other

2.2 Starting to Lecture in English. Taking Feelings Seriously

When EMI started up in Spain, we became aware that a lot of university teachers welcomed this change – but a lot of others were quite worried about what would happen and how it would affect them. To find out more about the way people experienced this major transition in their working lives, we carried out a survey of sixty university EMI teachers at five different universities here in Spain, in which we asked them to narrate their experiences of starting EMI, and to respond to a number of questions (Breeze & Roothooft 2018; Roothooft 2019). We found several typical patterns in the way these university professors experienced the change to EMI.

In one part of our research, we asked the university EMI teachers how they felt when they first learnt that they were going to be teaching in English, and how they felt now. In Table 2.1, their 'before' and 'after' responses are set out for you to compare.

Typical experiences

- *I felt afraid, but now I feel better*

By far the most typical response across the sixty people we talked to went more or less like this:

BEFORE: I felt afraid.
NOW: Now I feel better but still somewhat insecure.

What conclusions can we draw from this? For all the reasons we have discussed, almost everyone is nervous before they start. A large number of the people we talked to mentioned experiencing negative emotions when they were told that they would be doing EMI. They felt: nervous, worried, scared, overwhelmed.

TABLE 2.1 How Did You Feel before Starting EMI, and How Do You Feel about It Now?

When I first knew that I would be teaching in EMI, . . .	Now that I have been doing EMI for some time, . . .
'I felt very scared and I tried to overcome it.'	'I feel a little bit more comfortable but I need to spend a lot of time preparing my lectures.'
'I felt worried about my students! Frightened of the theory class, not of the practical class, because there you can talk, you can draw it if they don't understand.'	'Now I feel more confident. And I know that the students understand. And I know I know more than them, because I know all the terminology. Maybe they are bilingual but they don't know the subject, the words. And of course, the sources I use are in English, so it should be easier. When I was teaching *Instalaciones* I was worried because I know the students don't like this subject. It is not attractive. Lifts, heating systems. They like design, space . . . So I knew I had to work hard to make it attractive.'
'I felt nervous. I knew that I was able to have a conversation in English, but explaining a difficult concept in English is different.'	'Now I feel more or less comfortable. After some years lecturing in English I now know that I am able to communicate and that almost everybody can understand my explanations.'
'I felt interested, because that could be a serious experience for me, so consolidating my level of knowledge of English language in a way that is full of responsibility.'	'Now I feel as if it were a totally normal activity for me.'
'When I first knew about this, I felt overwhelmed but I felt it as a challenge (even an opportunity to improve my English).'	'Now I feel the same, better little by little (more confident).'
'I felt scared and overwhelmed, but also excited.'	'Now I feel still not terribly confident, but mostly ok about it.'
'When I first knew about this, I felt over overwhelmed preparing the notes in English.'	'Now I feel more comfortable, but delivering in English is still a challenge and it takes more time and energy.'
'Frightened!'	'Well, comfortable is not the correct word, but at least I am not frightened.'
'When I first knew about this, I felt that I lack confidence in my level of English and I studied a lot about the issues. I did a lot of work and I was really tired after giving the lectures.'	'Now I feel much more confident. I even can feel relaxed and tell jokes.'

But the very same people, after they had been doing EMI for a period of time, felt much better about it. They mentioned feeling: more comfortable, more confident, more relaxed and, in some cases, even happy.

It is clear that for most people, the pattern goes like this:

Phase One: You are told that you will be teaching in English. You feel worried. You lack confidence. But since you know that your professional future depends on this, you start making preparations.

Phase Two: You teach a course in English. You find out that it is not as difficult as you had feared. You start to see that your English is good enough to talk about the subjects you know well. You also realize that you still know more than your students. But you may experience momentary difficulties, such as when misunderstandings occur in the classroom, or when issues come up with particular students (e.g. because they feel that they are more fluent at English than you are).

Phase Three: You have been teaching EMI courses for some years. You have learnt how to deal with all the difficulties that come up, and you are starting to enjoy yourself. You have even started to incorporate some new jokes and anecdotes that work well in English with an international audience. You realize that EMI teaching in a globalized setting is not the same as teaching in your own language to a group of native speakers – it still occasionally takes you out of your comfort zone – but in general you are satisfied that you can meet this challenge well. Perhaps most importantly of all, you now feel that you truly belong to the international academic community!

- *Building confidence*

If we look more carefully at the people who said they felt better about teaching in English now, we can see that the changes are not just about becoming a better teacher, or about getting used to the new scenario. In fact, one of the most important aspects of these changes is the way your confidence increases as you gain more experience. One teacher answered:

BEFORE: When I first knew about this, in 2009, I felt ok. But I was afraid I wouldn't understand the questions that the students ask.
NOW: In fact, I still don't understand the questions. But now I feel confident, and when I don't understand the questions I ask the students to repeat them. I don't worry about doing that.

We can see that the teacher feels that he still does not understand the questions, but that this does not undermine his self-assurance. He no longer feels that he needs to have perfect English comprehension skills to cope with all the different accents that his students speak with. He has simply decided to be practical – and to toss the ball back into the students' court. If he does not understand what they say, then he asks them to repeat it or rephrase it!

> BEFORE: When I first knew about this, I felt worried because I knew I had to prepare a lot. I prepared the first classes a lot and so they were quite boring!
>
> AFTER: Now I feel more relaxed, my classes are more dynamic. In fact, in English I am more colloquial, more interactive, I have more 'banter' with the students than in Spanish. Perhaps that's because the English group is smaller.

- *My students don't respond as I hoped*

However, if you did not identify strongly with the general trends identified earlier, there is no need to worry. A lot depends on your own personality, and on your previous experiences of learning and teaching. One idea that came up several times in our research was: "My students don't respond as I hoped".

At first we did not know exactly how to interpret this comment, so we asked a few more questions to find out what was happening. One of the people we interviewed reported an experience of disillusionment with EMI:

> BEFORE I felt empowered.
>
> AFTER: Now I feel disappointed because the students don't follow my classes well. The students don't ask questions. They don't respond when I ask them. I think they don't have a good level in English.

In this case, the lecturer in question had started out in EMI in what was seemingly the most promising way: he had just got back from a few years in the United States, where he had been researching and teaching at a prestigious university. He felt very enthusiastic about being able to put his skills and experience into practice. So what went wrong? The local students were quite different from the students he had in the United States. His flawless accent and excellent fluency made him a confident teacher – but most of what he said in the classroom went over the students' heads. Most importantly of all, he did not factor the local students' intermediate level of English into the equation. The students felt intimidated by his dynamic teaching style, and by his fast speed of delivery. When he adopted the strategy of shooting out questions at his listeners, which had worked so well at an elite institution in the United States, the local students were confused, embarrassed and even frightened.

All in all, this EMI venture started out with great promise, but it failed because of a lack of adaptation on both sides. This lecturer needed to stop what he was doing, take stock of the situation and think out some ways of teaching his courses differently – factoring in the students' comprehension difficulties and lack of confidence. Some of the strategies this teacher could use to address these problems can be found in the section on 'providing support for students' later on in this chapter, and also in Chapter 3.

- *All my students are local!*

One of the teachers we talked to pointed to an important issue in his setting which many of us can easily imagine:

> It doesn't feel so natural for me to do EMI because my class is nearly all Spanish speaking students, with one Ukrainian Erasmus student, one Filipino.

If this reflects our own setting – a 95 per cent proportion of local students – then maybe it helps to try to see this in a wider perspective. We are somewhere in the early stages of the transition to a more international higher education system. Our students may not have the C1 level of English that would be desirable for academic purposes. But our students are young, they have potential, and we can help them on their journey. By encouraging them to work on their English and use it in your classes, you will be doing them a big favour.

And of course, depending on your university's language policy, it may be that we can sometimes use our L1 in the classroom too – always showing courtesy to international students. In a plurilingual world, it has to be acceptable to communicate in different languages. If you feel your students would benefit from some bibliography in their L1, or from a glossary where you provide bilingual wordlists or explanations of key terms, or from an occasional session given in the L1, this is unlikely to do them any harm. But exactly what you do is up to you, and has to be sensitive to context (for instance, see Chen et al. 2020, for an example of how EMI teachers systematically draw on the shared L1 in China). In our own sample, one extremely experienced, fluent and confident teacher felt that he should not be providing explanations in the L1, but he was also frustrated at the students' unresponsive behaviour when he taught in English, which left him wondering whether they had got the ideas that he was trying to teach – or not! We first suggested that he should provide summaries in the L1, and he felt that this was not appropriate. But then, the idea came up of spending five minutes at the end of each class asking the students themselves to summarize the contents back to him in the L1, using the notes they had taken. For this teacher, this solution seemed to be the most acceptable option – and when he applied it, it helped to bridge the communicative gap between him and his less confident students.

- *It is easier to teach my course in English*

We also found quite a few very positive responses, in which people found that the EMI experience brought many advantages. These included the greater availability of material (particularly multimedia material) for use in the classes or for setting work outside the classroom.

One teacher from the department of statistics answered as follows:

> I thought it would be difficult, because statistics is a subject that most students find hard. But in fact, I found that it is actually easier to teach statistics in English than in Spanish. There is a huge amount of teaching material available, and all the programs we use are basically in English. I have also found some backup videos in which different people explain statistical principles and methods. My students download the material and take it away, so I know they have got it even if they haven't understood the classes.

Several people commented that their own course worked well in English because 'it is natural to teach science/medicine/business in English' (see Roothooft 2019). This could be because most of the research is published in English, or because there is a better range of up-to-date textbooks in English, or because most of the terminology for that course is derived from English. So it is worth asking yourself if this applies to your own subject. Is your course a 'natural' subject to teach in English? Why might it be particularly useful for your students to get used to working on your subject in English?

- *It's more work to teach in English*

Among the sixty people we talked to, a fair number of them felt that the first year of EMI was uphill work, not least because they had to prepare all of their classes again. In fact, there is a consensus in the bibliography that teaching in a new language at any level places a greater demand on teachers' time (Dafouz et al. 2007; Vinke et al. 1998), at least at first. In fact, some universities actually factor this extra preparation time into the professors' contracts, allowing them to give fewer classes if they are teaching in English – but of course, this may not be practicable in all contexts. The good news is that the extra burden gets lighter over the years, as you build up experience and gain more confidence. However, some people, like this respondent, will always feel that teaching in English is more demanding than using the L1:

> BEFORE: When I first knew about this, I felt over overwhelmed preparing the notes in English.
> AFTER: Now I feel more conformable, but delivering in English is still a challenge and it takes more time and energy.

- *Overwhelmingly positive*

After all this, it is very important to emphasize that for some of the people we talked to, the transition to EMI has been an overwhelmingly positive experience:

BEFORE: When I first knew about this, I felt a little insecure because I was afraid that the quality of my lectures would not be as good as those taught in Spanish.

AFTER: I am convinced now that I am as good a professor in English as in Spanish.

- *Be ready to learn*

Whatever your initial reaction, it is clear that the experience of starting EMI is never exactly what you think it is going to be like. But remember that for many people, changing the language of instruction actually provides a good opportunity to question their teaching practices, rethink their priorities, internationalize their material and case studies, learn new methods and so on. In other words, it is a wonderful opportunity to become even better at what you do.

2.3 Starting to Lecture in English. What Do You Change, What Stays the Same?

So far we have talked about the way people feel when they start teaching in English, and about how their feelings evolved during the first few years of this experience. But what about their actual approach to teaching? We have seen that some people regard the transition to EMI as a way of renewing their courses, refreshing their approach, updating their material and becoming better teachers. Is this always the case? There is a certain amount of research that suggests that people's approach to teaching changes when they have to teach in a different language. But is that really true?

We asked the EMI teachers in our own sample how they thought their teaching had changed when they made the move to English. Their answers seemed to fall into two categories: the people who thought that the experience of teaching was basically the same in both languages, and the people who felt that there were some important differences.

- *What changes do you make when you teach in English?*

Everyone agrees that a number of changes take place when we start to give our classes in English. For example, Airey and Linder (2006) found that students asked fewer questions and had more difficulties taking notes when the class was in English. Some teachers had the impression that their EMI classes were less entertaining or less spontaneous, or that they were less capable of engaging in discussions or interacting with students (Airey 2011; Fortanet-Gómez 2012; Westbrook & Henriksen 2011). Tatzl (2011) explicitly mentions that some teachers report using fewer jokes! Other studies found that lecturers felt less capable of providing feedback on student work in EMI than when teaching in the shared L1 (Uys et al. 2007). Finally, the actual amount of material covered may be less in EMI than in the local language: in an empirical study, Thøgersen and Airey (2011) found that one EMI physics lecturer took longer to communicate the same message in English than in his native Danish, and his lecturing style was more formal and more repetitive.

These differences may not hold in the same way for everyone, though. There seem to be some different patterns in the experience of moving to EMI. For example, earlier studies also sometimes suggested that younger lecturers had fewer problems when moving over to EMI than older ones (Jensen & Thøgersen 2011), but it is likely that it is the amount of experience using English professionally, rather than the actual biological age of the lecturer, that is the determining factor here. Pointing to a rather more pervasive pattern, Kuteeva and Airey (2014) established that science lecturers accepted the move to EMI more easily than their humanities counterparts. At the same time, Roothooft (2019) found that humanities lecturers were more likely to feel the need to change their style of teaching when they moved to EMI, while professionals from science, engineering and technology often stated that they were not aware of requiring any changes in their teaching methodology. In fact, it is quite obvious that the experience of EMI is going to be different across disciplines, for two main reasons.

1. Some university courses are highly numbers-focused, with an emphasis on problems and/or equations, and with very little discursive language. Other courses may put language in the foreground, with lecturer performance – and student grades – determined by each person's discursive abilities and rhetorical skills. In the words of Kuteeva and Airey, subjects such as natural sciences tend to rely on a shared terminology, while in the humanities 'language serves as the means to construct knowledge and is therefore used in a more flexible and creative manner' (Kuteeva & Airey 2014, 538).

2. It is also clear that some university subjects are broadly similar across the world, while others are deeply embedded in a particular culture (Roothooft 2019). It is quite clearly not the same to teach physiology in English and to teach German law or Chinese history in English! It is obvious that the human body varies rather little from one country to another (and the terms used in English generally have direct equivalents in other languages). Legal and historical concepts, however, are embedded in cultures, and the vocabulary needed to talk about a particular aspect may simply not be available in English.

Here are some of the responses that the teachers in our own study gave when we asked them about how their approach to teaching had changed as a result of EMI:

In English I cover less material, but I stick to the point:

> I seem to go more slowly and cover less content than in the Spanish group.

> I use shorter sentences, my slides are simpler – I go straight to the point. In Spanish I perhaps talk too much!

> When giving lessons in Spanish I used to speak faster, but while when I did EMI I waited for students to understand what I was saying.

In English I am clearer, more organized:

> I think I change my style of teaching when I do EMI. My classes are clearer, more schematic. More visual.

In English I can take advantage of excellent international material for my course:

> I can use better means – the quality of the available books in English is much better than in Spanish, and there are some very nice videos.

> I think I change my style of teaching when I do EMI. Here are some examples: I have followed all the procedures used to teach a subject in an American University: developing a virtual course, adding many videos related to the subject, different syllabus and assessment systems.

The EMI groups have more highly motivated students:

> Since the features of English and Spanish groups (especially regarding size of the groups and motivation of the students) are very different, the way the class develops is different. It is easier to provide closer explanations and evaluations to the English class students because they are fewer, so at the end, to get in contact with all of them easily.

> The English group is smaller and they participate more.

In English I am less spontaneous:

> I have more subtlety in Spanish. In English I don't have so many possibilities, nuances. In English I stick to the script more.

> In Spanish I feel more comfortable, more natural. I can tell anecdotes in a more spontaneous way.

> When I teach in English the environment in the class is colder.

What Stays the Same When You Teach in English?

Of course, although almost everyone mentions some changes when they go over to EMI, there are still a lot of aspects that stay the same despite the change in the language of delivery – and that will probably always stay the same whatever we do!

Some people believe that even though there may be changes in the way we communicate with students, it is important to keep the contents of the course, including tasks and exams, exactly the same in English as in the local language. In some cases, there may be institutional or even legal pressure to make sure that this is the case:

> There is no change: Macroeconomics IV (International Economics) in English is fully replicated as *Macroeconomía IV (Economía Internacional)* in Spanish. Slides, homework, practice evaluations, mid-term exam, final exam and retake exam are all identical.

Other people make the point that the intrinsic difficulties of the subject they teach are in no way altered by the change in the language of instruction:

> I think it stays the same – the main problem my students have is the problem that mathematics is difficult! The English language doesn't make any difference to this.

But even if we do everything the same way, there is still a difference, because not everything depends on the teacher:

> I use the same contents, same style, same jokes. Same jokes – but sometimes the students don't laugh!

What Can We Learn from All This?

So just by way of conclusion, we can see that some things change – and some things really do stay the same. But on a positive note, we can see that some of these lecturers found that starting EMI gave them an impulse to reinvigorate their approach to teaching. The following example illustrates how one lecturer completely altered his approach to giving classes – and how he realizes that this has had a positive impact. After becoming a more innovative teacher in EMI (e.g. using more multimedia resources, or applying techniques associated with the 'flipped classroom'), he has come to the conclusion that this is what he should do in all his classes, including those taught in Spanish.

> I think I change my style of teaching when I do EMI. I tend to use videos more frequently, and make them available so that the students can watch them several times; I tend to 'invert' the class more frequently: the students have to read the material in advance, so that they have a first contact with the English technical words before we see them in class; I tend to go more slowly, and to repeat the same content in several ways; I use images, pictures, gestures . . . to complement my voice. Nevertheless, I suspect that these are good practices in any case, and I am incorporating them into my Spanish classes also.

This brings out a point that has often been emphasized by researchers who study the implementation of content teaching in English at school level

– moving to a different language leads us to challenge the way we have been teaching, reach out for new media and methods, and introduce more effective strategies for getting the message across.

2.4 Common Fears and Myths

Reading between the lines of what we have already seen in this chapter, there are some fears that a lot of people share – and some myths that need to be exploded.

One typical fear usually goes along the following lines:

The students all speak English better than I do!

But we have seen that this is really just a question of confidence. Perhaps some of them are native speakers of English, which would give them a certain advantage – but that's not the point! This is not a language competition, or a proficiency exam! They certainly don't know as much about your subject as you do – that's why you are the teacher, and they are the students! As far as speaking is concerned, the most important factor is the EMI teacher's own role as a competent, confident L2 English user. A good EMI teacher can become an important role model for his or her students. He or she may also sometimes have to struggle to understand students, but if he/she deals tactfully with breakdowns in communication, this also sets a good example and could encourage other students to participate. We all know that the students who are used to communicating in English often play a leading role in asking questions or making comments – but it is important that less vocal students should also gradually come to feel confident enough to play a more active part in the class. By understanding their fears and behaving in a supportive way, we can help our students overcome their difficulties with this.

Another typical myth that circulates when we discuss this issue with EMI teachers comes from the opposite perspective. Here is the sort of thing that people sometimes say when they are told they are going to teach their classes (of whatever specialized subject) in English:

So now I have to become an English teacher!

The answer to this is that you are a content teacher, and your job is to teach your subject, through the language that has been decided. Your role is *not* to teach students English grammar, or to correct their use of prepositions. 'But it is not so clear', you might say. 'I do need to teach them the terminology of my subject.' True, but of course, you would do that in your local language too. 'So do I have to correct their English when they write, or grade the language they use in their exams?' This is a complex question. The easy answer is that you could factor the students' communicative capacity or writing style into the grade that you give, much the same way as you would if they were performing the same writing tasks in, say, Spanish. But there is no need to go into more detail, or to provide detailed correction and feedback addressing all their language problems. We will see more about this in Chapter 5, but for the moment, the answer is: if you are afraid about having to take on a new identity, don't worry, you don't have to become an English teacher!

Finally, one myth that often circulates is that the EMI classes somehow have to be exactly the same as the ones you give on the same subject in your first language. From everything we have seen so far, it is clear that the answer is: no! The change in language of delivery triggers a chain of developments affecting the material you use, the way you relate to students, the way students communicate with you, the way that you evaluate them, and so on. So rather than trying to produce a perfect replica of the classes you give in English, look upon the change to EMI as an invitation to do something new!

To put it all together, here is a diagram that might help you to visualize the development of EMI teachers' cognition (Figure 2.1), modelled loosely on Borg (2006). Before you start EMI, your development as a lecturer (in the middle) has mainly progressed through the top-right bubble (training and experience as a content specialist) and the bottom rectangle (contextual factors and classroom experiences). It is clear that both of these aspects influence your development as a lecturer. But now, a new factor has been introduced, namely the left-hand bubble (experience of learning and using English, including your beliefs about language learning). In

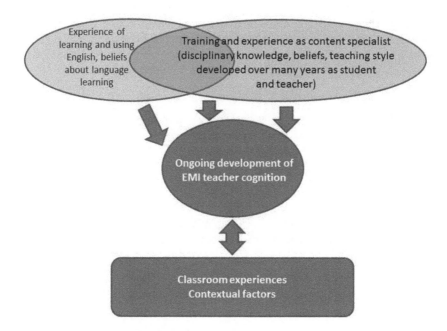

FIGURE 2.1 *Model of EMI teacher cognition.*

part, this bubble overlaps with your professional training and experience (you probably read professional literature in English, communicate with colleagues from other countries in English, publish in English, etc.). But now that we have added this bubble to the 'mixture', the diagram has become more complicated. Your teaching will still grow as a result of interaction between your disciplinary training and experience and your classroom experience – but English is now part of the mix! Any major new factor (like the introduction of a new technology, say) is likely to destabilize your classroom practice for a while. So it will be important to think about how your ideas about English, and about language learning and language use, may have an impact on your cognition, and how these may interact with your classroom experiences or affect your teaching style. But remember that the part that is developing is the 'you' in the middle. This will be a product of the interaction between all these different elements – but you also have free will and agency to determine how far each one of these is going to be a negative influence that holds you back, or a positive influence that takes your teaching forward.

WORKSHEET 2.2: TEACHING IN ENGLISH: GOOD PRACTICES

From all the things we have seen so far, we can already start to draw some conclusions. And one of these conclusions is there is no 'one fits all' solution – just a set of ideas and principles that can inspire us to become better EMI teachers. Here is a list of 'good practices' identified by people in different institutions. Which ones do you agree with? Which ones have worked for you?

1. Provide English-language tuition for university teachers.

2. Organize courses and seminars for university teachers, to help them to improve their teaching skills and adapt their style of teaching to the new situation.

3. Encourage the teachers to provide more written information and make the PowerPoints available to their students.

4. Get someone to video classes/lectures, and then analyse the video later. It will help the teacher to see what is really happening in the class, and to solve problems next time round.

5. Suggest that teachers should give the students a glossary of key terminology that they are going to use in the course.

6. If the students seem not to understand the teacher, tell him/her to offer a summary of the class in the local language at the end.

7. If a faculty member is going to teach in English, send him/her on a teaching exchange to another country for a while.

8. If a faculty member is going to teach a course in English, that course will count 1.5 times its credit weighting on that person's contract (e.g. teaching 30 hours in English is equivalent to teaching 45 hours in Italian/Spanish/Chinese).

9. Distribute the Erasmus students across different groups/classes. This will force the local students to speak English.

10. Put the Erasmus students together in a separate class, so that they do not disturb the local students, and so that the 'problem' of offering courses in English can be dealt with efficiently.

Can you add at least two more good practices to this list?

11.

12.

WORKSHEET 2.3: TEACHING IN ENGLISH: CHALLENGES

Just as we can learn from some good practices that other people have recorded, we can also take note of some challenges that are frequently mentioned in the contact of EMI. Here are some challenges mentioned by the people in our study who had been teaching in English for a while. Can you add to the list with challenges that people have mentioned at your institution? How can they address these challenges in a positive way?

1. 'I feel that the students don't understand me. But they don't come to consult me, probably because they are afraid of having to speak English.'

2. 'I want to get them to write lab reports in English, but I am worried about doing this, because even in Spanish they have lots of problems with writing reports.'

3. 'Students don't pay attention to each other's presentations.'

4. 'I don't know how to grade students' work. I don't know to what extent their communication skills need to be taken into account.'

What were the biggest challenges when your university first started to give courses in English?

And now?

2.5 Setting Priorities: Rethinking Your Teaching

Since most EMI lecturers have already been lecturing in their L1 for some time (maybe for many years), and they are always working as part of a system (a degree course, a national education system, an educational culture), it is not our intention here to explain university teaching from scratch. We know that you know your subject and your students, and we know that you have plenty of practical experience about what works and what is needed when you are teaching in the first language that you share with your students. If anything, we hope here to provide you with some rules of thumb that will help you make the tricky transition from where you are now to successful EMI. So the ideas we include here are intended to prompt some straightforward thinking about how to rethink your teaching in the EMI context, and how to go about preparation in a practical way.

All good teaching needs to be carefully thought out and well planned, and EMI is no exception. So when you set out on the adventure of EMI, one of the first things you have to do is revisit the aims of your course. Perhaps these are set out in terms of formal 'learning outcomes' (see Chapter 5 for more details on this). Perhaps they are expressed more traditionally in the form of a 'Course Programme' with a list of the topics to be covered. Or perhaps they are just embedded in the notes and PowerPoints that you use for your lectures. Perhaps the truth is that essential aspects of our course are somehow woven into all of these things, and there are moments when we find it hard to separate them!

But before we start to make preparations for EMI, it would be a good idea for us to sit down with a piece of paper (or the electronic equivalent) in front of us, and just write down what we intend our students to have by the time they finish our course. The following straightforward scheme can be useful to follow:

- What are the aims of the broader degree programme that your students are taking?

- What are the main competences they are supposed to acquire?

- What are the objectives of your specific course, and how do they fit into the overall design of the degree?

- What competences do you focus on in your course?

- What do your students need most in order to benefit from your course?

- What is the 'take away'; that is, what will the students know, or be able to do, when they finish your course, that they do not know or cannot do now?

- How might the use of English in the classroom affect the way you pursue your course objectives and define the students' learning outcomes?

If we have these points clear in our minds, it will help us to set priorities for our EMI course, at least the first time that we give it. So just as an exercise, we need to start by writing down the 'take away' – what the students will know and be able to do by the end of our course – and then take a few minutes to jot down the different elements of our course that will ultimately come together to enable them to know/do that.

Once we have these two points, we can look at what we usually do in the course when we teach it in our L1, and start to think of ways of prioritising (see also Chapter 5 for more details on this). Some of the things we teach may not be essential – or even particularly relevant – to the actual aims of the course. They may have crept in there over the years, because we liked them, or because we thought the students would like them, or because we needed to fill space (!). So now the time has come to do some spring-cleaning. One of the lessons that EMI research has taught us is that at least at the beginning, EMI courses tend to advance more slowly (either because of greater difficulty with the language or because international groups are more heterogeneous and it is not possible for us to take the students' previous knowledge base for granted in the same way as we do with local students). We should treat this apparent reduction in the course contents positively, because it also means that we will have slightly less material to cover, and thus rather less preparation to do, than if we just try to reproduce our L1 course in English in its entirety.

So now we have a description of the aims of the course, and a list of the essential contents. We should take a long, hard look at these, and at the material we use to teach them. If we are setting readings in the L1, we should look for readings in English – this is also a good opportunity to bring the material up to date. It might be a good idea to keep the L1 readings in a separate file, to give to any students who are having difficulties with the volume of content in English. If we are using multimedia material in the L1, we can easily find similar multimedia contents in English: there is an abundance of videos, podcasts, interactive exercises, and so on, available in English on the internet, and much of it is open access. This search for new, English-language material will have the additional effect of enabling us to update and internationalize our course: now that we are not limited to our L1, it will make more sense to use a wider variety of international examples in our classes, and to draw on readings, videos and other material from different countries. This will not only help us to connect with an increasingly international audience – it will also make us, as researchers and teachers, more aware of what is happening in our field in the wider world, which will in turn have positive effects on our development as academics and researchers.

Then, once we have located enough material (readings, videos, audios, etc.) we need to turn to the actual material we have developed ourselves for our courses. If we rely on PowerPoints in the L1, we need to redo our most important PowerPoints in English. 'Redoing' the PowerPoints does not necessarily mean translating them, because when we prepare for EMI we need to think about the priorities of our (new) course, and also about the specific challenges that students are going to face when they take our course in English. This might include consideration of the difficulty of technical vocabulary in English, for example, which means that we need to consider seriously how we are going to provide support for our students with this (e.g. by providing a glossary, recommending a dictionary, or devoting more time early in the course to helping the students master key terminology).

Once we start EMI, it is important, also, to be honest and realistic, and to reflect on our practice in a positive spirit. One way to do this is to make a plan for each class, and then take notes after each session. This kind of 'teaching diary' is a useful tool that can help us to optimize our EMI courses, and to build up our confidence as EMI teachers. Once we have given the course once, we can revisit the content matter, material and PowerPoints again, take a look at our notes and adjust the material, timing and overall plan if necessary. We can think about which aspects or sections of the course went well, and which did not. We can reflect on why we, personally, found one particular aspect or element of the course more difficult than the others. And we can try to do the same for our students, by taking stock of the parts of the course that caused them most difficulties, with a view to factoring in more support for future students in these areas.

2.6 Providing Support for Students

In all of this, there is a certain danger that we will become obsessed with our own problems and identity as teachers, and not reflect enough about what our students really need. Despite all the myths about how 'young people all speak English perfectly' and 'teenagers all leave school with a high level of English', we saw in Chapter 1 that a large proportion of the young people signing up for EMI courses at university do not have the C1 level of English competence that would be desirable. Many of them may even fall short of a functional B2 competence.

Thinking on an institutional level, then, we can imagine that universities, faculties/schools or departments should try to factor in some types of support for the students on EMI programmes. Of course, this is an institutional decision, rather than something that should be left to individual teachers – not least because it requires a different range of competences and skills from those of the EMI content lecturers. Nonetheless, EMI teachers should have an overview of the kind of support that should be on offer, so that they understand their own role as part of a complex system.

First of all, since our students are not all proficient English users, it is likely that some of them would truly appreciate more help with the language. Often they have opted to take a degree with a large EMI component in the hope that this will help them to improve their English, and they find the experience of EMI rather frustrating in this respect. Occasionally, our students may not have made an active decision to take EMI courses – they may have entered the degree programme and then discovered to their alarm that the EMI component is obligatory. Such students may feel overwhelmed, or perhaps annoyed. In other cases, the students we encounter may be international students – exchange students who are with us for one or two semesters, or students who are going to take their entire degree programme at our university. These international students may find living in your country exciting and studying at your university stimulating – or they may not! In their case, issues of intercultural communication, knowledge of other languages (i.e. the local language), educational styles and personality are all major factors that can affect their experience.

In all of this, there is no 'right' answer about what support the university should provide for students. But we can make some reasonable assumptions about the needs that the different groups will have.

At the very least, the *local students* should be given support to raise their general level of English language, and to acquire the academic and specific professional language skills that they will need to be successful in their course. Many universities increase the language learning provision made for students by offering general language courses, Academic English courses taught across a range of degree programmes or focused English for Specific Purposes courses for students within one degree programme. It is also a good idea for lecturers to provide their local students with references to useful resources, such as online dictionaries or encyclopaedias, textbooks and other subject-related materials in internet or the university library.

The *international students* may also appreciate support with English language and disciplinary language. It is not true that 'people from outside our country speak English perfectly'. In fact, other countries' education systems may lag behind our own in terms of English-language competence. However, international students also have some special needs. They should be given the opportunity to equip themselves in order to get by in the local language. They are also very young, and often away from home for the first time. So they also need proper induction courses in which your university system (courses, evaluation, facilities etc.) is explained to them, and they are given an introduction to the local culture. They will also benefit from having a range of resources – from local 'buddies' who can help them if they need it, and explain things from the student's point of view, to events designed specially for international students where they can meet people in the same situation as themselves.

2.7 Understanding the Development/ Empowerment of EMI Teachers

Sometimes people talk about EMI as though it were an isolated phenomenon, something happening just in their own classes. But we have seen that it is part of a much wider trend across much of the world. It is also important to think of EMI on the meso-level, that is, not the micro-level of your class, or the macro-level of education in Europe, but the 'in-between' level at which different institutions establish plans for incorporating EMI as part of their internationalization strategy. Academics worldwide often complain that they have had insufficient support and training for EMI (Mancho-Bares & Arnó Macià 2017). But what kind of support and training do you need? And how could these be put into place without straining resources that are already scarce?

Think about your own institution. How do you see that it is implementing EMI in the:

- Short term?

- Medium term?

- Long term?

One example could be:

- **Short term**: English-language training for teaching staff and administrative staff. Erasmus+ exchanges for teachers and administrative staff, in order to explore how universities work in other countries. More general and specific language courses for local students, with the particular aim of selecting some local students with a good B2 level to go on one-semester Erasmus exchanges. Designing and launching a few specific EMI courses in key schools (business management, engineering, education), with volunteer lecturers who have an international background, with a view to setting up Erasmus exchanges with neighbouring countries. Monitoring the progress of EMI courses, and interviewing teachers and students involved to learn more about what goes well and what can be improved.

- **Medium term**: Moving towards a larger EMI component in key degree programmes with an obvious international dimension: for example, establishing a degree in economics taught 50 per cent in English. Setting up a pilot MA/MSc programme taught entirely in English, in a subject in which your university has a number of prestigious experts who are happy to teach in English. Since this MA/MSc will be open to students from all over the world, this means exploring ways of publicizing this programme far beyond your usual catchment area. Discussing/negotiating entry criteria for students applying for these different (undergraduate and graduate) programmes. Organizing certification processes to ensure that students will be able to demonstrate that they have taken courses taught in English. Setting up a training programme for a large group of future EMI teachers. Encouraging this group to discuss the preparations for EMI with people already involved in it, and arranging for them to participate in Erasmus+ exchanges. Arranging Erasmus exchanges for large numbers of students. Identifying areas in which EMI is going to bring added value to your university in the future, and making plans to implement EMI in these areas.

- **Long term**: Rolling out EMI across a range of Schools and degree programmes as planned earlier. Publicizing these programmes, and monitoring them closely during the first years of implementation. Setting up regular exchange programmes for students on these degree courses, and for university teachers involved in them. Continuing to provide appropriate English-language support to both groups where required, and organizing appropriate linguistic and cultural support for incoming students. Building a structure to enable young academics (PhD students, teaching assistants and young professors) to spend at least two years abroad, preferably in universities where English is a working language (not necessarily in the English-speaking world), so that they acquire a more international outlook, learn intercultural skills, build a network of contacts and identify good practices that could be implemented when they return home.

On a final note, and without wanting to add to the complexity of this panorama, we would also like to point to some of the additional skills that EMI teachers need to have or acquire in the course of their preparation. Räsänen and Klaassen (2006) conducted an in-depth study of teachers transitioning to EMI, not just from the perspective of what the teachers need to know and do but also taking into consideration their communicative and pedagogical skills. Their list of 'new' abilities and skills needed by EMI teachers are not really 'new' in EMI – reflective teachers probably have acquired them over the years in the non-EMI classroom – but they take on new importance in EMI contexts. Their list includes:

- being able to assess the language demands/requirements of the discipline one is teaching, and knowing how to help the students achieve these.
- being aware of one's own teaching style, and knowing how to adapt it to new circumstances (e.g. EMI).
- knowing how to structure and communicate content in such a way that comprehension and processing are possible at different levels of language proficiency.

- knowing how to facilitate content and language development through appropriate instructional designs, materials and approaches.

- being able to monitor and assess learning and distinguish between conceptual/cognitive issues and language-related issues (i.e. the student who masters the content but is unable to express it, as distinguished from the student who has superficial fluency but does not engage effectively with content), and knowing how to redirect students appropriately.

2.8 One Suggestion I Would Like to Share

Chapter 2 has set the scene for the rest of the book, by presenting some experiences, bringing up some challenges, and setting out some good practices. We would like to end this with a preliminary list of suggestions that could help you when you take up the challenge of EMI. In our own survey of EMI teachers in Spain, we asked them if there were any ideas they would like to share with other people who were just starting out on EMI. These suggestions might be advice directed towards individual people who are starting to get involved in EMI, or they could be ideas about how the institutions (departments, faculties/schools, universities) could support staff and promote effective EMI. Here are some of the things they said.

Suggestions for EMI teachers:

- I would like to share the idea that it is possible, and you will enjoy it!

- Make sure you put in plenty of short breaks – and make good use of all the videos available in English!

- Try to say the same things in different ways – explain with words, but also with images, or by writing on the board.

- Get hold of a good textbook for your course in English – don't try and reinvent the wheel, because there is plenty of material out there.

- Remember that the students who take the EMI courses are usually the best students. It will be more rewarding to teach them!

- Make good use of the exchange students. They enrich the class a lot because they have different opinions, they participate a lot.

- I think that perhaps we need to emphasize the 'acting' dimension of teaching, and just enjoy the show. I think we must not look for a particular 'point' of the classes in English, but just take it as it is. I have to teach in English, I'll do my best!

Suggestions for departments, faculties or institutions:

- Create a community of EMI teachers within the university, so that you can exchange ideas and experiences.

- Ask to have the same course for several years, so that you can really build up experience. It is more work to teach in English – but the big investment of time is the first year of any subject, so the second year you can relax more.

- Ask your university to give you sabbatical leave to spend a year in the United States, Canada, Australia. That would be a great way to get used to using English!

- Set up a mentoring programme for new EMI teachers.

- Organize speaking activities in the university where teachers can improve their fluency and vocabulary in an informal way, and build up confidence. These activities would be free for the teachers who want to learn.

Case Study: Teaching Physics in Sweden

John Airey, a physics lecturer and researcher in Sweden, asked the lecturers in his university about how they felt when they learned that they had to give their courses in English (Airey 2011). From what they said, he was able to identify nine main themes that seemed to be important to many of the people he talked to.

Here are the nine recurring themes identified by the Swedish lecturers in his study, with some of the things they actually said. Do any of their comments reflect the experience of lecturers in your institution? Which points do you think are the most important?

Theme 1: Short notice

'All of a sudden I was supposed to teach in English.'

Theme 2: No training

'We were very nervous. We had no preparation.'

Theme 3: More preparation

'You need to plan more carefully in order to communicate what you want in the given amount of time.'

Theme 4: Less detail

'I think that I, in some ways, are losing some depth as I have a feeling that it's much easier to be precise in my native language.'

Theme 5: Less flexibility

'In a "normal" situation, in Swedish, I would probably try to tell some funny stories connected to marketing but I don't think I would dare to do that in English.'

Theme 6: Less fluency

'In Swedish my presentation is quicker and much more lively than in the English version. In English I have to struggle with pronunciations and use more time to find the right words, even though I have written a "manuscript".'
'I turn to the students with questions more in the Swedish version and I feel much more relaxed. In English I don't move so much, I put my arms behind my back and I use fewer gestures. So my body language does not work – either.'

Theme 7: Impossible to give corrections

'During the lessons or at examination I do not correct the students if they are using a wrong expression or making any mistakes when using English. In my opinion I am not that skilled in English and have not the confidence to correct another person.'
'I avoid making language a factor when it comes to the grades. I am not a teacher of English. I've also stopped correcting their mistakes.'
'I am frightened of not being able to function as an English language expert but maybe it's not our job to correct their work like a "traditional" English teacher. Maybe it's enough if we provide the students with the typical language, e.g. technical vocabulary and specialised expressions.'

Theme 8: Not so many differences

'I was maybe expecting more differences, but at the same time I am quite pleased with the result even though there are always improvements to be made!'

Theme 9: Confidence boost

'I'm a bit surprised that it wasn't as terrible as I thought it would be. This has clearly strengthened my self-confidence – and I'm very happy and thankful for that!'

POINTS FOR REFLECTION

1. Can you remember who were the best teachers you ever had? What subjects did they teach? What was their predominant teaching style (please see below)? Was that style determined by the subject matter they taught, by their personality, by the students' background or by any other external circumstances (furniture arrangement, lack of certain resources, etc.)?

Here are the most common types of 'teaching styles':

VERBAL ➜ Mainly based on reading, writing and oral exposition and reporting.

LOGICAL-MATHEMATICAL ➜ Based on analysis, questioning, reasoning, calculation, problem resolution.

VISUAL-SPATIAL ➜ Based on graphics and illustrations, slides and videos.

KINETIC ➜ Based on physical movement: gestures, touch, dance, etc.

MUSICAL ➜ Based on rhythm, rhyme, etc.

INTERPERSONAL ➜ Based on relationships, communication of content among learners and between them and others, such as staff from other departments and disciplines, companies and external audiences.

INTRAPERSONAL ➜ Based on reflection, meditation, planning, self-evaluation, planning, imagination.

What type or combination of types would characterize your teaching style? Can you give approximate percentages? Here is a diagnostic bar chart:

My teaching style(s)

```
100 ─────────────────────────────────────────────



%




  0 ─────────────────────────────────────────────
         Teaching styles (pure or combined)
```

Some extra questions for reflection:

1. Does your teaching style coincide with your students' average learning style?
2. And with your own learning style?
3. Do you teach using the same style that you were taught with in your university years? Why or why not?
4. Have digital technologies broadened your repertoire of styles?
5. Does your teaching offer a balanced combination of teaching styles?
6. What styles could you incorporate in your habitual teaching to make it more vivid and memorable?
7. Does something prevent you from doing this? If so, what?

CHAPTER 3

Lecturing in English

3.1 Lecturing in English: Some General Ideas

As we saw in Chapter 2, when lecturers with experience of teaching in their first language are told that they will be expected to teach in English, they react in a number of different ways. Some people react with fear and trepidation, while others welcome the chance to capitalize on their good command of English, or the opportunity to teach a more varied student group. Whatever your first reaction is, it is important to be practical and consider how you can go about preparing for this new challenge. We propose that before you start your preparations, you dedicate a few minutes to thinking about what really matters when you are teaching, so that you can set some priorities for preparing your EMI classes.

So what makes a good lecture? In our lives we sit through thousands of hours of class, and we all form our own ideas about what aspects contribute to a good lecture – and what features we should try to avoid. It is important to reflect on this, because even though we may not agree on everything, there are some general ideas and principles that we should be aware of.

Now have a look at Task 3.1, which is designed to provoke reflection on what matters when you are lecturing. Take some time to write a list of the factors that make a good lecture, thinking specifically of an informative presentation of new material to a large group of students, rather than a class in which you are trying to provoke discussion or revise concepts studied previously.

WORKSHEET 3.1: WHAT MAKES A GOOD LECTURE

What do you think makes a good lecture? Make notes for each point. You should reflect about:

- contents
- quantity of information
- speed and timing
- organization
- visuals
- style of delivery
- body language
- voice
- language

Now think about how these factors vary according to the type of lecture or class that you are giving. Do the same principles apply to small classes, discussion groups or seminars?

Research on university lecturing in general tells us that – perhaps contrary to some popular beliefs – lectures are not only well organized and packed with information, but also highly interactive, personal, persuasive and involved (Biber 2006). Look at these two authentic transcripts A and B (below) from lectures by native speakers in the British Academic Spoken English (BASE)[1] corpus, and find examples of some of the features of natural conversation listed in the box below:

- Repetitions
- Fillers (er, em, sort of, yeah)
- Attitude markers

[1] The British Academic Spoken English (BASE) corpus was developed at the Universities of Warwick and Reading under the directorship of Hilary Nesi and Paul Thompson. Corpus development was assisted by funding from BALEAP, EURALEX, the British Academy and the Arts and Humanities Research Council.

- Rhetorical questions
- Contractions/abbreviations
- Incomplete sentences
- Onomatopoeic language
- Interjections
- Many linked clauses
- False starts
- Personal pronouns

Lecture transcript A

Thomas Ray has actually produced what he calls the Tierra Project which are these are not viruses these are actually computational organisms that live on the internet and they they transmit themselves and reproduce themselves in different computers wherever they can get and he sort of generated them and let them loose and now they are they're out there reproducing with slight variations evolving some of them die some of them find it easier to survive if they mutate slightly what are these things well they're they're they're digital organisms it's been found that they tend to follow the shadow of they they they tend to hover the the the the the internet covers the globe and they tend to be found in the dark part now why is that it's because then people go to sleep and the computers have got more room to host these organisms so they've actually developed organic patterns robots that learned to control their bodies.

Lecture transcript B

Well there's a two two other things that we have to worry about with measuring rainfall it's very easy to put a rain gauge out on the on on the land but how any ideas how you'd measure rain in the o on the ocean so two-thirds of the planet is covered by ocean and we need to know the rainfall there buoys maybe yeah do you think that would work very well 'cause the one of the problems these things are rocky you need to keep keep your gauge level and you've got a lot of a lot of waves splashing in and things like that so they don't tend to work terribly well any other ideas measuring rain in the ocean put them on ships pardon put them on ships well you can but you've got a real problem there is keeping the ship steady and it it tends to be many metres above the surface so it's not really regarded as very reliable I mean there's two things that tend to be done one is just to use stations in island re island stations and hope that they're somehow representative of the surrounding region which is a a a big assumption a another thing that's being thought about is actually just measuring which wow is amazing is is measuring the noise due to the raindrops hitting the surface so there are now people trying to develop acoustic techniques of actually having little microphones under the ocean literally listening to the pitter-patter of the rainfall so they're very much at the at the research level.

So lectures are not a kind of language test, or a demonstration of perfect language skills. First and foremost, lectures are a pedagogical genre concerned with the transmission and acquisition of knowledge (Crawford Camiciottoli 2007). They are fundamentally about communicating with an audience in an educational setting. This means that they have expository aspects, but also other aspects concerned with the building and maintenance of relationships, or the socialization of the students into a discipline through co-participation. And this complex ensemble of communicative acts will naturally build on the way we use language with our colleagues, with other professionals, as well as with people in other areas of our lives. If our lectures tell an interesting story, give insights into a difficult concept, or transmit enthusiasm and love for our subject, then our students will value them positively.

At the same time the bibliography on EMI teaching also tells us that certain formal aspects of our classes are particularly important when we teach in English to groups who come from other language backgrounds. These are:

- structuring the lecture/class in a logical way
- providing adequate signposting
- interacting with the PowerPoints and other visuals
- supporting students by providing extra resources

In this chapter, we will go through each of these points, and then provide some case studies that illustrate good practices in this area.

3.2 Structuring the Lecture

To help students understand your lectures, it is important to try to see your teaching activity from the students' point of view. Students like clarity. They like to be able to take notes that make sense. They appreciate order. If you can make the structure of your class visible to them, it will help them to follow. In fact, even small things, like using discourse markers (on the one hand/on the other hand, first, second, last), have been shown to have a positive effect on the amount of information that students understand and retain. Many years ago, in a study of student recall from lectures in English, Chaudron and Richards found that students were more likely to remember information from lectures that contained 'explicit expressions of the planning of the lecture information' (1986, 123). Following on from this, some other researchers found that explicit metadiscourse indicating how the information in the lecture is organized is most helpful for students whose level of English is lower, since use of explicit discourse organizers helps lighten the cognitive load and build connections to their previous knowledge (Aguilar Pérez & Arnó Maciá 2002). Crawford Camiciottoli (2007, 89) points out that these organizers fall into two categories, namely macromarkers (phrases that guide the listener in a relational manner, such as 'what I'm going to be doing today') and micromarkers (elements like 'well' or 'ok then', that indicate the relationship between phrases, but also give listeners time to process changes in the ongoing information flow and communicative purpose). We are going to look at the structure of lectures in more detail, to see how all these elements fit into the bigger picture.

How Are Lectures Structured?

Although times are changing, many lecturers still follow a classic pattern for lectures that has proved effective over many decades. The typical structure of such lectures was analysed by Young (1994), who divides the phases of the lecture into two types:

- Phases in which the lecturer talks about what he/she is trying to achieve through the lecture. These could be called 'organizing phases'.

- Phases in which the lecturer conveys information about the contents of the subject itself. These might be termed 'content phases'.

Each of these phases can be subdivided into many smaller categories, as we will see here. However, first, so that we are all in the picture, we think it would be helpful to look at the broad overview of the main phases in a typical lecture, illustrated here with extracts from an authentic medical lecture available in the British Academic Spoken English (BASE) corpus.

From the example provided in Table 3.1, we can see that organizing tends to be particularly prominent at the beginning and the end of a lecture, or when the lecturer wants to change the type of activity going on in the classroom. Each of these brief organizing phases may have several different components. For example, according to Lee (2009), the initial organizing phase of the lecture consists of a warm-up (housekeeping, looking ahead), setting up the framework (announcing the topic, structure and aims) and putting the topic in context (relating 'new' to 'given', referring to previous lectures). An analysis of EMI lectures carried out by Dafouz and Núñez (2010) showed that there are three principal metadiscoursal/organizing phases (phases in which you talk about what you are trying to communicate):

- introducing what you are going to say

- guiding your listeners through the lecture (NOTE: Dafouz and Núñez call this 'interaction' but we avoid this term here, because interaction encompasses aspects beyond the lecture hall and forms the subject of Chapter 4)

TABLE 3.1 Overview of the Lecture Structure (Example from Medical Lecture in BASE)

Phase	What you want to do	What you say
Introduction (O)	Recap on previous material and set the scene for today's class	I think as part of your biological training to date you should have covered some of the molecular aspects of malignancy, some of the aspects you'd have covered, I believe, in some of the basic science courses, so today we're really going to concentrate on some of the clinical aspects of patients with leukaemias and lymphomas and see how that ties in and builds together with what you've learnt from the biological sciences.
Part 1 (C)	Explain the first part of the topic	So really I'm going to start off with leukaemias and leukaemias are conditions whereby you have an abnormal proliferation of primitive cells in the bone marrow. The bone marrow is the site where different blood cells are made, and there are a whole variety of different leukaemias, acute and chronic, would be the main types of leukaemias that we're going to be looking at.
Transition (O)	Change to new part of topic or new activity	So for a start we're going to have a presentation on a patient who has recently been at Warwick Hospital presenting with an acute leukaemia and I think we'll just go straight into that.
Part 2 (C)	Explain the next part of the topic	I'll go through these in a bit of detail, it's full blood count obviously we're looking for a normochromic normocytic anaemia, so just because there's less red blood cells being made also thrombocytopenia you may also find that the white cell count is either decreased or significantly increased.
Trailing (O)	Mention what you are going to discuss later	Cytogenetics and molecular studies will be talked about more later, but they can have a great impact on the prognostic and diagnostic values and also lumbar puncture in acute leukaemias.
Asking questions (O)	Find out how much students know	And I was just wondering if anybody can tell me how long a platelet actually survives routinely in a normal circulation.

Phase	What you want to do	What you say
Rephrasing (C)	Use different words to explain a term or concept	Up to 70 to 80 per cent of patients will go into a remission; in other words there'll be reconstitution of the normal blood counts.
Checking under-standing (O)	Ask for questions or feedback	Are there any questions that you want to ask quickly about this because we've got all the other ones to go through?
Transition (O)	Change to new part of topic or new activity	So we're going to move on now and learn a little bit about chronic myeloid leukaemia.
Summarizing (O)	Remind students about what they have seen	So chronic myeloid leukaemia is a condition which at the end of the day is really quite chronic and insidious in its onset but at the end of the day is something which ultimately will transform to a blast crisis.
Alerting to evaluation (O)	Relate the content of the class to the questions that may be in the exam	If you are in an exam and you had a patient who had splenomegaly what would be your immediate clinical differential diagnosis? It's the sort of thing you're bound to get in your finals isn't it so you need to be able to say something vaguely sensible about it. And it would be sensible in your clinical exam to actually not just look at the spleen in sheer amazement that you've found it but to actually have some sort of plan as to how you're going to impress the examiner.
Recapping and reformu-lating (O)	Show students what kind of answers they should be giving in exams	And if you want to really impress your examiners again when you've found the spleen not only do you look for evidence of chronic liver disease and you can say, well, this patient's got splenomegaly there aren't any signs of chronic liver disease, the other thing that would impress them would be if you actually went and were seen to be examining as to whether the patient had any enlarged lymph glands because if the patient has something like chronic lymphocytic leukaemia then you might score some extra points by actually showing that you actually are thinking one step ahead.

(Continued)

TABLE 3.1 (Continued)

Phase	What you want to do	What you say
Eliciting main points (O)	Check that the students have understood the main ideas	You've had an hour's worth of being drilled with information about high- and low-grade lymphoma patients with acute and chronic leukaemias, so I think, yeah, this was mentioned before but can you say again the difference between Hodgkin's and non-Hodgkin's?
Concluding (O)	Signal the end	I'm going to have to bring it to an end today. Can I just say thank you to all of you who have taken part?

- summarizing what you have said

And there are also three content phases (phases in which you communicate information), which are interspersed between these organizing phases and connected together by them, which we will explain in the following order:

- explaining new information, including theories, models and definitions

- evaluating the importance or relevance of the material under discussion

- providing examples to illustrate the new concepts

Obviously, although these phases may sometimes follow a strict sequence, they generally do not. For instance, in the course of a lecture, we may go through two or three cycles of new concepts with definitions, followed by examples. However, it is interesting to think of these as different 'discursive actions', because we use different types of language structure in order to perform them.

Organizing Phases

Here, we are going to look in detail at the organizing phases, since these are crucial to ensure that your lecture makes sense and your students understand your explanations. Moreover, they will probably be similar each time – whereas the content is likely to be very different.

Table 3.2, adapted from Dafouz and Núñez (2010), presents the different organizing phases with examples of the kind of language that lecturers can use in each one.

TABLE 3.2 Organizing Phases, with Purpose and Examples

Phase	Action	Function	Examples
Introducing	Opening	Signal the formal opening of the class	Today, we're going to take a look at . . .
	Sequencing	Indicate the order in which topics will be presented	First, second, next, finally
	Topicalizing	Draw attention to new topics	Another important issue is
	Recalling	Refer back to previous classes or previous points	As we saw yesterday/As I pointed out earlier
	Trailing	Hint at what is going to come later	As we will see later in this class
Guiding	Connecting	Establish rapport with listeners	We already know about this I'm sure this has sometimes happened to you
	Checking comprehension	Find out if students are following your explanation	Are we on the same page here? What do you think will happen next?
	Activating previous knowledge	Encourage students to build connections with what they know already	If you have read *Great Expectations* you will remember the churchyard scene.
	Providing feedback	Evaluating students' responses and correcting if necessary	Right! Not exactly
	Prompting	Make it easier for students to respond	So if animals with a backbone are called vertebrates, the ones without a backbone are called . . .
	Managing	Organize activity within the lecture hall	So could you discuss this in pairs, for about five minutes? Then I'm going to ask you what you came up with.

(Continued)

TABLE 3.2 (Continued)

Phase	Action	Function	Examples
Summarizing	Recapitulating	Summarize what you covered	Today we have seen the impact of the Wall Street crash on the US economy
	Recalling	Refer back to previous classes or previous points	As we saw in previous lectures, the US economy had enjoyed sustained growth up to 1929
	Trailing	Hint at what is going to come later	And in the next class we will see how the United States managed to pull out of the recession
	Closing	Show you are going to stop	I will finish here. Have a good weekend!

Working on Each Phase

In what follows, we will take the order of a 'typical' lecture. This can be adapted in many ways, but it helps to start with a straightforward plan. We will look first at the three organizing phases (see Table 3.2), and then at the content phases.

Organizing Phase 1: Introducing What You Are Going to Say

We usually begin our lecture by stating what we are going to be doing in the next hour/two hours. We can call this our 'introduction'. The introduction needs to be appropriate to the occasion – even though there are some shared features, the introduction to a lecture is not the same as the introduction to a speech, or a conference paper. Introductions to lectures need to be brief and focused, but they also need to remind students what your course is about and help them to connect with what you are going to say.

WORKSHEET 3.2: EVALUATING INTRODUCTIONS

For each of the following lecture introductions (A to E) decide the following:

- how appropriate the introduction is (Use a scale of 1–5: 1 is very bad and 5 is very good).

- what you like or do not like about the introduction
- what information is either superfluous of missing

Introduction A. Today I'm going to talk about the new building regulations to prevent heat loss. The first of these is the recent Technical Guidance Document. It states that . . .

Rating: _____

Introduction B. Good morning students. Firstly, I would like to say that it is a great pleasure for me to be here to give this lecture on sustainability and natural resources. We all know that finding sustainable sources of energy is a priority for the world in the twenty-first century. Non-renewable fuels are likely to be exhausted within the next fifty to one hundred years. Moreover, use of traditional fuels such as coal and gas causes many serious environmental problems. For these reasons, there is increasing interest in natural energy sources, such as wind and water power. In today's lecture I will be covering the chief advantages and disadvantages of wind power, and then considering how the situation is likely to develop over the next five to ten years.

Rating: _____

Introduction C. My name is Zhu Wang and the title of my lecture is 'A pilot project in waste recycling'. I'm going to talk about the methods used, the results we obtained and the general conclusions which can be drawn from our research. So first the method. . .

Rating: _____

Introduction D. The topic of today's lecture is the state of the art in wind turbine technology. In the last few weeks we have compared different kinds of conventional and alternative energy sources, and looked at their cost, and their impact on the places where the energy is generated. We already know that wind is a clean, inexhaustible energy resource that can generate enough electricity to power millions of homes and businesses. However, we have also seen that the main challenge is to find ways of exploiting this resource that are efficient and cost-effective, but have a low environmental impact. Today, we are going to look at two different models of wind turbine, evaluate their cost-effectiveness and weigh up the extent to which they might cause disturbance in the rural environments where they are situated. . .

Rating: _____

Introduction E. I'll be talking to you today about the 'The Wind Energy Program' and its goal for small distributed wind energy systems, which was to reduce the cost of energy to 10 to 15 cents per kilowatt-hour (kWh) in a Class 3 wind resource from a 2002 baseline of 17 to 22 cents per kWh. In 2007, the programme met that goal through collaborative efforts with industry partners that included Southwest Windpower, Windward Engineering, Abundant Renewable Energy and Wetzel Engineering, reducing the cost of electricity produced by residential-sized turbines (10 kW or less) to 9.9 cents per kWh.

Rating: _____

When you are introducing your lecture, it is very important to contextualize what you are going to say, and to activate students' previous knowledge.

You probably noticed that in Worksheet 3.2 you gave a better rating to the introductions (B and D) in which the speaker has attempted to put the information he/she is going to give into a wider context, and specifically into the context of what the students have already seen in the course. In all lectures, you will find that your students benefit from receiving some brief background information on what you are going to say. This should explain where the subject of today's lecture 'fits' on the landscape of the course you are teaching. This will help the students to build connections with their previous knowledge, and organize the new information in their minds.

When you open your lecture, you can facilitate this contextualization process and help students to connect the new information to their previous knowledge in various ways:

1. by reminding them of what they have seen so far in the course, and particularly, what they saw in the previous lecture (recalling)

2. by emphasizing the importance of what you are going to cover today (topicalizing)

3. by providing a preview of what you are going to cover in today's class (trailing and sequencing)

Look at the examples in Worksheet 3.2, and see which introductions do this.

Organizing Phase 2: Guiding Your Audience as You Go Along

In many cases, a lecture can be understood as a conversation between the lecturer and the students. In this dialogue, the lecturer has control, but the role of the students is also important. Some of the strategies useful in the 'guiding' phase are shown in Table 3.2: connecting, checking comprehension, activating previous knowledge, providing feedback, prompting and managing. You can see that a lot of different things go on in the course of a lecture while you are also trying to teach new ideas and facts to your students! In Worksheet 3.3 we will take a look at an imaginary class, in which the lecturer is establishing a dialogic interaction with the students.

WORKSHEET 3.3: LANGUAGE AND STRATEGIES FOR GUIDING YOUR AUDIENCE

Complete the transcript of an imaginary class, using an appropriate phrase from the box below.

Lecture on economic policy (extract)

Teacher: Now, the topic we're going to start on today is known as EPA. (A) . . .?

Student: Economic Policy Affairs.

Teacher: (B) . . .?

Student: Economic Policy Analysis.

Teacher: (C) . . . So there are lots of reasons why we should be interested in Economic Policy Analysis. For one thing, economic policies affect our daily lives in lots of concrete ways. (D) . . . One of those ways is tax, which I think you have studied before. (E) . . .?

Student: Income tax, for example. Or sales tax, like VAT.

Teacher: That's right. Any more? What do we call things like disability allowances or social benefits? (F) . . .?

Student: Transfers.

Teacher: Good. That would cover all kinds of public social assistance including pensions, unemployment benefits. (G) . . .?

Student: Housing allowances, perhaps?

Teacher: Yes, indeed. Those are also a form of state aid. So now we are going to imagine the government is going to introduce a new economic policy related to transfers – for example, let's imagine they are considering extending paternity leave to 6 months . . .

Students: Yes.

Teacher : I would like you to look at the figures on the handout, and calculate the impact of this overall on the economy as a whole. (H) . . .

1. *Economic Policy . . .?*

2. *Who knows what EPA stands for?*

3. *You can work in pairs to do this.*

4. *Is there a general word for this?*

5. *Do you get that?*

6. *Right.*

7. *Any more?*

8. *So what kind of taxes might affect us?*

Now think about why the teacher said each of these things.

Connecting
Checking comprehension
Establishing previous knowledge
Providing feedback
Prompting
Managing

Answers

Connecting	If you don't believe me now, just wait for a couple of years until you start working!
Checking comprehension	Do you get that?
Activating previous knowledge	Who knows what EPA stands for?
Prompting	Is there a general word for this?
Providing feedback	Right.
Prompting	Economic Policy . . .?
Prompting	Any more?
Managing	You can work in pairs to do this.

Organizing Phase 3: Summarizing What You Have Said

At the end of a lecture, or perhaps at the end of an important section in the lecture, it is usual to provide a summary of the main points (recapitulating). This is not redundant – it is an important strategy to ensure that students have understood your class, and to encourage them to make useful notes. You may also want to remind students of things they learned in previous classes (recalling), or talk about what you are going to do next week (trailing). Last of all, often people use a conventional formula to end the class (closing), such as 'Well, that's it for today' or 'I'm going to finish here'.

In its most basic form, the summary is a mirror image of the introduction you gave at the beginning. So the summary of the lecture that was introduced by example D, aforementioned, might look like this:

So in our course so far we have examined different types of conventional and alternative energy sources. And today we have looked at two current models of wind turbine that we can see around us as we travel across the country. We have learnt about their different advantages and disadvantages, and we have seen a way to evaluate their cost-effectiveness. What's more, we have also learnt to weigh up the extent to which they might cause disturbance in the rural environments where they are situated. When we come to look at different types of biomass next week, this will provide us with some interesting material for comparison. Anyway, that's it for today – see you all next week!

WORKSHEET 3.4: ELEMENTS OF THE SUMMARY

Can you identify the different ingredients of the summary section (see Table 3.2) in this? These were:

- Recapitulating
- Recalling
- Trailing
- Closing

So in our course so far we have examined different types of conventional and alternative energy sources. And today we have looked at two current models of wind turbine that we can see around us as we travel across the country. We have learnt about their different advantages and disadvantages, and we have seen a way to evaluate their cost-effectiveness. What's more, we have also learnt to weigh up the extent to which they might cause disturbance in the rural environments where they are situated. When we come to look at different types of biomass next week, this will provide us with some interesting material for comparison. Anyway, that's it for today – see you all next week!

Notice that in the example given in Worksheet 3.4, the largest segment of the concluding words is dedicated to recapitulating, that is, to giving a brief overview of what you have done in the class today. Above all, don't be frightened of a bit of repetition – your students will thank you for it. As the American public speaking experts are fond of saying – 'Say what you're going to say. Then say it. And then say what you've said.' If people hear something once, they are unlikely to remember it, or even to pay much attention. If they hear it three times, there is a much stronger possibility that they will get the idea.

LANGUAGE PRACTICE BOX 1: Stating Your Purpose

English has a wide range of phrases that you can use for stating your purpose. They can be tricky until you get used to them. Use this box to practice saying what you intend to achieve.

Language practice 1. Phrases for stating your purpose.

Below you will find a number of ways of stating the purpose of your presentation. Complete them using the words given. If you combine the sentences by using the right verb, you will get a complete introduction.

Good morning, everyone. OK let's get started. This is our fourth lecture in the course on Employment Law. This morning I'm going to be:

showing talking taking reporting telling

1. .... to you about the law concerning how employees can now be fired legally.

2. .... you about the different types of unlawful dismissal.

3. .... you how to determine whether a dismissal was unfair or not.

4. .... a look at the recent boom in cases going to the Employment Tribunal.

5. .... on the recent changes in Employment Law in our country.

...so, I'll begin by:

making outlining bringing giving filling

1. .... you in on the background to the law concerning termination of employment.

2. .... a few observations about the events leading up to the recent changes.

3. .... some important recent precedents from the Employment Appeals Tribunal.

4. .... you an overview of the different types of dismissal contemplated by the law.

5. .... you up-to-date on the latest legal thinking in this area.

... and then I'll go on to:

put discuss make highlight talk

1. .... what I see as the main advantages of the new legislation.

2. .... the new legislation into a historical perspective.

3. .... you through a simple procedure for deciding whether a case is viable.

4. .... detailed recommendations regarding how to approach such cases.

5. .... in more depth the implications of these changes for employers and employees.

ANSWERS: 1. talking; 2. telling; 3. showing; 4. taking; 5. reporting. 1. filling; 2. making; 3. outlining; 4. giving; 5. bringing. 1. highlight; 2. put; 3. talk; 4. make; 5. discuss.

Introductions have to be delivered with confidence, and especially if you are an invited speaker! Even if you don't feel too confident, there are some golden rules that you can follow to give the impression that you do:

- Keep eye contact with the audience (or, if you can't face looking at their eyes, look at their foreheads, because it will seem the same to them).

- Keep it slow! When you rush, your pronunciation will become less clear, and you might give the impression of nervousness.

- Prepare your talk carefully (although it is better not to read, there is no harm in having the whole talk, or parts of it, written down, so that you can refer back to the page if you forget what you were going to say, or get a sudden attack of nerves).

When you are preparing your introduction, it is a good idea to think carefully about what you are going to say, but also about how you are going to say it. You can even mark the words that you want to stress, and indicate where the pauses in the text should be, to show you where you can afford to take a deep breath.

This is the introduction of a guest lecture given by Pierre Dupont from Dazz Engineering. To give this introduction well, he needs to emphasize certain words, and break the text up into suitable segments. Can you underline the stressed words and put in the pauses? Prepare, and then practise delivering the introduction.

Good afternoon, ladies and gentlemen. It's a pleasure to be here with you today. First, I'd like to introduce myself. I'm Pierre Dupont from Dazz Engineering. Dazz Engineering is a small but growing company based in Grenoble, in the heart of the French Alps. Our main activities are in the field of waste management. You may be familiar with some of the techniques we've developed for recycling plastics. One of the main problems facing the field of waste management worldwide today is that of the sheer quantity of municipal solid waste being generated. Moreover, this phenomenon is directly linked to economic growth: the wealthier a society becomes, the more waste of this kind it generates. Unlike industrial waste, this kind of waste is difficult to collect and treat. This afternoon, I would like to describe some positive developments in this area, and show we have succeeded in reducing the municipal solid waste in the Grenoble area to manageable proportions. To begin with, I'll be speaking about the major aspects of the problem. Then, we'll take a look at some of the technological options for handling this type of waste, and the logistical problems involved. Finally, I'll review three pilot projects that our company was involved in, and how the results of these were used in coordination with Grenoble local government in order to redesign the waste management system to cope with increased volume. My talk will last for around half an hour, and after that I'd be delighted to answer any questions. Well, so let's make a start on . . .

Attracting and Keeping Students' Attention

Although it is often suggested that the best lectures or presentations have 'arresting' or 'dramatic' introductions where lecturers/presenters immediately grab the attention of their audience, it is not really practical to do this every day. However, from time to time you might want to test out a different strategy to capture students' attention. Here are some ideas to help you:

- Hook: Tell your audience what your talk is about, and where you aim to take them. You might be able to use a rhetorical question, an anecdote or some other kind of 'hook' to attract their interest. An example might be: 'Muhtar Kent once said that "a brand is a promise". But we all know that not everyone keeps their promises. So what happens if the promise is broken?'

- Connect: Introduce the subject by posing the issue you are going to address in the context of what (you can reasonably assume) is already known. For instance: 'I'm sure all of us can think of Coca Cola's most successful advertising campaign, way back in 1971: "I'd like to buy the world a Coke". But I would like to bet that you don't know that Coca-Cola Europe originally rejected this campaign for being "too American". It was only when an Italian film company stepped in that the legendary version familiar to us all was finally produced.'

- Feeling: If possible, make a positive, complimentary connection with the local culture: 'I know that here in Venice you love carnivals – in fact, you have one of the most famous carnivals in the world! So when I talk to you about the carnivalesque in magical realism, you probably understand this concept better than most of my students do in Kentucky.'

- Benefit: 'Sell' your talk by telling your audience how they are going to benefit from listening to you. You can use phrases like 'By the end of today's talk, you will be able to. . .' or 'What you'll get from today's session is. . .' For example, 'By the end of this morning's talk, you'll know how to say "no" and feel good about it.'

- Credibility: 'Sell' yourself by giving the audience a good reason to listen to you by boosting your own credibility as speaker: 'My experiences with the WHO in the front line battle combating Ebola in the Democratic Republic of the Congo last year taught me a lot about public health planning.'

Content Phases

The content phases also contain a number of different aspects. The type and amount of content that you are teaching will have a strong bearing on the way you present it, and there is much more variation between subjects and classes in these phases than there is in the organizing phases. However, it is clear that all of us, at least from time to time, do the following things in our classes:

- explaining new information, including theories, models and definitions
- evaluating the importance or relevance of the material under discussion
- providing examples to illustrate the new concepts

Content Phase 1: Explaining New Information

New information can take a variety of different forms. According to Deroey and Taverniers (2011) the type of informing activity carried out in a lecture can take the following forms:

- describing
- recounting
- reporting
- interpreting
- demonstrating

Each of these can be accompanied by a specific range of tenses and structures, as illustrated in Table 3.3 (classification of informing activities, adapted from Deroey and Taverniers (2011)).

When we are explaining a topic that the students do not already know, it is obvious that we have to organize our information in such a way that maximizes their possibilities of understanding this. Probably without knowing it, we set up verbal signposts in our discourse that help students to find their way through the forest of new information.

Signposting

From time to time, all teachers need to remind themselves that what is obvious – even boring and mundane – to them is probably quite new to their students. That is the whole point about teaching!

TABLE 3.3 Explaining New Information, with Language and Examples

Action	Typical language	Examples
Describing	Present tense, adjectives and prepositions	The Japanese economy is the third largest in the world in terms of GDP
Recounting	Past tenses, narrative sequences, adverbs of time	During the Meiji period (1868–1912), Japan's rulers set up a new Western-style education system for all young people, sent thousands of students to the West and hired foreigners to teach science, maths and technology.
Reporting	Reporting verbs, reported speech	Aristotle tells us that we become virtuous by doing virtuous acts. Boyle's law states that the pressure of a gas varies inversely with its volume.
Interpreting	Modal verbs, suggest, illustrate, show, use of 'seem' or 'appear'	Shakespeare seems to use Macbeth to show the appalling effects that ambition may have on a man with a weak character.
Demonstrating	Imperatives, personal pronouns (you, we), deictics (this, here), if, so, therefore	Let's say the corporate tax rate in the United States is 35 per cent, so if I stay there I would pay 350k. But if I move here, you can see the rate is only 5 per cent, so here I pay this lower rate, only 50k.

For this reason, we have to be sure that we order the information we give carefully, and emphasize what is important. As we have seen, our language offers us ways of helping students to understand and assess what we are trying to communicate. If you don't agree, just take a look at Explanation A (in the following), about how the legal process of buying/selling real estate works in the UK. Then read Explanation B. Which one do you find easier to follow?

Explanation A

The seller accepts the buyer's offer and the seller's solicitor drafts the contract outlining the conditions of sale, terms (e.g. price). The buyer's solicitor checks the seller's legal title to the property, organizes a survey of the property to check its condition, looks into any outstanding issues with the local authority and contacts the seller's solicitor to clear up any doubts about the draft contract. The two parties' solicitors finalize the terms in the draft contract. The parties sign in readiness for exchange. The buyer pays a deposit and a date for completion is fixed. On completion the payment is completed and the keys are handed over. The buyer's solicitor checks the deeds, pays the duties and registers the purchase at the land registry. He/she ensures the right papers are sent to the right people.

Explanation B

The first important moment is when the seller accepts the buyer's offer. At this point, the seller's solicitor drafts the contract outlining the conditions of sale, terms (e.g. price). After this, the buyer's solicitor checks the seller's legal title to the property, organizes a survey of the property to check its condition, looks into any outstanding issues with the local authority and contacts the seller's solicitor to clear up any doubts about the draft contract. You should note that in the UK it is the buyer's solicitor who is responsible for making the local authority checks. Once this process is complete, the two parties' solicitors finalize the terms in the draft contract. Now, the parties sign in readiness for exchange: the draft contract has been approved! But there are still some further steps to be completed. The next major event comes when the buyer pays a deposit. At this point, we know that he is fully committed to the purchase, and so a date for completion is fixed. Completion, you will remember, means the point when the actual transaction – the purchase and sale – is done. Completion happens on the day when the payment is completed and the keys are handed over to the buyer. But this is not the end of the story. After this there is still some work to do. In the days that follow, the buyer's solicitor checks the deeds, pays the duties and registers the purchase at the land registry. The conveyancing process ends when he/she ensures the right papers are sent to the right people.

You probably found Explanation B much less confusing, easier to follow and somehow more engaging. The use of ordering devices ('now', 'at this point', 'the next important event', 'after this', 'in the days that follow') is crucial, but notice that some other types of signposting are also used:

- *Keeping the listener's attention*: But there are still some further steps to be completed. But this is not the end of the story. After this there is still some work to do.

- *Emphasizing importance of key points*: The first important moment is when . . . The next major event comes when . . .

- *Adding dramatic effect*: The draft contract has been approved!

- *Reminding*: Completion, you will remember, means the point when the actual transaction – the purchase and sale – is done.

- *Pointing to areas of difficulty*: You should note that in the UK it is the buyer's solicitor who is responsible for making the local authority checks.

Overview of Typical Signposting Phrases

Some research on EMI classrooms has shown that EMI teachers feel confident when they have a good range of signposting phrases at their disposal. These include phrases for making the organization of the lecture more obvious to the listeners. They also include ways of directing the students' attention to aspects that are particularly important or interesting. There are also phrases that can be used to engage listeners and make them get more involved in what you are explaining.

Two of the most typical ways of making your lecture clearer and more interesting for the listeners are by making the order of your information more explicit (e.g. when you are explaining a process or sequence), and by joining ideas together using linking words that show the relationship between them (e.g. to show causality):

Ordering Points
First, you need to be chosen as a candidate.
Second, you need to get elected.
Finally, you have to make a speech in the House of Commons.
In conclusion, it's not easy to become a member of parliament.

Cause and Effect
People in this population group eat large quantities of fatty food, *so* they are likely to have high cholesterol.
Crash diets usually make people's blood sugar drop drastically. *As a result*, people usually feel hungrier and tend to eat more over the next few days.
Global temperatures are rising. *Therefore*, when droughts occur, they tend to be more severe and last longer than in the past.
The peasants lost their land. *As a consequence,* they became very poor.
These plants are allogamous. *Consequently*, they are subject to great variety.

Giving Definitions

Definitions are statements of the meaning of a word or word combination. In many of our courses, we rely on students understanding the definitions we give them of key terminology. Sometimes we can be shocked, when we look at their exams at the end of the course, to see that some of them have failed to understand a basic definition, and that this has led to serious misunderstanding of some essential aspects of the course.

Let's think for a minute about how to prepare definitions that will be useful for our students. Experts recommend the following principles for a good definition:
Define only one concept at a time.

Use words that your listeners will understand.

Don't make it too complicated.

Concentrate on the main point – don't get bogged down in detail.

Give a useful example.

Give a comparison.

Yes, but how does it actually go? Definitions usually break into two parts:

1. category of concept
2. differentiating characteristics

(if you are a scientist, it might help you to think about genus + differentia)

So you generally start by saying what kind of thing you are talking about – so the listeners will pick this up and think, yes, we know what this is. And then you go on by saying how it is different from other, similar things. To take an easy example, if we want to define a tiger, we might say:

A tiger is a mammal (category)

or, if we want to be more specific:

A tiger is a member of the big cat family (category).

A tiger is the largest member of this family, and is distinguished from other members by its dark vertical stripes on orange-brown fur (differentiating characteristics).

We might also want to add a useful comparison:

A tiger is heavier and more muscular than a lion, and it doesn't have a mane.

Of course, lions and tigers are reassuringly concrete and visual. It is much harder to give definitions of abstract concepts – although we know perfectly well that we can.

Let's take the example of preferred stock (sometimes known as 'preference shares' or 'preferreds'). What category do they belong to? How can we distinguish them from other members of this category? Our explanation might go something like this:

Preferred stock is a kind of share in a company's capital.

But it is different from other shares of this kind, such as common stock, because it has a special combination of features: its holders get their dividends paid first they often receive a fixed dividend, but they usually have no voting rights. They have priority over other shareholders if the company is liquidated.

It is obvious that a comparison between ordinary shares and preference shares would help:

So holders of preference shares have no voting rights, whereas holders of common shares can vote at AGMs. The dividend on preference shares is fixed, while the dividend on common shares will vary according to the amount of profit the company has made that year. And if the company enters bankruptcy proceedings, the owners of the preference shares will be reimbursed first. The owners of the common shares are entitled to a refund of their capital investment only after the company's other creditors have been paid.

Content Phase 2: Evaluating the Importance or Relevance of the Material

Ideally, your lecture should not just be a dry explanation of the subject. Most lecturers want to excite their students' interest. You can do this simply by transmitting your own enthusiasm for the subject (students can easily notice if you are bored) (see also Appendix 3 "Fluency worksheets").

Other strategies that you could use are: adding emphasis, expressing reactions or emotions, or telling stories:

Emphasis

Dickens was a great writer. *In fact*, he was probably the greatest English novelist.
James is *actually* the first person I have known who has been to Africa.
This sample size is insufficient. *In other words*, we need to try to get a bigger sample.
The plan needed only two things to succeed—*namely*, time and money.
The most important point is that Russia has huge supplies of natural gas.
It is essential to realize that Japan has to import natural resources.
I'd like to highlight the increase in purchasing power during the 1960s.
The main thing here is the change in direction.
What I'm going to do is talk about the methodology we used.

Reactions or Emotions

Surprisingly enough, the most important thing for employees is not money.
It's truly amazing that almost every child in Britain has read Harry Potter.
The existence of slavery in the twenty-first century is a *shocking* fact.
Today we'll take a look at one of *the most fascinating* areas of IP law.

Telling Stories

Another idea that some teachers have suggested as a way of holding attention is telling stories, as stories are what people remember most. As Jerome Bruner, the famous educational thinker, pointed out (1996), most of our early education takes place through narrative. But our love of the story does not stop there. Throughout our lifespan, the human mind is peculiarly receptive to stories of all kinds. So if we can find a few stories that will illustrate the points we are trying to make in our classes, this will have a positive effect.

Remember, stories also have a particular structure that we can recognize and use:

- setting the scene
- action starts
- climax
- resolution
- and sometimes – moral

Content Phase 3: Giving Useful Examples

Another very important strategy that genuinely helps students to understand and remember important concepts is providing plenty of examples. Look at the three extracts from lectures on economics in BASE:

A.   Finally, this analysis of sequential games also provides a discussion of issues relating to credibility, and credibility is an important issue in modern economics. *For example*, we're told that the independence of the Bank of England gives credibility to monetary policy, we're told that countries that enter into treaties through the World Trade Organization give credibility to their competition and trade policies because if they were to change them at some future time they would suffer severe penalties and everybody knows this.

B.   All right the thing about this particular form is if you look at it not only does it give you the variable but it also gives you where the variable is in the dataset. Is that okay? So if you look at age, *for example*, you'll find that in columns one and three, and also you'll find the data type.

C.   In other words if we're dealing with unit elasticity then that's just the same thing as saying that the proportional increase in quantity demanded will be exactly equal to the proportional change in price, okay, so in other words if *for example* prices go up by ten per cent and quantity demanded falls by ten per cent then we're talking about unit elasticity.

Which of these examples is intended to help students to understand visual information? Which one helps the students to understand a theoretical concept? Which one gives some concrete situations to illustrate the importance of an abstract quality?

ANSWERS: B, C, A.

3.3 Creating Rhythm and Flow

In all of the ideas we have seen, it is important to remember that the lecture is also a kind of performance. All the different aspects come together to make a cohesive whole, which has its own dynamics. Good lecturers know how to adapt the 'pace' or 'rhythm' of the lecture to keep students' attention. To do this, they take care to plan their classes so that they include a variety of different phases in which the demands made on the students (and the teacher) are subtly different.

Varying the Classroom Dynamics

To attract and maintain your listeners' attention, try using certain strategies to change the pace. This is something that you become more aware of as you gain more experience as a teacher/lecturer.

- *Varying the activity*

It can be very useful to vary the kind of activity that goes on in the classroom, or the type of attention that you are demanding from your students. Most people have an attention span of TWENTY MINUTES, and will find it impossible to concentrate through a lecture lasting, say, fifty minutes, in which they only have to listen and take notes. It will help these students if you engineer different types of activity over the course of the fifty minutes, including whole-class discussions, question-and-answer sessions, reading, problem-solving, doing exercises, or watching video material, as well as listening and looking at PowerPoints. It is not a bad thing if the class is sometimes noisy, active and engaged, and sometimes quiet, calm and reflective.

One way of looking at your class is to think of it as a sequence of activity types. Graph 3.1 shows the amount of active engagement by students – in this case, there is an initial discussion in which students get involved,

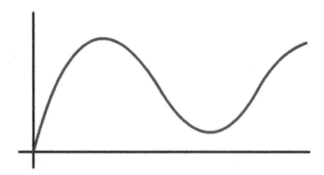

GRAPH 3.1 *Dynamics of a class over fifty minutes (x=time, y=visible student activity).*

but then there is a longer explanation by the teacher in which the students are mentally engaged in silent concentration, and finally a problem-solving exercise related to the content being studied, in which students have to first read and concentrate to understand the problem, and then discuss and decide on the way to resolve it in pairs.

- *Involving different language competences*

You can also look at your EMI class in terms of the language competences it requires the students to use: in the example illustrated by Graph 3.1, the class begins with interaction (listening and speaking), which is then followed by listening comprehension and note-taking. After that, the students have to read the problem (reading comprehension), and finally they discuss it in pairs in order to resolve it (speaking).

- *Pacing the material*

Pacing is an important aspect of teaching. Good pacing means including the right amount of information in each class – not too much, and not too little. It is important to include some new material in each lecture, but don't overdo it. Many lecturers have mentioned the idea that they go slightly more slowly when they start to teach EMI – perhaps because a more varied international group of students progresses more slowly than a homogeneous group of local student, or perhaps because the use of English makes everyone slow down. If you are worried about not covering all the important content material, then you can think about recommending some reading, or setting more homework.

- *Interacting with PowerPoint*

In this, the PowerPoint is one of your best friends, because you can make the structure of your lecture visible to everyone. Some people remember best what they read, while others remember what they hear – by giving them both, you will be helping more people to use their strengths.

There is nothing particularly difficult about the language used to present visuals. Indeed, it may even be a good idea to keep this language as simple as possible. Here are some typical examples that people often use:

- Here you can see . . .
- Here's the data from . . .
- This (next) slide shows/summarizes . . .
- What this slide shows is . . .
- This just illustrates . . .
- If we look at . . .

When you are using PowerPoint, one of the challenges is to ensure smooth transitions from one slide to another. It is very important to think carefully about these transitions between slides. You need to move seamlessly from one slide to another, taking your students' attention with you.

One good idea for this is to promise a reward or pose a new question or problem that will maintain students' interest from one slide to the next. Here are some ways of doing this:

1. Promising a reward:

So far, we've seen a lot about . . . But in my next slide, I'll show you the solution to . . .

2. Hinting that something really interesting is coming:

Now, that we've seen . . ., it is time to look at something truly impressive. In my next slide, . . .

3. Raising a question in the listeners' minds:

So how does this fit with what we know about global warming?

But you must always remember the golden rule for using questions: You must ask the question before you click to the next slide, and not after!

So you would do it like this:

So how does this fit with what we know about global warming? Any ideas? Yes? Any more ideas? Good!

Ok, so now let's see what the recent data actually show – in this next slide you see that . . .

- *Answering questions*

In principle, we know that it is a good thing if students ask questions in our lectures. And we probably like to think that we know how to deal with pretty much all the questions they can ask. After all, students' questions recur, and after we have been teaching a course for a few years, we can probably make a reasonable prediction about what is going to cause most difficulty – and about what kind of questions students are likely to ask at what point in the course.

When we start to teach in English, particularly if we have international student groups, we may find that the questions themselves, and their style of delivery, undergo some changes. There are several reasons for this:

- The students may have language difficulties, and find it harder to follow your classes. This means they might ask questions that seem very obvious, or that reveal that they misunderstand basic points.

- International students have different educational backgrounds. You can no longer make safe assumptions about what they already know.

They may have a less solid background than local students in some aspects – but they may sometimes know more! It is also possible that exchange students have studied the material for your course before, and seem to have an alarming amount of knowledge at their disposal!

- What is considered appropriate behaviour for students tends to vary from one culture to another. In some cultures, there is great respect for teachers, and students are afraid to ask questions. In other cultures, teachers like to foster a more egalitarian relationship with their students, and encourage them to participate in the class. In some cultures, students' questions are thought to be impertinent intrusions, while in other cultures, students are penalized for not asking questions!

- Depending on what you teach, the subject itself may be approached differently in different cultures. For example, in English-speaking countries, it is usual for literature classes to centre on specific works of literature, which students are expected to read and discuss. However, in other cultures, literature classes often consist of an overview of authors, works and literary movements. International students might be confused if they have experienced a very different approach to the subject, and ask questions that seem to you to be irrelevant to the course you are trying to teach.

Added to this, there is the point that you, the teacher, feel less confident when you are teaching EMI courses than when you are lecturing in your first language. All of this can lead to some embarrassing moments – particularly if there are questions that you don't understand – or questions that you feel incapable of answering!

But there is also some good news. Since we know that questions can be a problem, we can actually develop some strategies for dealing with them.

When someone in the audience asks you a question, it's a good idea to comment on it before you actually answer it. This gives you time to think. There are four basic types of questions (see Worksheet 3.5 below, and Worksheet 4.3 for further practice):

Good questions
Thank the questioner for asking them. These questions help you to get your message across to the audience better.

Difficult questions
These are the ones you cannot answer or just prefer not to answer. Sometimes teachers don't like to say they don't know. If you want, you can offer to find out, or you can ask the questioner what they think the answer is.

Unnecessary questions
These questions are not needed, because you have already given this information. Point this out, answer very quickly again and move on.

Irrelevant questions

Find a way of letting the questioner know that this question is not appropriate. Be polite, but move on as swiftly as you can.

> ## WORKSHEET 3.5: RESPONDING TO DIFFERENT TYPES OF QUESTION

Put the following responses (1 to 14) into four groups:

A) responses to good questions

B) responses to difficult questions

C) responses to unnecessary questions

D) responses to irrelevant questions

1. I'm sorry, I'm afraid I don't really see the connection with what we were talking about.
2. Well, as I mentioned earlier today. . .
3. I'm really pleased you asked that question.
4. Can I get back to you next week on that?
5. I think I answered that earlier, didn't I?
6. Good point!
7. Interesting. What do you think?
8. Well, as I said in last week's class. . .
9. I'm afraid I'm not in a position to comment on that.
10. I wish I knew.
11. I don't know that off the top of my head.
12. Sorry, I don't follow you there.
13. To be honest, I think that raises a completely different issue.
14. That's a very important question, and I think it deserves a full answer.

POSSIBLE ANSWERS: A: 3, 6, 14; B: 4, 7, 10, 11, 14; C: 2, 5, 8; D: 1, 9, 12, 13.

● *Asking questions*

Sometimes, there might be occasions when you yourself want to ask questions. For example, if you have asked a student to present part of the course material, or if students are presenting their projects or theses.

When asking questions, you should speak up so that people can hear you. Try not to talk too quickly, because you may run the risk of nobody (neither the presenter nor anyone in the audience) understanding just what your question is about.

A good way to make sure that your questions is clear to everybody is to use the following three-part structure:

Contextualizing the question	*When you were talking about the population sample used for your study*
Focusing the question	*You mentioned that you had some difficulty obtaining a large enough sample for quantitative analysis.*
Asking the question	*Could you give us some more details about that?*

Here are some more phrases and expressions that you could use for each of the three parts:

Contextualizing the question

When you were talking about/dealing with/discussing/describing . . .

Focusing the question

You referred to . . .

You commented on . . .

You said/mentioned that . . .

You made the point that . . .

Asking the question

Wouldn't you agree that . . .?

Isn't it also true that . . .?

Isn't it just possible that . . .?

Could you explain what you mean by . . .?

What exactly did you mean by . . .?

How did you arrive at the figure of. . .?

I think I misunderstood you. Did you say . . .?

If I understand you correctly . . . Is that right?

I'm not sure I fully understood. Did you say that . . .?

WORKSHEET 3.6: ANSWERING QUESTIONS

Here is a list of suggestions that one expert came up with for dealing with questions. Think about them, and mark any advice that you do not agree with or that you think should be qualified in some way.

Eight points to remember when you answer questions:

- When you are writing your class/presentation be aware of the questions that you may be asked. Then get your colleagues to ask you difficult questions so that you can practisce this aspect too.

- Listen to each question carefully. Do not interrupt the questioner before they have finished. Take your time in responding, that way you not only show some respect for the questioner but you also give yourself some extra time to formulate your answer.

- It is a good idea to repeat or summarize the question so that everybody knows what you have been asked, and again you win yourself a little extra time for thinking.

- Keep your answers as short and concise as possible.

- Do not engage in lengthy discussions or extended answers to only one person. Offer to discuss the matter on a 1 to 1 basis at a later time if necessary.

- Always respond in a positive manner no matter how hostile, stupid or irrelevant you think a question may be.

- If you do not know the answer to a question then just say so. Do not apologize. As a follow-up strategy you can:

  ○ offer to find an answer and then get back to the questioner

  ○ suggest sources where an answer might be found

- Avoid the temptation of returning to the person who asked the question to check if you have answered to their satisfaction or not.

3.4 Providing Support for the Students in Your Classes

So far, our attention has mainly centred on our own performance as lecturers: how we organize the information in our classes, how we explicitly signal the structure we are following, how we maintain students' attention. It is understandable that sometimes we are most concerned with ourselves! But we must always keep in mind that teaching in English is not just some kind of performance that we do in order to show that we are international academics with an excellent level of English. EMI teaching is just like other sorts of teaching: it is a form of communication designed to help students acquire knowledge and skills. And students sometimes have difficulties too! As we have already mentioned, not all EMI students have the C1 level of English that might equip them properly to take your course. So it is extremely important to consider their needs.

In reality, it would be a good idea for us focus more on the students, and try to solve the most frequent problems they have. Worksheet 3.7 gives you the opportunity to think about some of the typical problems that students mention, and some proposals about how to address these problems.

WORKSHEET 3.7: ADDRESSING STUDENTS' PROBLEMS

Match the problems (a to f) with the proposals (1 to 6):

a. Students say that you speak too fast.	1. Give them a one-minute break every 10 minutes.
b. Students have difficulty concentrating for 50 minutes.	2. Write the difficult word on the board.
c. Students find it hard to make notes.	3. Give the students a written summary of each class.
d. Students seem to be confused by a word you are using.	4. Provide the students with an outline of what is in each class at the beginning of each session, so that they can use it as a structure for their notes.
e. Students lack essential background knowledge.	5. Remind students that English is a global language, and that they are going to encounter many different varieties of it during their careers.
f. Students complain about your accent.	6. Recommend some easy reading material or videos that will help them get into the subject.

ANSWERS: a3, b1, c4, d2, e6, f5

Sometimes, it is interesting to think of the students we have in our courses over the years, and try to imagine ways that we could make their learning process easier. For example, if terminology is important, we should emphasize this more, and provide students with resources (glossaries, online dictionaries, wordlists) in order to help them learn it. We could give a short test on the terminology near the beginning of the course, which will help the students to focus on the essential words. Here are some ideas that we have tested in different courses:

Glossary: When it comes to the language, one resource that some teachers use is the subject glossary. This consists of a list of words or expressions that are important in your course, and that students probably will not know beforehand. Some universities provide platforms such as Blackboard, which have a glossary option. To encourage students to use them, you could include a quiz in which they have to match terms with definitions, or complete the definitions themselves using words provided.

PowerPoints and Readings: It makes sense to provide the students with your PowerPoint (best in PDF format) and recommended reading in the form of PDFs of articles and chapters. If you think this makes sense, ask the students to download the PowerPoints before the class, and use them as a structure for making notes. It also makes a lot of sense to recommend a good textbook.

Group Study: Some universities promote study groups as a way of helping students to acquire study skills and to support each other. You could help students to organize study groups in which international students from different areas work together on specific tasks, or simply meet in order to go through the class material and exercises. In groups of this kind, the students whose English is stronger will often help those whose English is weaker.

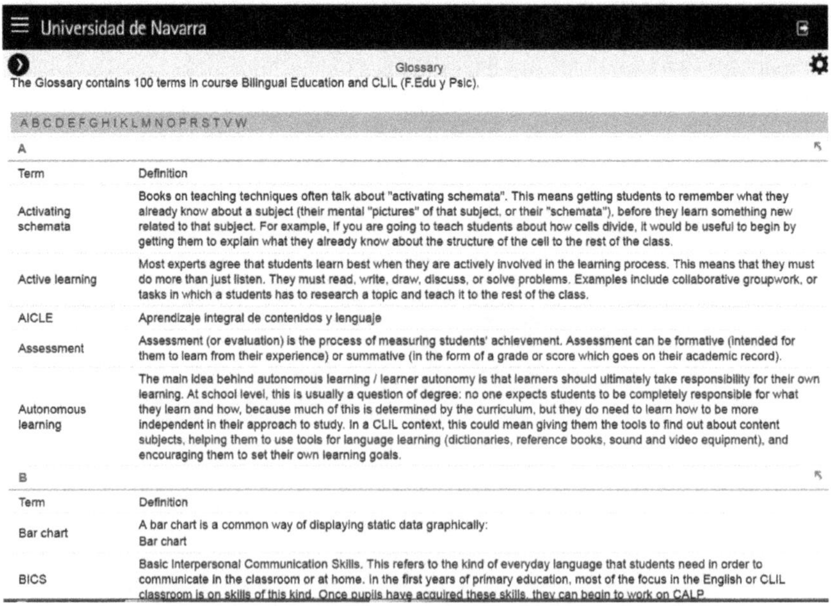

Universidad de Navarra

Glossary

The Glossary contains 100 terms in course Bilingual Education and CLIL (F.Edu y Psic).

A B C D E F G H I K L M N O P R S T V W

A

Term	Definition
Activating schemata	Books on teaching techniques often talk about "activating schemata". This means getting students to remember what they already know about a subject (their mental "pictures" of that subject, or their "schemata"), before they learn something new related to that subject. For example, if you are going to teach students about how cells divide, it would be useful to begin by getting them to explain what they already know about the structure of the cell to the rest of the class.
Active learning	Most experts agree that students learn best when they are actively involved in the learning process. This means that they must do more than just listen. They must read, write, draw, discuss, or solve problems. Examples include collaborative groupwork, or tasks in which a students has to research a topic and teach it to the rest of the class.
AICLE	Aprendizaje integral de contenidos y lenguaje
Assessment	Assessment (or evaluation) is the process of measuring students' achievement. Assessment can be formative (intended for them to learn from their experience) or summative (in the form of a grade or score which goes on their academic record).
Autonomous learning	The main idea behind autonomous learning / learner autonomy is that learners should ultimately take responsibility for their own learning. At school level, this is usually a question of degree: no one expects students to be completely responsible for what they learn and how, because much of this is determined by the curriculum, but they do need to learn how to be more independent in their approach to study. In a CLIL context, this could mean giving them the tools to find out about content subjects, helping them to use tools for language learning (dictionaries, reference books, sound and video equipment), and encouraging them to set their own learning goals.

B

Term	Definition
Bar chart	A bar chart is a common way of displaying static data graphically: Bar chart
BICS	Basic Interpersonal Communication Skills. This refers to the kind of everyday language that students need in order to communicate in the classroom or at home. In the first years of primary education, most of the focus in the English or CLIL classroom is on skills of this kind. Once pupils have acquired these skills, they can begin to work on CALP.

FIGURE 3.1 *Screenshot of course glossary.*

Language Support: If you detect particular problems in your student group, it might be a good idea to consult the university's language teaching experts. You can establish collaboration of an informal kind (invite one of the English teachers to come and give your students some advice about their writing, or suggest that the students should go and take an academic English course). Many universities have also set up collaboration on a more formal level: an English teacher can give a couple of sessions from your course, near the beginning of the year, or when you are setting a long written task. This teacher can also help you to devise the evaluation rubric, because he or she will have a good practical grasp of what students can be expected to achieve, and he or she will also know how language requirements should best be described in the rubric. In problematic cases, the language specialist may also be able to administer a test to find out what the students' strengths and weaknesses are as far as English is concerned, and recommend help where necessary. (See also our suggestions about team teaching, in Chapter 6.)

Writing Centres: A special word will be devoted to writing centres in Chapter 6. Here it is enough to mention that many universities in English-speaking countries have writing centres, which are designed to be a resource for undergraduate and graduate students. These centres are staffed by experts in academic writing who can help students with the written assignments required on their courses, and with the writing of MA and PhD theses. They usually also organize seminars and courses, and have reference material available. In some cases, they also provide online resources for academic writing.

Understanding Students' Difficulties

We have seen that students sometimes have difficulties with EMI lectures. Some years ago, we conducted a survey to find out what our local students found most difficult about the courses they were taking in English. Here are some of the items that *students* ranked as 'difficult' or 'very difficult' in a survey that we carried out (Breeze 2014a):

Difficult or very difficult:

- How easy is it for you to understand chunks of language and remember them long enough to take notes?

- How easy is it for you to understand lecturers who speak fast?

- How easy is it for you to maintain your concentration over longer stretches of time?

- How easy is it for you to deduce the meanings of words that you do not know by using the context and what you already know about the subject?

- How easy is it for you to identify the key words/terminology related to the content of the lecture?

- How easy is it for you to deal with the more colloquial aspects of the lecture (jokes, asides, anecdotes)?

Students were also asked to write down the aspects that they found most difficult. Many students wrote down the following points:

- Vocabulary (mentioned more by first year students)

- Speed of delivery

- Lecturer's accent

- Slides in one language, lecture in another

Think about what you could do to help the students with these problems. Then look at Table 3.4 to see some possible solutions.

Finally, let's take a look at some positive evidence about what students feel works for them. Costa (2016, 108–109) asked 134 EMI students at Italian universities what they found most useful or positive to aid understanding in EMI classes. The use of examples was overwhelmingly reported to be the most important strategy, followed by use of summaries, synonyms and definitions, all of which were selected as useful by more than 85 per cent of EMI students. Many students also gave a high rating to use of visual material and PowerPoint, and to 'friendly behaviour' on the part of the teacher. (See also Appendix 2 "Pronunciation practice" and Appendix 4 "Guidelines for visiting speakers".)

3.5 Online Lectures

Recent events have probably left many of us wondering whether the traditional lecture is still the most efficient way to deliver our teaching. During the Covid-19 pandemic the university world seemed to be divided into those who believe that online teaching needs to replicate face-to-face teaching as closely as possible, and those who think that the radically different affordances available in digital environments should be exploited to the full, even if this means discarding time-honoured formats like the one-hour lecture.

The supporters of the traditional class point out that it is a compact, convenient way of transmitting knowledge and promoting learning. The lecture helps to order students' and teachers' working day, build social relationships of various kinds and structure the educational process in a time-tested manner. Its detractors, on the other hand, point to the inconvenience of having to travel to a specific place, or be available at a particular time, and advocate new formats such as streamed lectures that can be accessed conveniently by students in their own homes, or recorded ones that are still available at the

TABLE 3.4 Students Who Don't Understand. Problems and Solutions

Problem	Solutions
Students find it difficult to understand chunks of language and remember them long enough to take notes.	1. Schedule in a brief pause after each main point, and encourage the students to complete their notes. 2. Make your PowerPoints available to the students so that they can use them as the basis for note taking. 3. Take a look at the notes students are taking. This might open your eyes to what you need to emphasize more! 4. Record short versions of your PowerPoint presentations – it isn't difficult and it will help the students master your subject.
It is difficult for students to understand lecturers who speak fast.	1. Slow down!! It is not a race to cover as much material as possible. 2. Don't be worried about repeating the main points at the end of the class. Most students will thank you for this.
Students find it hard to maintain their concentration over longer stretches of time.	It really is harder to concentrate when you are listening to someone speaking in a foreign language. Schedule breaks every twenty minutes, instead of every hour.
Students find it difficult to deduce the meanings of words that they do not know by using the context and what they already know about the subject.	1. Provide students with a glossary for the course. Emphasize the usefulness of the glossary in your lectures. 2. Make specialized vocabulary one of the focuses of your course, and test the students on it in the first few weeks, so that they get the idea that it is important to work on it.
Students need to learn to identify the key words/ terminology related to the content of the lecture.	If your lecture contains a lot of new/difficult words, you could draw the students' attention to them at the beginning of the class, give them special emphasis in the slides (e.g. by putting them in a different colour) and then test them on these words at the end of the class, or the beginning of the following lecture.
Students have problems with the more colloquial aspects of the lecture (jokes, asides, anecdotes).	1. Take care with colloquial aspects. If they are not essential, leave them out. 2. Visual humour based on cartoons or photographs might be easier for students to understand than verbal humour.

(Continued)

TABLE 3.4 (Continued)

Problem	Solutions
Students say they do not find it easy to understand your accent.	1. Slow down! Don't get nervous and speed up, because that will make things worse. 2. Concentrate on pronouncing the technical words correctly. Check the pronunciation with an online dictionary, and say them slowly. Emphasize them by writing them down the first time you use them. 3. If students seem puzzled by one of your explanations, ask one of the more confident students to explain it again to the whole class. This is a good way to make good students feel useful, and to find out how much your students really understand!

end of the term for revision purposes. Still more radical departures include the reduction of one-hour classes to ten-minute talks, 'learning modules' or 'bite-sized lectures', to name just three of the numerous formats on offer. These reduced formats, which have been used on MOOCs and other distance learning platforms for years, respond to the difficulties that arise for students when concentrating on longer online videos, coupled with the insight that the most important contents of a longer class can usually be conveyed in a brief, but focused, manner if there are no interruptions.

In the middle of this controversy and whatever the lecture format (traditional or abridged and synchronous or asynchronous) or the more innovative 'anti-lecture' options available, online learning (also known as 'e-learning' and 'distance learning') is expected to fulfil a series of pedagogical requisites. It must seek the *empowerment* of students as lifelong learners (Dawley 2007), offer them time and space for *cooperative socialization,* and promote the development of *higher-order mental skills,* such as critical thinking, creativity, and a sense of initiative or proactivity. Online learning is also supposed to be *transformative* in a double sense: on the one hand, through peer contact students may enrich their points of view and thus learn from others. They can also create learning tools or tune up existing technologies with their own strategies and ways of use, exploring possible synergies and simultaneously letting their learning habits be shaped by them. On the other hand, learners need to become 'knowledge transformers' able to transfer skills and knowledge across situations, contexts and disciplines. However, there is no 'recipe' or prototypical teaching experience for achieving all these desirable learning outcomes, even though online instruction is certainly no longer a novelty (Ko & Rossen 2017).

So we can see that online teaching/learning is complex and difficult to pin down. Perhaps we can start from what it is not: it is neither an online library (even less a digital bookshop charging fees for document downloads) nor a repository of exercises and tests for self-study. This has been the great mistake of many teachers during the pandemic: they uploaded documents and activities in their institutional platforms or in some cloud storage service on the internet and expected students to cope individually by themselves, without any class session or teacher presence – at the most some consultations via email. Too much learning autonomy was taken for granted, and nothing can be really assumed in online teaching: students do not automatically know how to learn online, even though we might think they are 'digital natives'. The early definition put forth by Ko and Rossen (2004) that online teaching/learning means 'conducting a course partially or entirely through the Internet' is currently dated and needs to be expanded to embrace a number of key concepts, among which are those of 'constructivism', 'learning community', 'transformation', 'active learning' or 'lifelong empowerment'.

So what do specialists agree on? Let us look at a few features that constitute the 'backbone' of online teaching/learning:

1. *Promoting deep lifelong learning:* while surface learning gives students an idea of their progress through exercises, exams and quizzes, deep learning encourages learners to manage and share information and to reflect on it and on their own learning process. This is possible through typical collaborative activities such as (a)synchronous discussions, collective blogs and wikis, and group challenges, which provide a balance between action and reflection. The sense of achievement resulting from successful group work helps to maintain a positive attitude towards learning and technologies during the course – and during people's lifelong, ongoing development.

2. *Peer collaboration:* the activities mentioned above reflect this principle. Learning needs to be not only social or interactive, but also collaborative among peers. Let us not forget that every collaboration is interactive but not the way round: not every interaction is necessarily collaborative. Collaboration should be part of the course assignments and happen within small work teams, where it is easier to connect up more quickly than in large groups. Chapter 4 will comment more on online collaborative learning.

3. *Challenging authentic tasks:* online assignments should be multidisciplinary, connected to the real world, and integrated within a larger picture that includes the course's learning goals. They should be designed to promote higher order thinking skills (HOTS): from the application of information to new situations and

the analysis of ideas and their interconnection, to the evaluation conducive to decision-making and ultimately to the creation of a new or original product.

5. *Diversity of learning styles:* different styles of learning should be not only respected but also encouraged. Authentic collaborative tasks tend to require the convergence of multiple learning styles.

6. *Adequate and timely feedback:* It should come from both instructors and peers. Rubrics for the evaluation of group achievements and performance with clear criteria are advisable.

Now, we may wonder what class time should be devoted to, what we can do with the traditional lecture, if information can be presented readily online. Scholars researching online teaching suggest investing time in group work monitoring during the lessons. They emphasize that the more time-on-task, the more and better learning chances (Palloff & Pratt 2015), which hints at structural changes in the conventional lecture when online. Bach et al. (2007), for example, hold that the lecture 'needs to move beyond its traditional boundaries' towards increased student interaction, and encourage teachers to break up the delivery of content by means of activities such as group discussions, problem-solving in small teams or

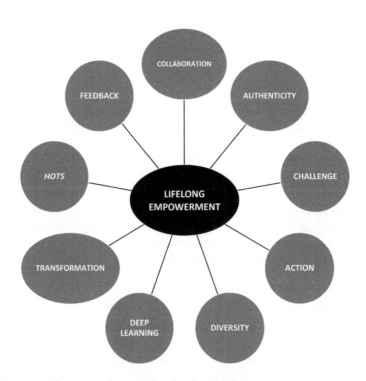

FIGURE 3.2 *The aim and essentials of online teaching.*

even formative tests. In our own experience, it is especially fruitful to divide class time into fixed bands:

- INPUT TIME by means of slideshows or brief texts and quizzes to be read/done on the spot and immediately discussed. Slideshow viewing is usually an assignment to do at home, so that class time can be reserved for clarification and discussion.

- WORKSHOP TIME, during which the different groups tackle new tasks or resume the ones pending from previous sessions.

- REPORTING TIME, in which results and procedures are presented to the whole class.

- QUERIES AND QUESTIONS TIME, for teacher and students to check understanding.

- CLOSING SESSION, in which student volunteers are asked to verbally summarize the highlights of the session, or the teacher may show a written recapitulation or a relevant visual to elicit concepts and stimulate the interrelation and encapsulation of ideas.

Closing summaries may stem from a direct question asked by the teacher, of the type: 'What have we learnt today?' or 'What have been the main points of today's class?', or from instantaneous quizzing tools such as the one in BbCollaborate (Moodle), with Yes/No and multiple-choice questions. This sort of tool can put an end to the class with quick comprehension tests that display the number of students choosing a certain answer.

Other 'tips' that work to enhance the online lesson(s) (some inspired by Dawley 2007) are the following:

- SCREENSAVERS: before and after the class, as students are gradually logging on/off, images, brief texts, outlines and infographics can be projected as 'wait materials'. They can also contain the day's lesson plan (overview + objectives + resources + activities) or a final verbal or visual summary. They can serve as practical 'lecture pills' on important concepts and problems.

- 'AHA! BOARDS': areas where students can share those 'aha moments' of enlightening revelation that may occur during or after the class.

- 'BUMPER STICKER SUMMARIES': they condense the student's experience or knowledge gained at the end of a lesson or unit as it would fit on a bumper sticker.

- LIKERT-SCALE SURVEYS: completed at the end of a unit or of the course, they inform the teacher about the students' opinions on the instructional methodology and strategies, the syllabus, their own learning satisfaction and the degree of effectiveness in the use of the learning environment.

3.6 Take-Home Message

As we have seen, there is no reason to be nervous about lecturing in English, as long as you take time to prepare your classes properly. But don't let intensive preparation make your classes longer and heavier than before – when you are preparing for EMI the most important thing is to have clear priorities. It is better to get three important ideas across properly, than to swamp your students with details that they are never going to remember. Sometimes less is more!

And here is a second point to think about. Remember the saying about getting the message across in public speaking: 'Say what you're going to say, then say it, then say what you've said.' The same principle applies to lectures. Near the beginning of your class, you should say what you are going to talk about, then spend most of the time explaining it, and finally you should summarize the subject briefly at the end. Don't be afraid of repeating your main ideas – those should be the ideas that students take away at the end of one day's class, and that you can start off with at the beginning of the next one!

WORKSHEET 3.8: PERSONAL OVERVIEW

When you start doing EMI, the aspect that probably worries you the most is the idea of lecturing in English. Lecturing is a formal performance, often in front of a large audience, and so it is important to prepare your lectures well (and if they don't go as well as expected, to try to learn from that experience). Here are some questions for you to reflect on or discuss, now that you have read this chapter.

In your experience (or opinion), what is the most difficult aspect of the lecture? Rank these aspects in order of difficulty:

- Starting the lecture and engaging the students' attention
- Structuring the lecture in a logical way
- Keeping the students' attention throughout the lecture
- Integrating different activities (video, discussions, formal explanations, exercises)
- Answering students' questions
- Dealing with problems (student behaviour, students who cannot follow the lecture, or who ask difficult questions, etc.)
- Ending the lecture

What ideas from this chapter can help you with the aspects you find most difficult?

Case Study 1: Experiences from Nursing and Genetics

When people start lecturing in English, their whole approach is conditioned by factors such as their previous experience in lecturing, the way they have learned English and the extent to which they are used to using that language for professional/academic purposes, the kind of subject they have to teach, their lecturing style, the level of English among their students, whether their students are local or international, homogeneous or heterogeneous, undergraduates or graduates, and so on. Another factor that is rarely mentioned in this context, but which is extremely important, is personality. Consider these two accounts of the first year of teaching content courses in English. Which factors do you think influenced these teachers? What advice would you give to them?

Loreto is a qualified nurse and has taught in a nursing school in her country for many years. After working there for many years, she was given the opportunity to take a master's degree and then a PhD in Edinburgh, an opportunity that she welcomed with some trepidation. She had some problems at first adapting to the UK university, but with the help of her tutors and advisors she was able to complete the master's, and she then spent three more years completing her PhD, which was written entirely in English. When she learned that she was going to be teaching a theoretical course in nursing, she immediately signed up for an advanced-level English course, and decided to study hard to take the Cambridge Proficiency exam. As she herself put it, 'When I start teaching in English, I am concerned that my performance will not be good enough. I may make some mistakes. And my pronunciation is not perfect.' However, after the first term of teaching in English her attitude had modified somewhat. 'I now see that the problem is the same as in Spanish. I need to go back to the beginning and find ways of engaging my students in the subject. My students get bored, and they get distracted easily. And it is more difficult now, because the students have a lot of difficulties expressing themselves in English. I was very worried about myself, about my English. But now I know I have to think about myself less, and about the students more. In the end it's not about English, it's about teaching.'

Miguel is a highly distinguished research scientist who spent many years researching at a lab in Oxford. When he returned to a position at a large Spanish public university, one of the ideas was that he should teach genetics in English. He had never taken any English-language exams, but he felt 100 per cent confident that he could teach his subject effectively in English, since he never had any communication problems in that language and he used English all the time for research projects, writing, etc. However, when he started lecturing in English, he realized that things were not so simple. His native-like English and total fluency enabled him to express complex ideas with ease – but his classes went above the students' heads. They were simply not on the same level as his colleagues in the Oxford lab or at the international conferences. 'I had to slow down, go back to basics,' he said. 'I somehow fell into the trap of thinking that because I was teaching in English, my students would be like my colleagues in Oxford. No way! They are still undergraduates, and some of them really have problems understanding English. And my subject is a very difficult one conceptually speaking, which means that I have to explain everything twice, and even then, I'm worried that they haven't understood.' One of Miguel's solutions has been to ask students to do more reading before the lecture, and to make students responsible for explaining some parts of the course to their peers. Another has been to ask them to summarize the contents of the class back to him at the end of the session – in English if possible, in Spanish if necessary. 'Above all, it's about finding solutions. We know our subject, but when it comes to teaching it in English, we have to be prepared to learn new approaches.'

Case Study 2: Distributing Class Time

In the biannual in-service training seminars for content teachers held by the ICE (Institute of Educational Sciences) at the Universidad Politécnica de Madrid, one of the participants' biggest fears is not being able to bear the discursive burden of a whole class session, normally of one hour and a half or two full hours. Insecurity and anxiety increase if the subject matter to be taught is more verbal than numerical and, therefore, its discourse is not as controlled as that of mathematics-, physics- and chemistry-based disciplines.

In every edition of the course, the teacher proposes that the participants should brainstorm how such fears could be minimized. They crave for classified repertoires of discursive functions, for the exposition of content (e.g. definition, cause-and effect relationships, comparison, hypothesis, deduction, discussion, conclusion, summary) and for personal interaction (e.g. comprehension checks, floor-giving and taking, interruptions, encouragement, constructive criticism, etc.), as well as for class management routines (e.g. distribution and collection of materials, instructions of any kind). This type of repertoire is usually applied to each of the phases of the conventional lecture: start, introduction, content delivery, summary and closure. But, how about dividing class time into yet more controllable segments?

So far, brainstorming has yielded three alternative class-time distribution models: *fixed-slot-based*, *radial* and *task-based*. Those teachers who have implemented them have noticed that the application of linguistic repertoires of connectives and expressions for marking different discursive functions becomes clearer and more orderly, and, of course, less discursive load is to be borne by the teacher, since student-led modes give learners much more opportunity to talk. While the fixed-slot-model provides scheduled bands for certain types of activities, several of which almost do not require teacher talk and lend themselves to a flipped format (e.g. for background facilitation), the radial model pivots around some central aspect of the teacher's exposition and just involves him/her talking at the demo and discussion stages. In the latter, he or she is the moderator in the presentation and feedback sections held after the students' group, pair, or individual work. Below are the graphical summaries of these two models:

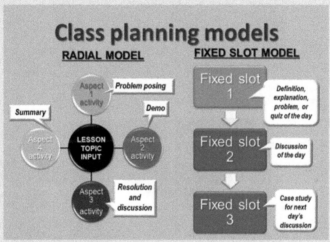

The task-based model may revolve around the construction of a professional document (a specific textual genre such as a report, an abstract and a grant application) or the resolution of a problem. The sequence of actions in the diagram is not completely original but adapted from Feez (1998). The teacher should just contextualize the task and show how the problem is solved or the text constructed. Finally, (s)he may link it to other problem types or texts or leave that as a documentation assignment for students, who previously should have tried to solve the problem or construct the text in groups or pairs and individually.

TASK-BASED MODEL

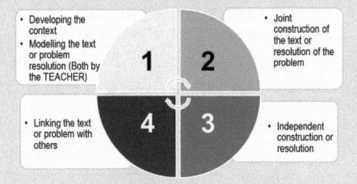

- Developing the context
- Modelling the text or problem resolution (Both by the TEACHER)

1

2

- Joint construction of the text or resolution of the problem

4

3

- Linking the text or problem with others

- Independent construction or resolution

With this class plan model, students' discourse takes up from half to two thirds of the class time, which saves teachers a considerable amount of discursive stress. If the contextualization and modelling are flipped, then teachers' discursive investment can be minimal.

POINTS FOR REFLECTION

Class beginnings and ends are crucial: the former to capture students' attention and raise their interest in the topic to be explained, and the latter to make them leave the classroom with a strong 'take-home message'. In other words, with a clear idea of the content taught and motivation to continue working on it, learn outside the class and eventually do something practical, such as identify the content's possible applications in real-life situations and try to solve everyday problems. These objectives, however, are hardly met if the teacher finishes the class with vague colloquial expressions of the kind 'And that's all', 'And that's it', 'This is all I wanted to say', 'or just by saying farewell' ('See you tomorrow/ on Thursday/next week').

1. WHAT ARE YOUR CLASS CLOSURES LIKE?

Many teachers quickly *summarize* what has been explained or done towards the end of the session. Summaries are always desirable, as we have seen, but they do not need to fall always on us teachers. Here are several ways through which you may delegate the recapitulation of content and which allow you to check your students' comprehension and call them to action:

DISPLAY-BASED

- A *slide* with:
  - an effective outline (e.g. bullet points)
  - an effective diagram, optionally for eliciting a minimal oral explanation or a concept
  - a suggestive image (e.g. a photograph for diagnosis) for eliciting the content covered during the class session
- *Realia* (samples of any kind to be described, either voluntarily or by a group or by the individual student who receives the sample).

TASK-BASED

- An *on-the-spot oral summary* by a student or a group of students. It may be voluntary or scheduled beforehand (e.g. assigned to groups with a class session calendar).
  - *Quizzes* of various kinds:
  - *Gap-fills* to be completed by students
  - *Matching* of concepts, causes and consequences, methods and areas of application, etc.
  - *Labelling* of scenarios, symptoms, materials, components, etc. (all of them in visual form)
  - *Quick problems* to be solved, individually or in teams
  - Four or five *questions,* open or in multiple-choice format
  - A very brief *hypothetical situation or case study* involving the concepts and procedures explained in the class session and

requiring the student to sketch out a quick procedure (e.g. a medical treatment for a clinical history, a legal procedure fit for a given case, an equation or method suitable for solving an engineering problem, the application of a business idea)

- A *graph or table commentary* (e.g. for diagnosis or discussion on the evolution of a certain treatment or management of a specific situation) involving the concepts and/or procedures explained

- *Error detection* in diagnoses, calculations, legal and business procedures, the labelling of concepts and procedural stages, etc.

- *Riddles or guesses* whose answer is one of the concepts or terms explained (e.g. 'What is the X that produces Y and has such-and-such features?', or 'Which two viral diseases share the symptoms of fever, rashes and blisters?'). A final slide with a graphic organizer may function as an effective mnemonic:

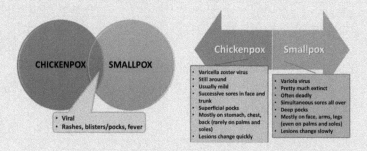

- *Logbook blog assignment:* the class may agree to keep a blog to report on the major class difficulties and highlights and provide summaries of class sessions. Each work team may be in charge of the summary of a particular session in the class calendar. This initiative would facilitate catching up by students who have missed a class and help the authors of the blog entry to differentiate important from peripheral information and become more concise writers.

- *Disciplinary bingo game:* the teacher may give one card to each work team, which contains the information delivered in class, and then read aloud a term, a question, an equation, a concept definition, a description of a case, a scenario or some symptoms, or a mini-narrative. Team members must pay attention and check whether what has just been read matches any of the items on their card. The relationship between the written information and the items on the card is not always immediate and may require some processing, as cards may contain images (photos, drawings and synthetic diagrams), terms, definitions, small datasets, formulae, equations, calculations, graphics/charts and tables, brief scenario descriptions and minimal narratives.

The following example combines the verbal and visual learning styles. For the sake of illustration, it gathers items from a variety of disciplines (physics, dermatology, botany, architecture/art history, epidemiology) at a very basic level of knowledge. The circles show the information originally read by the teacher. Note that the 'malaria' item not only demands visual identification but also cause-and-effect knowledge (female *anopheles* mosquitoes transmit the disease). Complex formulae, equations and some scenario descriptions and case studies likewise need some mental processing before the aural-visual matching.

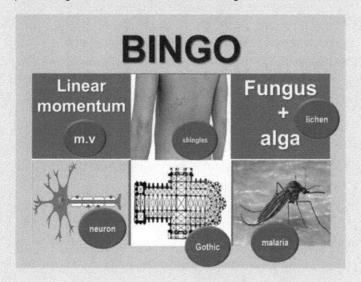

2. YOUR 'OVERALL TEACHING RADIOGRAPHY': WHAT ARE YOUR MOST COMMON PRACTICES DURING THE LECTURE?

CLASS START (especially when introducing a new topic)

- **Inductive** (presenting concrete data or some particular phenomenon or element)

- **Deductive** (presenting the general law, principle or macrostructure)

- **Tangible** (presenting realia (a piece of alloy, an engine piece, etc.), a balance sheet, a medical history, a legal case, a geological map, etc.)

- **A combination of the three**

INTRODUCTION

- **Reminder** of the **last class** session
- **Elicitation** of knowledge from students by:
  - asking **direct questions**
  - asking for **voluntary contributions**
  - starting a **casual conversation** with students
  - **sparking a discussio**n with a case study or a snippet of news. Work teams may be allotted time for internal discussion and their views may be communicated by spokespersons.
- **Brainstorming** (for example, with the aid of mind maps on the blackboard or whiteboard) See Sancho Guinda 2010.
- **Description or narrative of a real-life situation** related with the content to be explained next. Work teams may be allotted time for internal discussion and a spokesperson communicates their views to the whole class.
  - **Presentation of a problem** to be solved or minimized with the content to be explained later on
- **Your own explanation/lecture** (your monologue)
  - **Anecdotes and stories**
  - **Definitions**

CONTENT DELIVERY

Predominant type of discourse in your exposition of content:

- **Contrastive**
- **Argumentative**
- **Descriptive**
- **Narrative**
- A **combination** of . . .

SUMMARY

Your recapitulating habits are:

- **Progressive** (as the lecture progresses, or after each important concept)
- **Final** (towards the end of the session, sometimes as a closure device)
- **Both**

CLOSURE

- **Visual** (slide, photograph, diagram, video clip)
- **Verbal message** (e.g. a brief oral or written summary in a slide or a handout)
- **Quiz**
- Quick on-the-spot **assignment** or for the next class
- A famous **quote** pertinent to the content
- A **game** (e.g. the 'disciplinary bingo' described above)

CHAPTER 4

Interacting with Students

4.1 Interacting with Students: Some General Ideas

We all spend part of our day talking to students on an individual or group basis: explaining, reformulating, encouraging, listening, redirecting – all of these are the way we build and maintain our ongoing relationships with our students. When we are teaching in our own language, we know how to manage these interactions: we understand the roles we (and our students) are supposed to play, and we feel comfortable in them; we know whether the students are polite and respectful, and when they cross the limits; we know how to deal with most of the problems that come up; we have no difficulty rephrasing what we mean, or communicating information in a more informal way if necessary. When we are dealing with international students, the problems often become more complex. We sometimes feel that a student (or group of students) has a negative, hostile or aggressive attitude. We sometimes have real problems getting through to him/her/them – either because of different expectations or because of real language problems. In this chapter, we take a look at the different kinds of interactions that come up in our day-to-day lives as university teachers, and provide some ideas that can help you manage these successfully.

Teacher Roles

One of the factors that shape our interaction with students is the kind of role that we are expected to play. Cultural expectations – the culture of our country, and more specifically the educational culture in our university – have a major influence on the way the different participants in higher education understand their roles.

Here are some of the main roles in university teaching – these are *roles* that any university teacher might have, and are not to be confused with your actual job title (e.g. professor), which probably has to do with your status within the academic community:

Lecturer: The lecturer is essentially a provider of knowledge. He or she stands up in front of a large class, and delivers that knowledge in the form of formal lectures, perhaps accompanied by visual information, so that students can take notes. This is still the backbone of university education in many countries. The lecturer is expected to explain his/her subject clearly, in a structured way. Students are expected to learn the content material, and their knowledge will be tested in the final exam.

Instructor: Outside the university world, the term 'instructor' is used to mean the person who directs people as they learn a practical skill. We talk about a 'skiing instructor' or a 'driving instructor'. In both cases, the instructor provides information and guidance, and takes learners through a structured programme so that they can acquire the necessary skills and expertise. Some universities give the name 'instructors' to the people who teach languages, composition skills or hands-on laboratory sessions. They are working with groups, rather than with individuals. But notice how their way of working is different from the lecturer's role: the instructor is focusing more on the student's progress, provides help where needed and withdraws that support when it is not necessary any more. A similar role to this is that of the trainer (for example, the 'teacher trainer'), who is someone who supports people as they take their first steps in their profession.

Advisor: An advisor is someone who gives advice – and we generally understand that this is happening within a one-to-one situation. Some universities have established formal systems in which students are assigned an official advisor (or 'tutor') and are expected to meet up with him/her once a term or once a month. The purpose of these meetings will vary, but in some universities these advisors play an important role in the first year of the degree programme, helping students to adapt to university life. They may also give students advice about choices they have to make (taking an exchange year, doing summer work experience, looking for a master's programme or a job).

Coach: We all know that the coach has an essential role in sport: many sportspeople rely heavily on their coach for personalized support and encouragement, as well as for an independent perspective on their performance. Just recently, the concept of the 'life coach' has become popular: these are professionals who know how to empower other people, helping them to form their goals in life and achieve them, overcome difficulties, handle relationships and so on. Importantly, the coach is supposed to encourage self-discovery, helping his/her clients to make their own decisions in order to maximize their potential. In the university, the advisory role (advisor, tutor) might sometimes encompass elements of coaching.

These roles are far from the only ones. In Figure 4.1, we have left some of the spaces blank, for you to reflect on other roles that you might find yourself performing with some of your students (e.g. friend, parent, police officer, psychologist, entertainer).

Although these roles are all different, and place varying demands on your linguistic skills if you have to perform them in English, they also overlap in a number of ways, and have various aspects in common. While the lecturer role is probably prominent when you are working with large groups, the instructor role takes on more importance in group work, and the roles of advisor and coach are generally found only in one-to-one sessions.

In this chapter we are going to focus on some of the main language functions that you will need in your overall interaction with students. For the sake of clarity, we will organize this by thinking about three big areas of higher education: lectures and formal classes with large numbers of students; group work; and one-to-one sessions. As you will see, the different roles that you may have in these situations are reflected in the different kinds of language that you are likely to use.

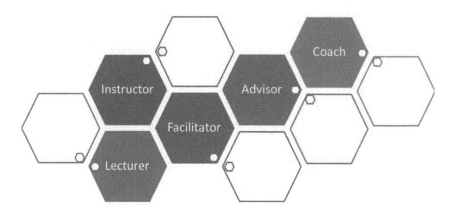

FIGURE 4.1 *Teacher roles.*

4.2 Interacting with Large Groups

Most university teachers have to give lectures to large groups. In Chapter 3, we talked about how to organize information and express ideas clearly in English. Here, we are going to think about how teachers normally interact with students in this situation, and what problems can come up. We will start by looking at questions – the questions you ask, and the questions the students ask you – and then go on to consider a few other aspects of classroom management that are important when you are dealing with large groups.

Teachers Ask Questions . . .

How do you know your students are following what you are teaching? How do you know what they understand and what they don't? How do you know what doubts and difficulties they have with your subject in general, or with particular topics or tasks? Questions and answers play an important role in all of this: the questions you ask them, and the questions they ask you.

So let's think first about the questions you ask the students. Researchers have found that using the right kind of questions plays an important role in motivating students, ensuring active participation, teaching students to think and helping them to develop problem-solving skills. In your own lectures, you might ask questions to test students' understanding, to elicit opinions or information or to perform certain classroom management roles. But you might also use them to push students' learning further, to encourage critical thinking or creativity.

Questions to Check Students' Understanding

Let's think first about the kind of questions you ask to check whether students understand what you are explaining. We all sometimes ask questions like 'Do you understand?' or 'Have I explained that clearly enough?' The problem is that the most vocal students tend to answer 'yes', and the students who really haven't followed what you were saying tend to keep a low profile.

In general, if you want to know whether students follow your classes easily, it is better to ask some very concrete questions based on what you have just explained, along the lines of 'So, on the basis of what I have just explained, if X goes down, what is likely to happen to Y? Will it go up, or down?'

There are plenty of other ways to check students' understanding. Here are some simple techniques:

- At the end of the class, project three questions related to what you have talked about in that class. Give students a minute to think and check their notes. Then, either allow three students to give quick answers (risky) or say that you will go through the answers at the beginning of the next class. Doing this helps to maintain the connection and dynamism between the different lectures in your series, and also helps to get the students 'on the page' when the next class starts. This is specially important in contexts where the lectures are being given in different languages, and your students may have, say, a formal lecture in Spanish in the morning, a lab session in Catalan at lunchtime, and your lecture in English in the afternoon. We all need a few minutes to acclimatize in a different language!

- At the end of the class, allow five minutes for the students to write down a brief summary, or bullet points, covering the topics you talked about in the lecture. If you see that they are having difficulties, elicit a brief summary from the better students, and share it with the whole class.

- At the beginning of the class, spend a few minutes reminding students about what you talked about in the previous class. This has the benefit of simplicity, and it also emphasizes the continuity and flow that links all your classes together. Education has been described as a 'long conversation', and within that, your course should also be a 'conversation' with continuity, flow and two-way communication.

Questions to Engage Students with the Topic

If you ask students how much they already know about an issue that you are discussing in the classroom, or what their opinion about it is, something similar usually happens. The students who are most confident in English, or who believe that it is important to give their opinions, will probably answer. Those who don't feel confident in English, or who are shy about giving their opinions in public, will not. Is this a problem? The silent majority (around 90 per cent of the student body at any given time) may already be irritated that two or three vocal students seem to monopolize all the teacher's attention. Moreover, if you have asked the question to find out what the general opinions are among this group of students, you will have failed in your objective: you will still not know what most people think. So the first thing to ask yourself is: why am I asking this question?

If you are asking questions simply in order to make students engage with the subject, to get them to think about it or respond on a personal level, then you need to consider how to achieve this goal. One good method is to allow students time to think about the question and practise their answers. Here are some ways in which you could do this:

> *Situation: Activating previous knowledge and generating interest.*
> You want to activate the students' previous knowledge and ideas

about the new topic that you are going to study over the next few classes. Let's take the example of the effects of urbanization. Your aim in asking questions is to get the students 'on topic', to help them to see what the key issues are, and to challenge their own preconceived notions so that they are receptive to new knowledge.

Dynamics: Ask the students to work with a partner to brainstorm a list of the advantages and disadvantages of the move to the cities, in the contexts that you are going to study. If you have a large group, it may be useful to break down this task so that different groups within the classroom discuss different aspects of the question (for example, in this case, some people could think about advantages and disadvantages from the perspective of people moving from the rural environment to the urban one, while others could think about what this means for city planners, or for the regional government). Set a realistic time limit for the task (e.g. 10 minutes). Suggest that since you will be asking them for feedback, they should keep notes about what they are discussing in English. Once the ten minutes is up, you can either get them to compare their ideas with another pair or you can go around the class quickly, asking each pair to contribute an idea. A good way to do this is to write down 'advantages' and 'disadvantages' on the board or PowerPoint, and add one idea to this from each group.

Take care: It is important to remember that the aim of this activity is not to teach the subject through group work, or to carry on until the students come up with the 'right answers', but to activate students' previous knowledge or experience of the subject, and to get them to see that there is a lot that they don't know! So once you have elicited all the ideas from the class, you can project your own overview of the topic, and show how you are going to address those points that the students mentioned, but also introduce some new ones that they didn't think of.

If you are asking questions in order to get students to respond on a more personal level, relate the issue to their own experience, and in general, adopt a more reflective attitude to life, then you need to think about your strategy more carefully. Nothing much will be gained by just asking students to volunteer answers to questions like 'When you started your teaching practice, did you have any problems with discipline in the classroom?' in front of all their peers. In fact, by doing this, you would run the risk of closing down the subject that you really want to open up! Here are some ways in which you could open up your discussion of problems and difficulties, and engage students on a more personal level:

Situation: Getting students to reflect on their experiences and feelings. You want to find out about your students' experiences, opinions and feelings during their first work placement in schools. You know that it might be invasive to ask a specific student a personal question in front of all the other students. You want them to engage with the subject on a personal basis, but also learn to share their experiences and see that they are not alone in having problems.

Dynamics: Ask the students to work in groups of three or four. Project a graph or some quotations that show typical problems that students have when they start their teaching practice. Ask the students to discuss these problems in their group, and think of ways in which they might address these problems in their next teaching practice. Allow sufficient time for this (10 or 15 minutes, depending on the amount of material to be covered). Elicit responses from each group, and write them on the board or PowerPoint. Another option would be to project or distribute a short survey, in which students have to evaluate their own feelings or responses to certain aspects on a Likert-type scale (i.e. 'To what extent did you find it easy to maintain your pupils' attention? Did you feel confident at dealing with challenging behaviour? Were you able to time your classes appropriately'?). The students should rate themselves quickly, and then discuss their responses with the other members of their group.

Take care: In this case, students should work with groups in which they feel comfortable. You should make it clear that it is important to reflect on our own experience as teachers, in order to learn how to do it better next time. If we were perfect, we wouldn't need to learn anything new!

Asking Better Questions . . .

One important point to think about is whether the questions we ask our students are really helping them to enhance their learning. Some researchers who reflected on this point came up with a Carroll diagram covering the different types of questions that teachers ask (McComas & Abraham 2004), displayed in Figure 4.2.

The quadrants in the diagram can be used to classify the questions teachers ask. The different classifications (lower order/higher order and convergent/divergent) can be understood as follows (please see also Chapter 5 for more about lower- and higher-order thinking skills):

- *Lower-order questions*

Questions that check a student's comprehension and ability to recognize and identify factual information. Questions that test a student's general background knowledge.

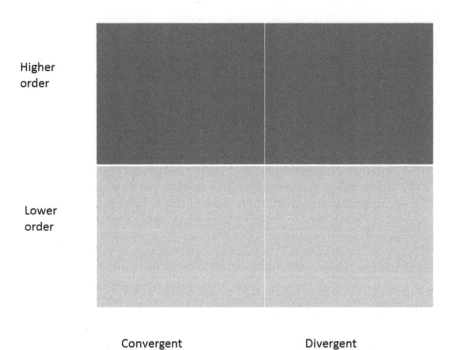

Higher
order

Lower
order

Convergent   Divergent

FIGURE 4.2 *Question types.*

Example: What countries does Italy have borders with on this map?
Example: Who wrote *Persuasion*?

- *Higher-order questions*

Questions that encourage the student to comprehend/recognize/identify information, but ask him/her to relate this information to wider factors.

Example: Why are Italy's borders on this map different from its present borders?

Example: Why do you think Jane Austen chose the title *Persuasion* for this novel?

- *Convergent questions*

Questions that have a rather narrowly defined correct answer – they ask students to recall relevant information but require little reflection, and the answers are generally quite short.

Example: What other countries' borders changed as a result of the First World War?

Example: Which other novels by Jane Austen have titles consisting of abstract terms?

- *Divergent questions*

Questions that are broad and open-ended. The student is required to recall some information from memory, but will need to apply that knowledge and other knowledge to explain a topic, situation or problem, or to analyse it further.

Example: What other effects did the First World War have on Italy?

Example: What trends in novel titles can you trace across the nineteenth century?

Now let's take a look at some questions from a chemistry lecture in the BASE corpus (mentioned in Chapter 3) asked (Table 4.1). This will help us to see how questions encourage interaction, but also fit into the flow of the class, providing the teacher uses them strategically. Notice how the lecturer asks questions to stimulate the students' interest and understanding of the topic and its wider importance, and encourages their contributions

TABLE 4.1 Questions Used to Maintain the Flow in a Chemistry Lecture

Lecturer	The question was why what other physical properties has the ruthenium complex got that make it a target for so much research? And the res the research is what what sort of research is it is it being used for?
Student	Renewable energy source sorry renewable energy source renewable energy source
Lecturer	Yes, it's used as a renewable energy source. It's been put in a number of target systems, one is photoelectrolytic cells that are driven by sunlight so you get perpetual electricity from a cell based on the ruthenium complex and the other one is splitting water into hydrogen and oxygen using the hydrogen as fuel so the big interest in this complex well we got got some answers from group D and it's it's got a high quantum yield
Lecturer	Now the I the last question was a bit nasty how can ruthenium complexes be tethered to to semicondu semiconductor services? Then it says why why should you want, to but let's let's hear it how you can tether them to start with if you want to tether a complex to a polar surface what's the best thing to do to it any any suggestions?
Student	Er a polar group
Lecturer	Yeah yeah put a polar group on it is a suggestion, that is that is a good suggestion actually. What we would want to do, I'll pick yet another one of these

WORKSHEET 4.1: CLASSIFYING TEACHERS' QUESTIONS

In which quadrant on the Carroll diagram (Figure 4.2) would you put the following questions?

- What are the symptoms of malaria?

- Why is it useful to drain standing water in order to prevent malaria?

- What other diseases are carried by mosquitoes?

- If you had an outbreak of malaria in your local area, what would be your first line of action in the short term? What other longer-term actions would you take and why?

Now write down some questions that you often ask your own students.

Are your questions mainly lower or higher order? Are they mainly convergent or divergent? Revisit your questions and think of ways to make them more stimulating.

WORKSHEET 4.2: UNDERSTANDING THE ROLE OF TEACHERS' QUESTIONS

Here is part of the transcript from a meteorology lecture in the BASE corpus. Put the students' answers from the box in the right gaps. What kind of questions is the lecturer using? Why? How does he encourage the students and support their attempts at answering?

Stefan   Density of material   Planck's law   Wien's law   emission

Lecturer	But of course remember there are two other things two other ways that energy is coming out the bottom of the slab what were they again?
Student	Scattering
Lecturer	Scattering and
Student	1.
Lecturer	Emission, thank you, it's one of these cases where everyone's whispering the answer but no one's saying it loud enough all right. So so the slab can be emitting radiation and also radiation that's entering the slab from other directions can be getting bounced into this direction so let's let's write down some expressions for those ones as well. So we'll start by taking emission, so energy emitted by the slab now once again this is going to depend on a couple of different factors so this depends on what's going to determine how much energy the slab is emitting at some given wavelength temperature is going to be a big one. So this depends on temperature and what's the relationship that tells us how much emission we're going to get at a given temperature?

Student	2.
Lecturer	Wien's law's going to tell us the wavelength where we get the most emission but what's going to give us the whole function at a as a function of any wavelength?
Student	3.
Lecturer	The Stefan-Boltzmann one is isn't the one I was looking for because that's giving you the total. I'm saying if you just have some arbitrary wavelength that's not at the peak what's the function that's going to tell you how much you get at that wavelength? We've done it in this course, we've written it out on the board, I've shown plots of it on the projector.
Student	4.
Lecturer	Planck's law, that's right, so the Planck function, so the energy emitted depends on the temperature and that's given by the Planck function. And well, what else is it going to depend on? So if if it's at a given temperature what else is going to affect the amount of emission that we get?
Student	Sorry is it the amount of material
Lecturer	The amount of material absolutely the amount of material does it depend on anything else?
Student	5.

And Students Ask Questions . . .

Of course, students also ask questions. And in reality, sometimes, these questions are not really welcome. There is, in fact, a massive difference between cultures concerning whether or not students are supposed to ask questions, and what teachers think and feel about this (see Section 4.5 for more ideas about international students and the cultural expectations they may bring with them).

In all of this, as we saw in Chapter 3 and Worksheet 3.5, there are different kinds of question. We identified four main kinds:

Good questions. These are the ones that you probably want, because they show that the student has understood what you have been explaining, that the student is interested in your topic, and that he/she wants to know more. These questions may also generate interest among the other students, and show how you can make your classes even more stimulating and informative. Don't be afraid to thank the student for asking such a good question! This will encourage others to ask good questions too.

Difficult questions. These are questions that take you into dangerous territory. It might be that you simply do not know the answer. Or it might be that in order to answer the question, you would need at least half an hour more. Or that the answer would be difficult even for fourth-year students, and the class you are teaching is in the first year. In this case, please do not feel personally threatened by the question. It is quite acceptable to say that this question is something that you will address next year (or in the master's). Most students will be happy with that answer. Above all, do not let this kind of question unsettle you as a teacher. You always know more than the students do about your particular subject.

Irrelevant questions. These are questions that you really do not need to answer. For example, it is common for international students to ask EMI teachers questions about their exchange programme, local transport, university administration, etc. If you feel that it is not your job to help them with these non-academic aspects, feel free to tell them that, and to point towards the appropriate office or person. There are also some students who ask irrelevant questions about your course or subject matter. These questions can be answered by other questions, such as 'How is that relevant to the subject we were talking about today?'

Unnecessary questions. These are questions that tell you that a certain student was not paying attention. For example, you have explained five times that the specialized vocabulary for your course is all available in the online glossary, and that there are also some dictionaries that can help. But one student still persists in asking you about a term that you have already explained. Either point the student towards the relevant resources or let one of his/her classmates do it.

WORKSHEET 4.3: RESPONDING TO STUDENTS' QUESTIONS

Take a look at the phrases for responding to students' questions, then classify them according to the four headings in the table.

Good questions.	Difficult questions.	Irrelevant questions.	Unnecessary questions.

- That is a very good question, but I think it would take too long to answer it today.

- Could you explain what that has to do with today's class?

- I think we covered that in detail in yesterday's session. Perhaps you could consult the notes and the PowerPoint.

- Thank you, that's an extremely important point. So important that we will be talking about it in detail next week.

- What an interesting question! Would anyone in the room like to suggest an answer?

- That's an important question, but I think you will find the answer in the glossary.

- Exam dates? Please consult the university website.

- That's certainly a fascinating question, but it is not one that we can deal with today.

- Thanks for the question. On the basis of what we've just seen, what do you think the answer is?

- Excellent question, but we don't have time to deal with it now. Can I ask you to check the answer yourself, and we can discuss it later?

Classroom Management

Questions and answers are a fundamental part of the way teachers 'manage' the classroom and exercise their authority. But there are also other ways in which teachers do this (see also Chapter 5 on setting work and giving feedback). Some teachers like to establish the ground rules at the beginning of the course. In formal lectures, there are certain types of behaviour that may be acceptable in some places, but not in others. It is therefore useful to give a few explicit rules about what is appropriate in your context.

Establishing the Ground Rules

Do you allow students to eat or drink in the classroom? Do you accept assignments after the deadline? Are students allowed to arrive late and/or leave early? Is attendance obligatory, and do students have to sign a list? One of the best ways to deal with these issues in an international context is to have an explicit list of rules, which you can publish on your course website, or simply communicate to the students at the start of the course. Of course, you should check whether the rules that you impose are compatible with the rules in your institution and country.

If a student breaks a rule, it is clear that you can draw attention to this in a constructive way. Among the advantages of doing this, it will make other students aware that the rule exists.

WORKSHEET 4.4: SETTING STANDARDS OF BEHAVIOUR

Here are some different things that a teacher might say when a student has overstepped the mark. What rule or norm of university behaviour has the student broken?

1. The class actually begins at 9 o'clock on the dot.
2. There is a cafeteria outside if you are feeling hungry.
3. As we said at the beginning of the course, all assignments have to be handed in before the deadline, so I'm afraid I can't accept this.
4. Absences from class need to be justified by a doctor's note.
5. Please see the guidelines about how the essay should be formatted.
6. Mobile phones should be on silent mode during class time.
7. In this country, it is normal for university students to address their teachers as 'Dr' or 'Professor', so you can call me 'Dr. Mackay'.
8. If you would like to explain your problem in English, then we can all help you to solve it.

4.3 Managing Group Work

Many European universities are currently encouraging students to work in groups. Various arguments are used to support this choice, the most important of which are instrumental, pedagogical, practical and motivational. First, in the world of work, many of our activities involve collaborating with other people. At university, we are preparing students for their professional future, and therefore we need to set up tasks in which they can learn the skills needed to work as part of a team. Second, there is a strong tradition in education showing that group work is beneficial in itself. It allows students to acquire different skills and competences that are valuable for their own sake. It has also been shown that in many cases students can learn better with their peers, because they provide useful scaffolding for each other: the support they provide for each other is somehow closer and more appropriate than the support provided by the teacher, and it is easier for them to understand each other's problems. Third, there is also a practical argument in favour of group work. If you have a large class, you often can't get to check each person's work individually. If they work in groups, not only do they support each other's learning, but they also generate one single piece of work per group, which you can then address in more detail. Also, some types of activity can really only be done in a group. Finally, group work is also a useful way of varying the dynamics of the classroom. In many countries, students are still expected to attend four to seven hours of classes in one day. If we put ourselves in their position, we will see that it is important to provide them with a variety of different activities and exploit different classroom dynamics. The more sociable and extrovert students find group work particularly motivating. However, group work is not a panacea, and in order to be useful, it has to be carefully set up, managed and evaluated.

Setting Up the Task

Group work is not easy to manage. But it is easier if we start off with a clear idea of the processes the participants should follow, the products they should produce and the roles they should play. For this, we need to keep the learning objectives and assessment criteria for our course in mind (see Chapter 5 for more details on this). We also need to make sure that students have the resources they will need to complete the task (including content knowledge and reference material, material resources and, of course, linguistic resources). Specialists who study task-based learning and group learning in schools have come up with some ideas that might be useful, providing we adapt them to the level of maturity of our students.

Explaining the Procedure

It is very important to provide guidelines about how to carry out the procedure. The level of detail that you provide will depend on the complexity of the task, the students' previous experience with group tasks of this kind, the timeframe and deadlines involved, and other factors.

For example, in a scientific English course taught during the third year of the degree in psychology, we thought it would be important for students to learn the procedure for conducting questionnaire-based research, and for writing up papers. This proved to be a useful exercise that would prepare them for writing up their final project, or later, for writing a master's thesis. In our experience it works best done in pairs, or in groups of three.

So how did we go about organizing this task? In order to sidestep the problems that will come up if we ask students to write original questionnaires, we always set out from a questionnaire in a published study. The students choose from three studies that we have pre-selected on the grounds that they were relatively short (no more than 5,000 words), had an accessible topic (general, but involving psychological issues) and were relatively easy for third-year undergraduates to understand (clear presentation of theoretical background, no complex statistics). For example, one year they could choose from short (4,000 to 5,000-word) studies about shopping habits and age, about language learning preferences and about attitudes to smoking.

Once each pair or group of students has selected the study that they are going to replicate, we ask them to extract the questionnaire used in the study and consider how feasible it would be to apply it in our local context. We ask them to adapt it or translate it if necessary (although we raise their awareness of the need for back-translation, owing to time constraints this is not always possible during our course). But we do insist that the students should pilot their version of the questionnaire with two or three subjects (usually fellow students), and then we organize a brief feedback session in which they can explain to the other members of the class how they might adapt the questionnaire to use it locally.

We then also discuss how students can make contact with their sample of subjects – stressing the need for the subjects to give informed consent. We debate the pros and cons of paper versus online administration, and ask the students to decide how they are going to administer their survey, bearing in mind the characteristics of their sample. Unsurprisingly, most of them opt for online distribution using Google Forms or Survey Monkey. However, we have had some more adventurous students who want to conduct their survey among populations that are less digitally savvy, and so we leave the option of paper questionnaires open.

Students then go away and put their survey online or produce paper questionnaires, make contact with their sample and obtain results. Since this is a learning exercise, it is not important for them to get a large number of responses. We usually tell them that ten would be enough (apart from anything else, it makes the statistics easier!). However, the nature of social networks being what it is, students often seem to have no difficulty getting much larger samples.

After allowing a week for students to obtain some data, we then ask them to bring it to the class, and we go through the different sections of the paper, encouraging them first to prepare their method and results sections, and then to write a discussion in which they compare their own results with those of the published study. In general, students do not conduct statistical comparisons between their own results and those of the model paper they are using, because of the unequal sample sizes, but if they want to do so, this should not be discouraged. Although in principle it is not necessary for the students to search for more bibliography, since their whole study is a replication of a previous study, we encourage the more enthusiastic students to conduct a bibliographical search, starting from the other works cited in the study they are replicating. The last sections to be written are the introduction and the structured abstract.

Once the research papers have been written, it is a good idea to share them online with the rest of the group. This usually sensitizes students to the characteristics of a good research paper, and helps them to understand the grade you have given them.

The five stages of our questionnaire study replication task can thus be set out as follows:

> *Stage One: Researching the bibliography and preparing the questionnaires.*
>
> *Stage Two: Drafting and trialling the questionnaires, and identifying the sample.*
>
> *Stage Three: Administering the questionnaires.*
>
> *Stage Four: Compiling the results in a database and processing the statistics.*
>
> *Stage Five: Writing up the final report.*

Defining the Product

Everyone needs to have a clear idea of what should be produced at the end of the task. You might want them to write a twenty-page report, or build a scale model, or carry out a laboratory experiment in which you compare several substances. In each case, you will need to make it clear what the characteristics of this final product should be:

> *Task: Final report. The final report should have the following sections: Abstract; Introduction; Background information; Method; Results; Discussion; Conclusions and limitations of study; References. It should be presented in Times New Roman (12), with 1.5 spacing, and with a line space between each paragraph and before and after section headings. It should be 4,000 to 5,000 words in length. It must be uploaded to the class platform in PDF format on 1 December.*

Assigning Roles

Some teachers prefer to assign roles to the different members of each group. This is a way of exerting a degree of control – or providing an element of structure, depending how you see it. It is not compulsory – many teachers prefer to leave the division of labour up to the students themselves. But it may be useful, in that it will draw the students' attention to the different aspects of the task and the roles that someone will have to play if they are to complete it successfully. It also serves as a way of communicating the message that everyone should contribute, but not necessarily in exactly the same way!

Some of the roles that you might want your students to take on in a given task are:

Manager: His/her job is to make sure that the task is properly carried out, and to solve any issues that come up.

Spokesperson: His/her task will be to communicate with the teacher, and perhaps also to present the results to the rest of the class.

Record keeper: This person has to produce a written record of what is decided at the group meetings, and send it to all the members of the group. This serves as a reminder for more forgetful or disorganized students.

Language expert: This student encourages the other students to use English, and helps out by looking up vocabulary or checking texts. This could be a good role for students with a stronger command of English.

However, there are probably as many different possible roles as there are different tasks, so it is not possible to provide a definitive list.

In all of this, remember that international students are your best ally! If you create groups consisting of people from different language backgrounds, you will guarantee that they use English when working together. If you create groups with members from different cultures, you will help them to maximize their international learning experience.

A final word about group tasks – when setting up the task, you should always:

- Give clear instructions, in clearly defined stages.

- Draw attention to the different task components and roles involved.

- Check students' understanding of the task.

Troubleshooting

Does group work need to be managed? Some teachers think that it does not. You can just send the students away to work in groups, and then evaluate the final product. At most, you might announce that you are 'available' for consultation if they have any problems. This kind of 'light-touch teaching' is perhaps appropriate at postgraduate level, with students who are serious and self-driven. It may also be suitable in the later years of a given degree programme, once students have learned how to collaborate effectively, and how to deal with problems that arise. It is probably not appropriate in the first year of a degree programme, or the first time that students undertake a new kind of activity (i.e. lab sessions, designing a product, etc.).

WORKSHEET 4.5: MONITORING STUDENT ACTIVITY

So let's imagine that we have set up some group work in the classroom or lab, and we want to ensure that students are contributing to their groups, learning from each other, learning from working together, acquiring new knowledge and skills, etc.

Here are some of the questions we might ask. Can you group them under the headings in the table?

Encouraging participants who have problems	Helping participants to manage their roles in the group	Praising participants who are working well	Getting participants back on task

- **a.** I like the way that you divided up the different aspects of the task.
- **b.** How does this discussion help us to solve the problem?
- **c.** Is that what everyone thinks, or just what two of you think?
- **d.** Could one of you explain exactly what you have done so far?
- **e.** Could you each explain to me what your role has been?
- **f.** Have you thought of approaching the problem from the perspective of the customer?
- **g.** That's is a very striking design!
- **h.** To finish the task, please write down each person's contribution to the overall activity.
- **i.** I notice that you were checking your social media. How exactly does that contribute to this task?
- **j.** That seems like a very promising solution.
- **k.** So what stage in the protocol have you reached?
- **l.** Why not stop and ask yourselves: Are we going about this in the right way? Is there a more efficient way?
- **m.** Can you explain exactly how that is going to fit into your final product?
- **n.** Why not go back to the second part of the task, and see if you can see any other way of moving forward.
- **o.** Why don't you divide up the different activities and assign them to different people?
- **p.** Are you all happy with that solution? Because if you aren't, there is still time to suggest an alternative that everyone can agree on.

Evaluating Task Participation

The key to reliable, fair evaluation of group work is to have a clear definition of what was expected (see 'setting up the task', aforementioned). In the name of fairness, it is also important to make it clear from the very beginning whether the grade is going to be a group grade, or whether there is some assessment of each individual's contribution.

Table 4.2 gives a rubric for evaluating students' performance during a group task. It breaks down the students' contribution and attitude to five components: collaboration, contributions, problem-solving, time management and attitude. Other rubrics might include a specific evaluation of each part/phase of the task, or include aspects such as efficiency, following instructions, concentration or creativity.

We should note that this is NOT a rubric for evaluating the final product – just for assessing whether our students have carried out the procedure in an appropriate way, working together in a collaborative spirit and solving the problems that have arisen along the way (for more about evaluating the product, see Chapter 5).

4.4 Interaction outside the Classroom: One-to-One Sessions

The amount of time university teachers are expected to spend talking to individual students tends to vary considerably. When one of the present authors was an undergraduate in the School of Modern and Medieval Languages at Cambridge University, most of the teaching took place through 'supervisions': one, two or perhaps three students would each write a long essay and deliver it to a teacher (a college fellow and professor in the university), who would then meet them for an hour-long discussion, in which he/she would listen to the students' ideas, comment on them, provide useful feedback and suggest how they should approach the reading and research for next week's task. When she went to Germany for an exchange year, she was surprised to see that students studying languages and literature spent most of their time attending lectures in large lecture halls, which often had hundreds of people present, and studying on their own for the exams at the end of the semester. It is quite clear that the type and quantity of contact between teachers and students is very different in each of these situations. Even now, in Europe after the Bologna Reforms, many universities follow the model of the 'magisterial class', in which most of the teaching is done by formal lecture to large groups. In developing countries, this is still the most usual way of teaching, and student numbers make any more personalized approach impracticable. Depending on the system in your university, you

TABLE 4.2 Rubric for Evaluating Student Participation in Group Work

Collaboration	1. Generally does not listen or share. Does not cooperate with the other members of the group.	2. Sometimes listens and shares, but sometimes is not cooperative.	3. Mostly listens, shares, supports others. Does not cause trouble for the other members of the group.	4. Always listens, shares, supports others. Tries to ensure that the group members all work together.
Contributions	1. Rarely provides ideas. Does not make an effort even when requested.	2. Sometimes contributes ideas. Makes an effort when requested.	3. Mostly provides useful ideas and usually makes an effort.	4. Always provides useful ideas and makes an effort.
Problem-solving	1. Does not try to solve problems. Leaves the work to others.	2. Sometimes follows suggestions proposed by others.	3. Rarely makes suggestions but is willing to try ideas proposed by others.	4. Thinks of solutions and makes suggestions.
Time management	1. Wastes time. Does not meet important deadlines.	2. Tends to delay. Often has to rush to meet deadlines.	3. Mostly makes good use of time. Generally keeps to deadlines.	4. Makes good use of time throughout the task. Always keeps to deadlines.
Attitude	1. Often criticizes the task, product or group members to others.	2. Occasionally criticizes the task, product or group members to others.	3. Hardly ever criticizes task, product or group members to others. General positive attitude.	4. Never criticizes the task, product or group members to others. Always has a constructive attitude.

may have to spend a lot of time engaging in one-to-one communication with your students. This may take the form of individual or small-group teaching, it may take the form of providing individual guidance and feedback for students writing their 'degree papers' or master's theses, or it may be what we could term a 'pastoral' activity, in which the tutor or advisor helps the first-year student to adapt to the demands of university life, then guides him or her through the ups and downs of the degree, helping with choice of optional courses, exchanges or work experience, and finally provides some advice about professional openings or further study. Some EMI teachers may also be closely involved in providing guidance for international students, who may well need a helping hand, particularly at the beginning of their stay.

In what follows, we will look at the different types of one-to-one or small-group interaction with students, and consider how we can prepare to make these sessions more useful.

Individual or Small-Group Teaching

Although individual or small-group class teaching sessions are rare, there are occasions when we might have to organize our teaching in this way. For example, when we were all working from home during the recent pandemic, one of the authors had students in different time zones, so sometimes sessions in Meet or Skype had to be conducted with groups of two or three.

The individual or small-group session is actually a wonderful opportunity to get to know our students better as people, and also to get insights into what they find easy or challenging about our courses. One particular experience is usually that those instructions that we thought were so comprehensive and explicit turn out to be confusing and vague for our students! Another is that students sometimes have knowledge gaps that we never suspected, and that can easily be rectified by prescribing some extra reading. One final insight coming from small-group teaching is that no two students are alike, and that the construct of 'the average student' that we tend to apply in our lectures simply does not exist. It is true that it is a useful construct, but it is also true that we are often blinded to the wealth of individual differences in culture, experience, education and ability in our classrooms. If anything, one-to-one sessions can help open our eyes to the needs of different kinds of student, and perhaps suggest possibilities for making our teaching richer and more varied.

Having said all of this, we also think it is important to control the time spent on giving one-to-one support to students, and to structure these sessions so that they are useful for everyone. If very small-group teaching forms part of your regular teaching load over a long period of time, it is

TABLE 4.3 Stages in a One-to-One or Small-Group Teaching Session

Getting up to date: A few minutes are spent on greeting each other, checking that everyone is fine, and making sure that no one has special difficulties. If someone does have special needs, the teacher can make a note of this and say that he/she will deal with this later in the session.
Setting the agenda: The teacher should explain what the group needs to achieve in today's session, and how it fits in the ongoing course.
Instruction: The teacher, or one of the students, presents new material or analysis.
Discussion or questions/answers: The students comment on the material and ask questions to clear up any doubts.
Practice: The students apply the new knowledge to an exercise or a practical case.
Feedback: The teacher provides answers, and comments on the way the students have handled the case.
Homework: Reading, exercises or other activities for next week are set for the next time.

useful to put measures in place to make sure that it is as productive as possible. Sometimes people think that when you are teaching one-to-one or one-to-two it is not necessary to have a class plan to organize the time – but this is not true for most people. Most teachers benefit from starting out with the idea that a certain number of points need to be covered, and that time needs to be made for each person present to listen to the other(s), ask/answer questions and give feedback.

Table 4.3 shows a plan that has been recommended for one-to-one or small-group (<4) teaching in face-to-face or online settings.

Support for Students Writing Undergraduate and Master's Theses

Students obviously need more individual support during the phase when they are writing their master's dissertation. In some countries, students also write a long piece of work in the final year of their degree, which we could call a degree project. In case you are worried about these names, it is useful to begin by saying that even in Anglophone countries, there seems to be no universally accepted names for these tasks. In the United States, a PhD is often called a 'dissertation', while a master's degree ends with a 'thesis'. In the United Kingdom, it is the other way around! But our troubles are still not at an end, because different universities also use different names for the same thing. A study conducted at the University of London by Paran et al. (2017, 271) found that even within one university, the following names were used to describe the final piece of long written work submitted for a master's degree: dissertation, report, project, written report, project report, scientific report and scientific paper. In this chapter, we will use the US term, referring to the text that students write at the end of their master's degree as a 'master's thesis'. For the end-of-degree paper, we will use the term 'degree project'.

But the complications do not end there. The expectations surrounding these projects also vary considerably. For example, the recommended word length can be anything from 4,000 words to 20,000 words, and the structure can be anything from 'introduction, main part, conclusions' to the formal 'abstract, introduction, material and method, results, discussion' found in scientific papers. The aforementioned London-based authors (Paran et al. 2017, 268) also describe the confusion around the role of the supervisor/director, who seems to have to fulfil confusing combinations of different roles in different institutions, from suggesting literature or proposing methodology to actually proofreading the text. A quick search of academic institutions worldwide also reveals a bewildering list of different activities that supervisors are expected to carry out in the course of one single master's project. In particular, there seems to be an expectation that the supervisor should take on an increasing number of different, and sometimes mutually incompatible, roles, ending up as 'both a mother figure who responds to emotional needs and a father figure who expects intellectual autonomy' (Firth & Martens 2008, 280). As if this were not enough, the globalization of higher education also means that intercultural differences are emerging as a further factor in this panorama, since mismatches emerge between what international students expect, on the basis of their home culture, and what they receive in their host country. In view of this highly complex situation, many people feel that the role of the supervisor in degree projects and master's theses needs to be clarified and streamlined. Above all, we should find ways of communicating to students what our role is, and what they can reasonably expect from us.

To streamline this as much as possible, here is a framework that we can use to define the roles of the supervisor in the master's thesis, based on the instructions for supervisors of master's theses published by the University of Otago Graduate Research School, New Zealand (University of Otago 2020). We should note that Otago, like many universities in English-speaking countries, asks students to complete a student-supervisor research agreement at the beginning of their collaboration, in order to bring a higher degree of definition to the relationship.

The supervisor and student should thus sign a binding agreement in which they explicitly set out the terms of the supervision agreement, including:

- the frequency of meetings
- responsibilities of the student and supervisor(s)
- workload expectations
- funding for the project (if appropriate)
- compliance matters (e.g. ethics and legal issues)
- intellectual property
- training requirements
- authorship for any publications resulting from the research
- how to resolve any issues if progress is unsatisfactory or there is a breakdown in the supervisory relationship.

Supervisors' responsibilities defined in the agreement would include holding 'regular formal supervision meetings' and providing 'quality, focused and uninterrupted attention to the student and the research'. The supervisors should be 'a reliable and well-informed source of guidance in all matters of sound research practice', and might eventually 'encourage the student to make seminar/conference presentations and to publish material'. On the personal side, they should also be 'sensitive to cultural, political or gender issues relating to the research topic or the student', 'assist in integrating the student into the academic and social life of the Department'. Their role also implies aspects of critical evaluation, as ultimately they have to apply criteria relating to ethical standards and quality control, by ensuring 'that work submitted was that of the student and that the data was plausible'.

For their part, students should be committed to 'being well organized and capable of setting and meeting deadlines for various phases of the research', 'maintaining frequent and regular contact with supervisors', 'establishing and maintaining a clear vision as to the overall aim of the research and of the intermediate goals', 'starting to write-up early and continuing to write sections of the work' and 'providing supervisors with draft written work at regular intervals'. It is the student's responsibility to ensure 'that the work of others is appropriately acknowledged and accurately cited and that the bibliography is accurate and complete'.

In the previous section, we looked at how many universities like master's students to meet their thesis supervisor and agree on important points related to their work together. Worksheet 4.6 provides some suggestions about the language you could use for carrying out these activities. For further ideas on supervising students' research, see also section 'Support for PhD Students' in Chapter 5.

WORKSHEET 4.6: SETTING THE SCENE FOR MASTER'S STUDENTS

Here is a table containing some of those points, and some phrases and expressions you could use to introduce a discussion of them. Which phrases could you use to discuss which point? In some cases you may find that more than one is relevant.

Discussion point	Phrases (letter)
Frequency of meetings	
Responsibilities of student and supervisor(s)	
Workload expectations	
Funding for the project	
Compliance matters	
Intellectual property	
Training requirements	
Authorship for any publications	
Resolving issues if progress is unsatisfactory	

a. You've been working on the MA/MSc for six months now. I was wondering if you felt there are still any gaps in your knowledge that need to be addressed.

b. One important point is to get ethics clearance. Have you filled in the application form for that?

c. Sometimes we can actually publish some of the research that comes out of your MSc project. If that happens, it's important to know that the normal rules of scientific publishing apply, and that you would not normally be the first named author on this paper.

d. It's really important to get the time frame for the thesis clear. You need to have a viable proposal by January, and I need to receive the first draft in April. Between those two points, you have to set your own internal deadlines so that you keep up the momentum.

e. I understand that you received funding from your own government for this MA. Do you need to acknowledge them in any papers that might come out of this?

f. I'm sure you're clear about the risks of plagiarism.

g. Any patents resulting from these experiments would be subject to the normal university rules on IP.

h. In May, I will expect you to hand in a first draft that has been edited and corrected. Good English is your responsibility, and I am not going to correct the language that you use.

i. Please feel free to make an appointment to talk to me if you get stuck. Remember, my consultation time is Friday from 3 to 5, and I'll need to know at least 2 days in advance.

j. There is a fair amount of reading to be done at the beginning. I would expect you to spend at least two hours a day reading and taking notes, so that you get an overview of the subject.

k. Quite a few funding opportunities come up in the course of the year. You should get on the mailing list for that.

l. I am happy to commit myself to meeting every two weeks, providing you can show me that you have new material to discuss.

m. It's a bit theoretical at the moment, but if we turned out to have some big problem – say, you just don't meet the deadlines or I am unavailable for weeks on end – you need to know that the course director is the person you (or I) should turn to.

Tutorial Sessions

In some universities, individual sessions are organized in which first-year students meet a particular teacher who is going to be their mentor throughout the years of the degree. The roles of these 'tutors' or 'mentors' vary from providing personal guidance and 'coaching' or giving help with study skills, to following a predetermined sequence of activities and discussions intended to socialize young people into the university's way of doing, being and thinking. Such sessions can be either extremely productive or somewhat frustrating, because there is inevitably going to be a strong personal component in any one-to-one relationship.

Worksheet 4.7 is based on a real situation, in which a university uses an online self-evaluation questionnaire to find out how the student sees him-/herself. This can be very useful, but of course, should not be used unless the students him-/herself actually consents to it!

WORKSHEET 4.7: HANDLING THE TUTORIAL

In some universities, students fill in an online questionnaire in order to define their stronger and weaker points. Here is the result of one student's self-evaluation questionnaire (self-rating on a scale from 0 to 5).

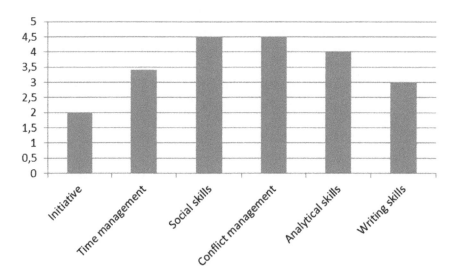

GRAPH 4.1 *Student self-evaluation.*

Choose a name for the student represented in Graph 4.1, and work with a partner to decide what you would say to this student. You will probably want to include some of the following phrases:

Being encouraging

- I can see that (COMPETENCE) is coming along nicely.
- You're on the right track with (COMPETENCE).
- Your marks so far are very good – keep up the good work!
- I'm happy to see that you organize your time well.
- It's good news that you know how to deal with conflicts.

Setting priorities

- So let's think about what you need to do first.
- Which aspect would you like to work on this month? Perhaps since the exams are coming up it would be a good idea to concentrate on organizing your study time.
- What is more important for you at the moment, writing skills or initiative?
- What do you think you should prioritize?

Suggesting areas for improvement

- I can see that you have given yourself a low score in (COMPETENCE). Why is that?
- Let's take a look at the graph. Your lowest score seems to be . . .
- People seem to think that initiative is not your strong point. Any comment?
- What has been the most difficult thing for you this term?

Following up on previous conversations

- Last time we talked you mentioned the problem with physics. How is it going now?
- You said last month that you were going to work on time management. How did it go?

4.5 Interaction in the Virtual Classroom

Based on an explicit constructivist approach to learning, most of the manuals on online teaching regarded today as 'classics' (Dawley 2007; Palloff & Pratt 1999, 2015; Stavredes 2011; White & Weight 1999, among others) stress its inherent interactional component, also termed 'community building' and 'engaged learning' (Conrad & Donaldson 2004). They point to the need to emulate, as far as possible, the social atmosphere of traditional face-to-face environments and build a 'learning community', a process which often takes longer than in the ground-based classroom and entails harder work. This difficulty is considered by many online instructors one of the major 'negatives' of virtual teaching. Some sources, such as the British Council and the BBC (on their joint teaching site), estimate that, whereas the socialization time necessary to 'get to know each other' is thirty minutes in face-to-face groups, online students spend at least one week trying to develop a sense of identity and collegiality.

The widely diverse models of online learning community are rooted in Wenger's (1998) concept of 'community of practice', which allows for the co-creation of meaning through 'doing' (i.e. in our case *action learning*) and the experience shared by a group of like-minded people who feel a sense of identity, distinctiveness or collective individuality. Action learning, as Bach et al. (2007) note, has consolidated the 'constructivist turn' in teaching and learning and not only includes practical pedagogical approaches such as TBL and PBL (task-based and problem-based learning, respectively) but also reveals what can be transferred to other situations, and raises awareness of group processes leading to effective ways of working together.

The idea is to go beyond the conventional lecture-oriented course and promote 'engaged learning' among participants. Engagement may occur at four levels of interaction, the first three of them being critical to ensure success:

- Interaction *between the learner and the content*
- Interaction between *the learners and the teacher*
- Interaction *between learners*
- Interaction *between learners and entities external to the course*

Successful interaction between learner and content demands clear learning goals, an appropriate design of didactic materials, an optimized storage area and authentic collaborative tasks connected with the real world, which frequently factor in different learning styles. The purpose of the course and its derived learning objectives must be part of the same picture showing the usefulness of the training: what skills learners are expected to acquire and where, when and how they can apply them. All students are supposed to learn the core concepts and procedures, but not all will learn all the course content and each comes to the virtual classroom with their own background of customized knowledge, interests and abilities. Teachers can help set learning priorities by asking students what they already know and want or need to learn and solve (e.g. curiosities, problems, challenges), what they will need and how they will know and show that they have learnt.

Content should be kept simple: brief lessons with limited text and graphic organizers and other types of visuals are very much appreciated. Yet it must be borne in mind that teaching online is not 'a contest to see who can create the coolest multimedia' (Dawley 2007, 28) but rather promotes an interactive learning experience. A consistent presentation of content in folders and subfolders in the least possible number of storage areas facilitates the comprehension of how knowledge has been sequenced and why, and may offer alternative paths for learning, by means of learning routes and course maps. Teacher-created summaries at the end of each lesson are an efficacious aid to improve comprehension, but even more effective are the ones co-created by students and the posting of their own reflections in forums, blogs, wikis and portfolios. Stimulating extra readings and additional task challenges usually arouse learner curiosity and may be hosted in a special area within the course webpage for easy access.

Teachers can know more accurately how students are interacting with the course content and at what pace if they provide a place for learner expression (e.g. comments and blogs), for interaction with other learners (e.g.

discussion forums) and for dialogue with the instructor (e.g. forums, chats, email) to let him/her know about their difficulties and overall progress. The interaction between learners and content, in any case, is largely mediated by their relationships with teachers and peers.

As for the second level of interaction, teachers and students ideally need to work to achieve engaged learning. This means that teachers must establish a social presence; that is, 'be there' to create a warm and supportive learning environment, explain concepts and clarify doubts, guide, model procedures, monitor teamwork, provide continuous feedback and in general be responsive to the learners' needs and concerns without exerting oppressive control. This balance is not easy to attain: two dangers of such 'social presence' on the teacher's part are an excessive investment of effort in class management and too much personal involvement. Gudea (2008) reports on the frustrating experiences of online instructors who fear not being able to effectively monitor and answer student questions, given the large number of messages they receive. These unfortunate teachers find themselves checking on emails and postings or analysing discussion threads several times a day throughout the week. They become so obsessed with making themselves permanently available that they end up investing much more time than in the same class face to face. The fact that technology use can be addictive also contributes to this effect.

To prevent this kind of overload, experts recommend small groups of five to ten students as the ideal class size for teaching online. In on-ground teaching one can have larger classrooms, but these tend to be limited to lecture mode, with more control by the teacher and reduced opportunities for active learning in the form of peer collaboration.

Some experts recommend that teachers in online formats should drop the 'lecturer' and 'grader' roles for a large amount of time to take on others which prove to be more democratic and productive in the long run (Gudea 2008; Ko & Rossen 2017), such as those of 'facilitator/provider', 'mentor/tutor/coach', 'moderator/conductor/director' and 'co-worker'. Of course, this does not mean that lectures should be scrapped, but rather that teachers should conduct them more dialogically than monologically and leave room for significant questions, posed either by the students or by themselves as 'food for thought'. Thinking of online contexts, Boettcher and Conrad (2016) distinguish three main types of questions, in order of increasing complexity:

1. *Questions on factual content*, which deal with data and knowledge bits implicit in core concepts.
2. *Socratic questions*, which make learners inquire about themselves.
3. *Problem-solving questions*, whose purpose is to make students think seriously about complex issues, take up challenges and customize learning to make it relevant.

Clearly, then, in addition to adopting different roles, a democratic interaction between teachers and students implies transforming or adjusting teaching methods. The traditional lecture as we know it, with the teacher positioned alone in front of a mass of students, connotes the idea of 'performance' and the image of a 'stage' where the audience is to be, above all, entertained. Another criticism against lecturing is that it is an elitist and paternalistic form of knowledge delivery (Bach et al. 2007) in which learners, out of respect, do not dare question the lecturer's judgements, experience and expertise. This is particularly problematic in online classes, where students may not have the chance to interact with the teacher in other ways (e.g. before and after the lecture). To remedy this, in online mode lecturers need to make an extra effort to be learner-centred and inspirational. In other words, they should pose questions and challenges key to the learning aims, suggest relevant and attractive reading, visual and multimodal materials, and kindle in students the wish to go beyond the basics and research into the topic themselves. Of course, none of this is possible without a crystal-clear structure around a few straightforward learning aims, a limited number of coherent and essential points and facts, and a conclusion that revisits the learning objectives enunciated at the outset (e.g. in the form of a closing verbal, visual, or audiovisual summary).

A last (and somewhat discouraging) aspect concerning online teacher–student interaction is the limitation of communication strategies and signals. In effect, teaching online is more formal than face to face, and therefore resources such as humour, storytelling and anecdotes are less used. Rapport must be set up entirely on the screen, where the teacher has less leeway for being spontaneous and jocular. Actually, there are teachers who change their persona according to the medium of instruction (Gudea 2008). To make matters worse, there is little opportunity to interpret the participants' paralinguistic cues, mainly gaze, gestures and body stances, since their faces and bodies may not be visible at all. Consequently, it is not always easy to detect boredom and tiredness or to gauge whether a concept has been fully understood. As a result, corrective teacher reactions, such as a change of pace and activity, elicitation, exemplification, reformulation or repetition, may not be as immediate as one would desire.

If we turn to online learner-to-learner interaction, we can see that this involves peer work and taking responsibility for one's own learning process, which in turn requires a strong sense of community to sustain student motivation (Hockly & Clanfield 2010). Teachers create an interactive scenario by designing or borrowing demanding collaborative activities central to the learning aims, and by fostering self-reflection, adequate and prompt peer feedback, as well as the analysis of group work strategies. In any collaborative task, student interaction starts with a joint processing of information, documentation and research, and continues in the appointment of roles and responsibilities within the group, the management of conflict and the development of norms, peer evaluation, decision-making and the communication of results and learning outcomes to the teacher or to the whole class. The pedagogical principle underlying this learning mechanics is Piaget's (1969) vision that learning is more likely to occur if two or more equal partners collaborate in finding a solution to a problem. From a Vygotskyan (1931) perspective, by contrast, learning would rather result from the guidance of a more skilled or advanced

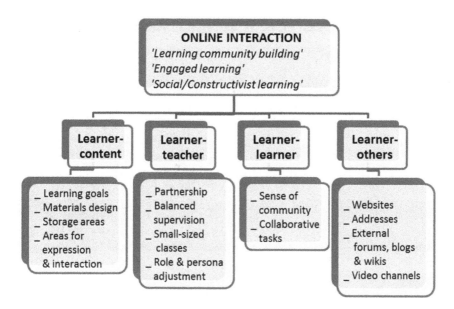

FIGURE 4.3 *Visual summary of the factors shaping online teaching/learning interaction.*

peer dominating the task, which offers certain learning opportunities, but may diminish the scope for exploration and risk-taking. Collaborative activities range from jigsaw activities, web quests and professional role-plays and simulations, to case studies (even student-generated ones), discussion forums, blogs, wikis, debates or small-group projects.

To conclude these reflections on virtual interaction, tools and addresses external to the learning platform of the course may also be hosted in the special area for 'extras' (readings, challenges, etc.) mentioned earlier. They may be related with authentic collaborative assignments and include websites of real companies, professional and academic networks, recorded lectures, interviews with professionals, social media, specialized blogs and wikis, relevant videos from different channels (of scientific video-abstracts and articles, industrial processes, etc.) and so forth. Students may be encouraged to leave their comments, ask for information, do webquests and exchange impressions with bloggers, YouTubers and so on.

In sum, this subsection has shown that the notions of 'learning community' and constructivist, engaged or social learning, together with adjustments to the course delivery style, are essential if we are to understand and promote online interaction. Such adaptations involve students, teachers, the course content and occasionally external entities (see Figure 4.3). Adjustments may affect teaching styles, course and materials design, lesson structure, in-class communicative strategies and many other things – all of which mean that teachers need to approach the transition to online teaching as a challenge, and be ready to learn from experience.

4.6 Supporting International Students

You probably find that international students have a different set of problems from your local students. Try to imagine yourself in their situation: they have travelled a long way, they have just moved into new accommodation, they may need to do extra paperwork, they don't know where to go to solve their problems and not everyone speaks English! Worksheet 4.8 gives a list of the problems that our own international students mentioned to us. Which ones would be a problem in your institution? How could the institution, or the teachers, help these students to deal with these problems?

WORKSHEET 4.8: SUPPORTING INTERNATIONAL STUDENTS

Here is a list of some of the things that international students in a Spanish university found difficult during their first weeks. Which ones do you think will be a problem for international students in your university? How can you help them to deal with these points?

- The timetable is different. We don't understand when we are supposed to eat our lunch.

- We went to the main office but there was a long queue, and it didn't seem to be progressing.

- I'm expecting an important call from my landlady. Is it ok if I go out of the class to answer the phone?

- I need to know how this course is evaluated. Where do I find that on the website?

- The local students are very quiet and they never ask questions. Is it prohibited?

- There isn't a proper programme for the course, just a general description. I need a list of all the classes with the contents of each one, to send to my home university.

- I had to meet up with my group, but they didn't arrive on time. How long should I wait?

- I can't find the classrooms. The buildings in this university are like a labyrinth.

- I need to know when the final exam is so that I can book my flight home.

- The local students don't want to talk to me.

4.7 Final Thoughts

Since interacting with students, one way or another, takes up a large amount of time, it is important to dedicate some thought to the way we do things. Have we got the right balance? Do we find constant queues of students outside our office? Are we bombarded with emails from students wanting to check points of fact or (more usually) details about the assignments and evaluation? Sometimes it is flattering to be in demand – but sometimes we also have other things to do. So if we find ourselves devoting an excessive amount of time to dealing with individual students' questions and problems, we need to think out the reasons why they are making such inroads into our time. Perhaps we could provide better written information? Perhaps it would be useful to provide examples of a 'good' and an 'average' piece of student work, so that students can understand better what we mean. Or perhaps, with the digital generation in mind, it would make more sense to record a video of ourselves repeating the main messages about how to get a good grade in our course – or a video of us talking them through the evaluation scheme. All of these things are useful, since our time is precious. But at the same time, we should not forget that individual contact with a teacher is one of the most important things that students gain from their university experience. And we teachers also benefit from those discussions with interested young people, who bring their own vision, enthusiasm and freshness and sometimes help us see our own subject with new eyes. So, clear information and organized systems are good, but we should never forget the importance of the human factor in the 'long conversation' of education!

Case Study 1: Benefits of a Student Mentoring Programme

Task monitoring in general, and within a formative assessment in particular, demands a great deal of dedication on the teacher's end, especially in massive classes subject to tight time constraints. Mentorship is one alternative for simplifying teacher–student interaction when following up learning and giving feedback. In the module of Academic Writing, taught as part of the compulsory fourth-year subject 'English for Professional and Academic Communication' within the Aerospace Engineering curriculum at the Universidad Politécnica de Madrid, the large number of students enrolled and the brevity and rotary dynamics of the module pose a considerable challenge.[1] Thanks to a voluntary mentorship plan, the teacher is relieved

---

[1] Over 400 students enrol in the subject only in the second semester and the module lasts six class sessions of one hour and a half during three weeks. Five applied linguistics teachers rotate with their respective modules in each group.

of much of the workload generated by sustained monitoring and feedback interaction.

The target skill and textual genre in focus are the impersonal writing of standard procedures for the methods section of scientific papers and dissertations. The abilities acquired are transferable to professional writing, since standard procedures are also present in the methods section of grant applications and technical reports.

Because an accredited B2 level of English proficiency is a requisite for enrolment in the subject, student mentors must have an accredited C1 or C2 level. Each mentor will monitor the learning of a maximum of four students. Mentoring duties comprise:

- Providing feedback on the texts produced by his/her mentees

  - The final versions to be sent to the teacher must have the mentor's final approval and incorporate improvements suggested by at least two other mentors

  - Therefore, the mentor must obtain feedback from other mentors (at least two) in the class.

- Evaluating the mentees' writing according to a specific rubric facilitated by the teacher

- Meeting weekly online with mentees for feedback and advice, discussing their performance in mock examinations and tasks

- Meeting with the teacher at least twice through the mentoring process to inform him/her of the mentees' progress

- Suggesting improvements to the texts of other mentors' mentees

- Submitting a 'progress grid' template (facilitated by the teacher) detailing the learning evolution of mentees and the suggestions made by the other mentors, if any, to their writing

In turn, mentees must:

- Write mock examinations and the tasks assigned and show them to the mentor

- Attend all the online meetings with the mentor for feedback and advice

- Successively rewrite the mock exams and tasks attending to the mentor's and teacher's corrections

- Keep a portfolio of all the written tasks accomplished and submit it to the teacher

- Keep a record of their own learning evolution in the 'mentee's grid' facilitated by the teacher and report what errors have been overcome and when (date register) and which persist

The teacher's supervising role involves:

- Organizing mentoring groups according to the number of mentors available
- Supervising the feedback given by mentors
- Meeting with mentors at least once a week (face to face or online)
- Facilitating mock exams and writing assignments
- Facilitating rubrics, and the 'mentor and mentee grids' for text assessment and self-evaluation, respectively
- Checking that mentees submit an orderly and complete portfolio

This activity brings about gains for every participant: mentors may boost their final grades from 0.1 to 0.8 points, become more critical, learn from mentee errors and help less advantaged classmates develop writing skills. Mentees get constant feedback in small groups, where learning conditions are more uninhibited, become more involved in their own learning process by keeping track of their progress and may boost their final grades from 0.1 to 0.5 points. Teachers delegate the bulk of their interaction for feedback and ongoing evaluation to advantaged students, and thus see a notable reduction of emails and visits during attention hours. They also contribute to the creation of an interdependent learning community, where solidarity is a key value and the role of expert is no longer exclusive to the teacher.

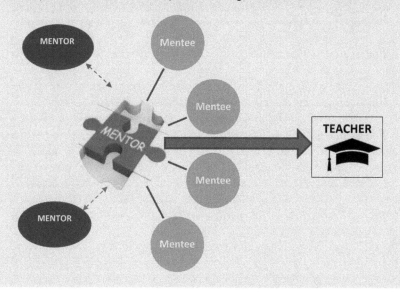

This mentoring activity was implemented for the first time in the academic year 2019–20 and, in light of all the aforementioned motivational benefits, it seems it has come to stay. It can be applied to any subject (text writing may be substituted with problem-solving, for example) and mentors may be selected through a diagnostic test or by their academic records in related disciplines.

Case Study 2: Facing the International Classroom

Juan teaches economics at a medium-sized public university in Spain. As his courses are taught in English, he generally receives a large number of incoming Erasmus and Erasmus Mundus students from other countries. In fact, the exchange students usually make up the majority in in his classes.

When he first taught these classes, he found the experience to be rather frustrating. In particular, he was struck by the different behaviour of the students from different backgrounds. The local Spanish students were rather quiet in the classroom, took notes during the lecture and were unwilling to participate in class discussions. After the lectures they usually went off together in groups, and they resisted working with international students, even in the kind of small-group work that Juan sometimes likes to use as part of his course. The Asian students behaved in a similar way to the local students, but Juan felt more intimidated by them: he could not work out whether they understood his lectures or not, and they seemed to spend a lot of time using their smartphones. Some North American and North European students, on the other hand, caused Juan great anxiety. They often asked questions that he perceived to be inappropriate, interrupted his explanations, argued about the evaluation given to their assignments and even proposed 'better' ways of teaching the subject. Juan perceived this as being highly disrespectful.

After discussion with his colleagues, Juan decided to adopt a two-pronged approach. First, he made it obligatory for all the students to have a short (5- to 10-minute) individual interview with him during the first three weeks of the term. He used this to find out about their background and experience, and was astonished to learn that students from some countries were studying a range of different degrees (financial accounting, liberal arts, economic history, etc.) in their home universities, and were taking his course simply because it was one of the few available in English. This led him to think of ways in which he could adapt the assignments he set, in order to make them more flexible for students of different backgrounds. Second, he was also very surprised at their expectations: some were used to lecture rooms with hundreds of students, while others came from universities where most of the day was spent doing small seminars and project work.

He realized that many of them simply did not understand how the Spanish system worked, and so he made a bigger effort to provide very clear course information, with a description of what would be covered in each class, what reading was required, how students should approach the assignments and – controversially – how students should behave in the classroom. In particular, he stressed that questions or suggestions should be held back until a formal 'question session' at the end of the class.

Juan was pleased with his solution: he had put in quite a lot of time, but he now feels less intimidated by the students, and his relationship with them is more constructive. (See also Chapter 7 on culture and cultures in EMI.)

POINTS FOR REFLECTION

1. This is your 'teaching pie-chart', which depicts your teaching behaviour: Have you ever thought what approximate percentages of teacher roles you undertake on average in your classes?

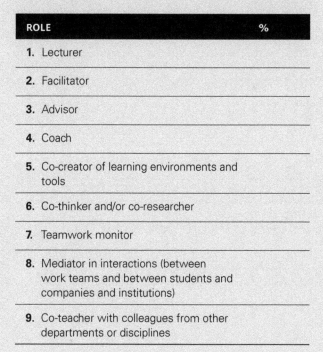

ROLE	%
1. Lecturer	
2. Facilitator	
3. Advisor	
4. Coach	
5. Co-creator of learning environments and tools	
6. Co-thinker and/or co-researcher	
7. Teamwork monitor	
8. Mediator in interactions (between work teams and between students and companies and institutions)	
9. Co-teacher with colleagues from other departments or disciplines	

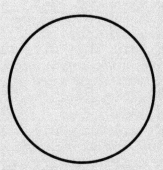

2. What other roles would you be willing to take on? What prevents you from doing so?

3. How does your relationship with students change when you move to online teaching? What are the advantages and disadvantages of communicating with students online?

CHAPTER 5

Assignments and Assessment

5.1 Assignments: General Principles

When we plan our EMI courses, we probably pay special attention to the tasks we set the students – assignments – and the way we evaluate these tasks, and the students' overall learning – assessment. Some teachers feel particularly nervous about doing this in English. Among the sixty new and experienced EMI teachers we consulted in our own study (see Chapter 2), around half expressed some concern about this, because they felt that language was important in their subject and they were uncertain about how to deal with evaluating written or spoken assignments in which students' language skills might have a negative impact on their performance. In this chapter, we will take a look at the role of assignments in EMI, review some strategies for setting and evaluating written work, and address the important topic of student presentations. At the end, we will suggest a few alternative types of assignment that could be appropriate in EMI contexts.

We all set assignments for our students, and in broad terms, the same principles apply to setting assignments in English as would apply to setting assignments in any other language: the task should be relevant to the students' academic and/or professional development, should be cognitively stimulating, should allow students to develop and deepen their knowledge of the subject area, and so on. But in addition to this, in situations where many students are going to complete the assignments in a language that is not their first language – in this case, English – it is actually very important to think more about the linguistic demands that the task is going to place on them. And once all this is done, we also need to think of ways in which we can evaluate the students' work fairly, and give some proper consideration to the ways in which their use of English might be factored into (or filtered out of) their grades for the assignments.

In this chapter, we are going to look at each of these aspects in turn, to see how student assignments can become one of the most powerful tools for EMI learning and teaching. But to do this, it is first necessary to start from the very beginning, and look at how we conceptualize what we want students to get out of our courses. In other words, we will begin by looking at what we want students to learn, and how to express this in the form of 'intended learning outcomes' – that is, what we want our students to be able to do by the end of the course. After that, we will look at the way assignments fit into this, and then examine the role of language in what the students do. In the course of this exploration, we will also point to ways we can help students to become better communicators and better English users – always within the framework of EMI, and bearing in mind that we are 'not English teachers'.

Thinking about What the Students Are Going to Learn

When we are planning our courses, we all probably have in mind what we want the students to be able to know and do by the end of the course, in other words, the 'big picture' of what our course contributes to the students' overall university education and preparation for their professional future. This aim to capture the 'big picture' fits together very well with the notion of 'intended learning outcomes', that is, statements that describe the knowledge and skills that we want our students to acquire by the time they complete our course and the tasks we set, which link up with the wider learning outcomes for the year and degree programme as a whole.

Expressing What Students Are Going to Learn

In their groundbreaking book *Teaching for Quality Learning at University* (4th edition 2011), Biggs and Tang emphasize the importance of defining the intended learning outcomes for a particular course. They explain how these learning outcomes should be described using specific verbs that state what students' learning will look like after they have succeeded in passing your course. They point out that using verbs like 'understand' is unhelpful, because they do not give much idea of the level at which the students should be able to understand the subject, or, indeed, of how you are going to find out what each student understands!

Since many people are familiar with Bloom's taxonomy, and particularly Anderson and Krathwohl's revised version of the taxonomy (2001), we think it is useful to start from this well-known framework to explore how these ideas can be applied in EMI settings. In its original version, Bloom's taxonomy is usually displayed as a pyramid, in which the lower-order thinking skills at the bottom (remember, understand) are understood to be more basic and acquired first, and higher-order thinking skills at the top (evaluate, create) are understood to be much more challenging, and can only be acquired after the lower ones are firmly in place. Although there is obviously some truth in this, Anderson and Krathwohl's updated version (2001) represents a considerable improvement, in that it takes into account different types of knowledge. This version, shown schematically in Table 5.1, represents an improvement on the original Bloom taxonomy because it takes into account that not all types of knowledge (and thus not all types of learning) are the same. It is obviously not the same to recall a set of facts as to remember a procedure, for example. This can help us to be clear about exactly what we are asking our students to learn, and about how they should demonstrate that they have achieved that.

So when we are expressing the intended learning outcomes for our course, it is useful to try to rethink our traditional 'course objectives' in terms of what students will actually be able to know and do by the end of the course, and how we expect them to show their mastery of those contents. Table 5.2 shows how a teacher from the Department of Urban Planning transformed

TABLE 5.1 Bloom's Taxonomy and Dimensions of Knowledge (Adapted from Krathwohl 2002)

Knowledge dimension	Remember	Understand	Apply	Analyse	Evaluate	Create
Factual knowledge						
Conceptual knowledge						
Procedural knowledge						
Metacognitive knowledge						

TABLE 5.2 Intended Learning Outcomes in Urban Planning

Urban Planning: Traditional Course Objectives
By the end of the course students will understand some of the main problems in urban planning and perceive how important these are in people's lives.
Urban Planning: New Intended Learning Outcome
By the end of the course students will be able to *devise* and *defend* a solution to an urban problem that is relevant to their own campus, town or city.

her course objectives into intended learning outcomes that make the goals more concrete and suggest how the students' attainment is going to be evaluated. Notice the changes in the verbs used: from 'understand' and 'perceive' (two invisible subjective processes) to 'devise' and 'defend' (verbs that suggest a product and a public process).

Now consider the difference between these sets of intended learning outcomes (ILOs) from a Macroeconomics course, a Genetics course and a Fluid Mechanics course, in Table 5.3.

Once we have the intended learning outcomes for our course it becomes more obvious what type of assignments we should be setting the students – and how each of these assignments will fit into the learning track for the course. This will also make it easier to understand the ideas that will guide the evaluation we are going to carry out.

Underlying all this, we need to consider the actual indications that we give to students before they approach each task. When we are defining the tasks students have to do, and explaining the process to achieve this, it is specially important to focus the instructions in the right way (see Breeze & Dafouz 2017). Obviously, the instructions have to be clear and explicit. But even more than that, the instructions have to push the students to apply the right kind of thinking. In other words, the students should be given explicit guidance that indicates how they should approach the task, what strategies they should use and what thinking processes will be important for completing the task successfully. One good way of doing this is to use prompts that contain certain key verbs that will indicate clearly what cognitive skills students should be using.

Table 5.4 shows a list of useful verbs that can be used to express what students should be able do, organized according to the macro-categories found in Bloom, and Anderson and Krathwohl. These can be extremely practical when we are writing intended learning outcomes (see herein), but also when we provide the detailed instructions for the pedagogical tasks that our students will carry out in order to acquire the knowledge and skills we want them to have by the end of our course.

TABLE 5.3 Traditional Course Objectives and Intended Learning Outcomes

Macroeconomics: Traditional Course Objectives

Students will understand Keynesian and Neoclassical approaches to understanding economics.

Macroeconomics: New Intended Learning Outcome

By the end of the course, learners will be able to *explain* the main tenets of Keynesian Economics and Neoclassical Economics.

They will be able to *compare* and *contrast* the Keynesian and Neoclassical approaches.

Introduction to Genetics: Traditional Course Objectives

To achieve a basic understanding of genes, chromosomes, mutation, natural selection, etc.

Introduction to Genetics: New Intended Learning Outcomes

Here are some ILOs from an introduction to Genetics course:

At the end of the course, students will be able to:

Locate genes on chromosomes

Describe fundamental genetic concepts (e.g. mutation, inbreeding, natural selection)

Describe and *analyse* simple inheritances

Analyse inheritance of multiple genes

Fluid Mechanics: Traditional Course Objectives

To *provide an overview* of fluid, its properties and behaviour under various conditions of internal and external flows.

To d*evelop understanding* about hydrostatic law, the principle of buoyancy and the stability of a floating body, and the application of mass, momentum and energy equation in fluid flow.

To *learn about* basic laws and equations used for analysis of static and dynamic fluid.

To *learn how to solve problems* related to fluid mechanics.

(Continued)

TABLE 5.3 (Continued)

Fluid Mechanics: New Intended Learning Outcomes

To *explain* Newton's law of viscosity and *describe* the mechanics of fluids at rest and in motion.

To *calculate* the force of buoyancy on a partially or fully submerged body and *analyse* the stability of a floating body.

Using given principles, to *solve* a problem that involves static and dynamic fluids. To *present the analyses and results* in such a way that a technically qualified person can follow them.

TABLE 5.4 Verbs for Expressing Intended Learning Outcomes

Creating: Create, design, develop, hypothesise, invent, perform, produce.

Evaluating: Assess, argue, critique, evaluate, judge, justify, predict, prioritize, rank.

Analysing: Analyse, distinguish, differentiate, deduce, organize, debate.

Applying: Apply, calculate, implement, show, use, put into practice.

Understanding: Explain, report, paraphrase, exemplify, demonstrate, classify, compare.

Remembering: Define, describe, label, list, identify, match, name, quote, tell, write.

One important point that we have to remember about these taxonomies is that they make sense as a general way for understanding how students learn, but they are not watertight cognitive structures that have been scientifically proven. For example, the bibliography shows considerable variation when it comes to assigning specific tasks to a particular level. It is not easy to say whether 'compare' is really just a low level aspect of 'understanding', or is perhaps close to the essence of what we mean by 'analysing'. The nature of the comparison, the amount of subject knowledge needed to carry it out and the degree of help that is provided – all need to be taken into account before we can determine exactly where a given 'comparing' activity should be placed. Often, adjacent levels seem to overlap. The inconvenient truth is that successful completion of a particular task often relies on the student's ability to combine aspects of two or more levels: to remember, understand and also evaluate, for example.

Table 5.5 illustrates this two-dimensional version and shows how it can be applied to a real case. In this example, in a history course, the teacher wants students to study the stages in the Industrial Revolution, and process this information through a variety of tasks.

TABLE 5.5 Application of Krathwohl's (2002) Adaptation of Bloom to a History Course

Knowledge dimension	Remember	Understand	Apply	Analyse	Evaluate	Create
Factual knowledge	(1)				(4)	(3)
Conceptual knowledge		(2)			(4)	(3)
Procedural knowledge						
Metacognitive knowledge						

1. Get an overview of the main events and stages in the Industrial Revolution in Britain, in the period 1760–1840.
2. Explain the consequences of the Industrial Revolution for different social groups.
3. Choose one social group and write a persuasive speech explaining their position. Edit those speeches, publish them on the class blog.
4. Read and give feedback to the speeches submitted by other class members.

Using the framework in Table 5.1, we could consider that step 1 in her plan involves simply knowing what happened, which places it in the first column (Remember) and the first row (Factual knowledge). Step 2 (explain) can be understood as requiring students to develop conceptual knowledge, that is, to 'make sense' of the facts and develop a coherent account. Since this is more to do with understanding than with simply remembering, we can put this in the second column (Understand) and the second row (Conceptual knowledge). The third stage involves other skills, particularly that of writing a persuasive argument. This involves a certain degree of creativity, as well as literacy skills and background knowledge of facts and concepts. For this reason, we can place this in the last column (Create), and the first two rows (Factual and Conceptual knowledge). The final stage of critically reading and giving feedback to other people's speeches is an evaluative activity, and involves the ability to check factual information and concepts that other students present. We can therefore put this in the fifth column (Evaluate), and again, in the first two rows, since both facts and ideas could be involved in students' critical responses.

Nonetheless, if we consider what we are trying to teach in the light of the verbs in Table 5.5, it is evident that using these words will help us to set out clearly what we expect students to learn. We should note that the learning outcomes focus on the significant learning that the students have achieved, and can reliably demonstrate at the end of the course or programme. In other words, they describe what the learner will KNOW and DO. But the more concrete we can make this, the better.

5.2 Setting Written Assignments

Naturally, the general principles set out in the previous section should underpin the whole of our course. But it goes without saying that they are particularly relevant when it comes to setting written assignments. If the instructions we give are clear, and the students understand how they are supposed to approach the task, how they should prepare or research for it and how they should present their results, then not only will their written work be better – their learning will be enhanced, and their level of satisfaction with our course will be higher!

When it comes to written work, we should have a clear picture in our minds of what the finished product should look like, and some idea of what the student needs to do in order to accomplish this.

It is not always easy to put our ideas into words, and so one strategy could be to take a piece of work that one of your students has done for you in previous years, or a model piece of writing from a textbook, and try to explain what it is about this work that makes it a good answer. For example, in the case of an essay:

This is a good essay because:

- it has an introduction that explains the relevance of the problem
- it has several paragraphs, each of which addresses a different aspect of the problem
- it cites five different sources appropriately and provides full references
- in the final paragraph, the writer's conclusions are clearly stated

It is then quite easy to translate this impression into a set of instructions for students who are going to write the essay:

Your essay should:

- have an introduction that explains the relevance of the problem
- contain several paragraphs, each of which addresses a different aspect of the problem

- be based on the work of the authors we have studied, and should cite these authors where appropriate and provide full references using the APA style (at least five citations are required)

- have a final paragraph in which you state your personal conclusion

In all of this, remember that the verbs for expressing intended learning outcomes (see Table 5.4) are extremely useful for explaining to the students what they are supposed to do.

Combining both these approaches, we could come up with the following instructions for a writing task for a business ethics course:

TASK INSTRUCTIONS: You are going to write a paper in which you compare two Financial Times Stock Exchange (FTSE) companies' Sustainability Reports:

- You will *summarize* the main features of each Sustainability Report in terms of the three pillars of corporate sustainability.

- You will *compare* the contents and discourses of the two reports in these three areas.

- You will *suggest explanations* for the similarities and differences that you identify, and *relate* these to the activities and ethos of the companies.

- Your essay will be presented in clearly structured paragraphs, with an introduction and conclusion. You will include references to the course material and bibliography where appropriate, using the APA style guide. All spellings should be checked.

You have probably noticed that these two examples give different names ('essay' and 'paper') to what is, essentially, a similar kind of writing activity. One of the problems is that in different countries or different fields, teachers and students give different names to the same kind of written genre – or use the same name to cover several different types of written genre! This can cause great confusion, especially among students who are new to your university. For this reason, rather than just saying 'write an essay of 2,000 words' or 'upload a three-page paper', you should be as explicit as possible about what you want students to write. The two examples would be a good starting point, but essays or papers are not the only kind of text you might ask your students to compose. In some courses, you might wish students to write texts that are closer to professional documents than to academic essays or papers. This demands a change of discursive focus, and you should try to make it clear to students what the objectives of each writing task are. By way of example, Class Handout 5.1 displays a list of 'key tips' that you might want to give students who are asked to write a 'report', that is, the kind of text that presents information, numbers and graphs in an ordered way, followed by some conclusions or recommendations.

CLASS HANDOUT 5.1: TIPS FOR WRITING REPORTS

Key tips for writing professional reports

These are some key tips that will help you write a good quality report:

Prepare an outline of the main sections/contents before you start writing – this is your plan, and it should be very clear.

Use headings for each section – these help the reader to know at a glance what your report contains and where to find the relevant information.

Tell a story! Don't just write down the numbers/facts, but explain them in an interesting way, showing what matters and explaining causal relationships.

Use good sources and say what they are: this will enhance the credibility of what you write.

If you have to make recommendations, you need to be careful that they emerge clearly from your results and analysis. Make sure your arguments are logical and well grounded.

Use graphs and charts to illustrate difficult concepts or show alternatives in a visually attractive way. Make sure that all the visuals you use are relevant and provide added value. And don't forget that every figure, graph or chart must be clearly labelled!

Before you finish, check the instructions again, and make sure you have included all the relevant points and focused on the important aspects of the task.

Use a neutral-formal style. Avoid personal, informal or slangy language, because that looks unprofessional. At the same time, you should make sure your text reads easily: avoid passive sentences, and use short sentences. If you want to present a list of points, it is quite acceptable to use bullet points.

Use a clear and consistent format throughout the report – poor design/format, careless writing style and mistakes in the English will prejudice the reader against you, while professional presentation will enhance your credibility.

If you follow these tips, this will help you to submit a high-quality report that makes a good impression on its readers. The skills involved in generating reports like this are highly sought after by employers in business, industry and consulting!

Another way to help your students with report writing would be to show them some examples of reports in the relevant field (e.g. market research studies, or business reports), ask them to analyse their key features (e.g. structure, sections, headings, register and tone, writer positioning, reference to visuals), and then talk them through the method for preparing their own writing using the same genre. If you feel uncertain about supporting students with their written assignments in English, this might be a good moment to establish collaboration with a professional from the English-language department, who could provide some backup on the target language and style, or help you to write the instructions and evaluation rubrics (see Chapter 6 on the advantages of teamwork).

5.3 Grading Written Work and Providing Feedback

When we asked the EMI teachers in our own survey about the subject of evaluation, we found three typical answers. The first answer was 'no problem', which is good news – the only thing about this was that this answer came mainly from people who were teaching mathematical, statistical or engineering subjects in which the exams were based mainly on doing problems or exercises with numbers. The second frequent answer was 'yes, it is problematic for me to evaluate my EMI students, so I have decided to use tests in which the students don't need to use any language'. These teachers advocated the use of true/false or multiple-choice formats, thus sidestepping the need for students actually to write text in English (and, accordingly, avoiding the task of grading student work written in English). The third kind of answer brought to light one of the aspects of evaluation in EMI that teachers often experience as problematic. This is the kind of thing they said:

> I sometimes find it difficult to grade my students' work and provide feedback in EMI classes because in a few cases it's difficult to get over language mistakes and focus on content.
> I find it difficult to grade my students' work because it is very problematic to differentiate between difficulties coming from the language, and coming from the (poor) understanding of the topic.

These answers all point to the question of how far the students' command of English actually influences the grade that teachers give them. If we think about it, it is obvious that students with poor language skills will find it harder to explain complex subjects in English, if the exam requires them to do so. Their answers may simply contain grammatical or lexical errors. However, they may also be incomprehensible at times. Is the teacher expected to 'guess' what the student means, in order to grade his/her exam? On the other hand, to what extent should the teacher penalize a student who seems to know a lot, but whose language skills are poor. Here is how one of our participants explained her stance:

> Of course, their language influences their grade. If they have a poor level of English, their answers are worse. The group with good marks usually have a high level of English. But I have also learnt to distinguish the people with poor English who have studied a lot. I now accept more 'schematic' answers, if they are complete.

Other people tried to systematize the extent to which language issues could affect the overall grade, by deducting some points for grammar or spelling:

> I find it easy to grade my students' work and provide feedback in EMI classes because I usually don't try to correct the language. But if the grammar or spelling is very bad, I take off some points for the errors.

Some others considered that terminology was the main issue in language control, and took away points if students failed to use the right terminology:

> I find it easy to grade my students' work and provide feedback in EMI classes because I use the same exam in English and Spanish, with the same 'bad' examples for them to correct (a badly designed page). But they do have to write some short answers. I take away points (in both language groups) if they don't use the correct terminology.

So do we have to correct or assess students' English? In our study we found that many content teachers felt uneasy about correcting student work, and they felt this aspect to be particularly problematic as far as their actual language (i.e. use of English) was concerned. Like the Swedish teachers we read about in Chapter 2, our Spanish teachers emphasized that they are not language teachers. They do not feel qualified to correct students' English, and they feel (sometimes rather strongly) that this is not their job!

But perhaps we should look at this in a little more detail. No, EMI teachers are not language teachers, in the sense that they are (generally) not expected to 'teach' students about English grammar, for example, or evaluate their grammatical competence in their writing. On the other hand, like all content teachers, EMI teachers really should made some demands on their students as far as communication is concerned.

In practical terms, this means that they should encourage students to write and speak English appropriately. For student writing, that means using an academic or professional style, presenting written work in a suitable way, using spell checkers and so on. When it comes to spoken language, EMI teachers can expect their students to express themselves using a suitably neutral or formal style, to be courteous in the way they address teachers, other students or support staff, and to be incisive or persuasive as appropriate.

We have already seen ways of setting and evaluating written work that take English-language skills into the equation. By making some stipulations about the language students are supposed to use, and by providing models and resources for them to improve their writing, EMI teachers can play a part in getting the students to work on their written communication skills. Although they are 'not language teachers', it would be reasonable for them to include an impression mark for clarity and readability as one of the criteria on an analytical rubric, for example. In the following section we will take a look at some useful ideas for giving feedback on students' assignments, and also at some ways that language could be factored into the overall marking scheme for an assignment or course.

Assessment: Providing Useful Feedback and Correction

When you give feedback to students, it is very important to try to find some positive angle. Students need encouragement! If they have done something well, show that you appreciate this. At the same time, they also need guidance about how to do better next time. In two easy steps this means: be positive as well as critical; and give useful feedback that will help students do better next time. One way of systematizing your feedback to students is by using a simple two-part framework like this:

- I really liked the way that you . . .

- Next time, I think you need to work harder on . . .

So in practice, this could mean that your responses are something like this:

- I really liked the way that you mention details of the different reasons for migration, and the difference between 'push' and 'pull' migration. You explained that very well!

- Next time, I think you need to work harder on providing an introduction and conclusion for your essay, and on presenting your references in APA format.

WORKSHEET 5.1: GIVING FEEDBACK

In general, the feedback we give to students should be constructive. Match the situation with an appropriate response from the teacher. There are two responses that you need not (or should not) use.

Situations

a. In your instructions, you told the students to write an essay of 800–1,000 words. One student handed in an essay that is 3,000 words long, which shows signs that she did a considerable amount of independent research. What would you say to her?

b. In your instructions, you stated that students should compare the situation in three countries. One student compared the situation in only two countries. Otherwise, her work met the requirements.

c. One student handed in a report that was full of spelling mistakes and grammatical errors. When challenged about this, he said, 'This is not an English course. I thought the content was the most important thing.'

d. One student submitted an essay that only included three references (you had stipulated that they should use a minimum of five) and did not use the APA system to present the references correctly.

e. One first-year student gave you a report that seemed to be excellent. However, when you put it through the university's plagiarism detector, it turned out that several entire paragraphs had been copied from published material.

Possible Responses

1. It is completely unacceptable to do this. Your behaviour is disgraceful. I will report you to the dean of the faculty and you will probably be kicked out.

2. You need to understand that the work you do in order to obtain credits in the university has to be your own work. If it is not your own work, how can I give you a grade for this? If this happens again, I will ask the Faculty to implement disciplinary measures.

3. When you do an assignment for me, I expect you to read and follow the instructions. In this case, one of the points of the assignment was for you to start using a proper referencing system. If you didn't understand how that system worked, you could have consulted me. As it stands, I will have to fail that assignment, because it did not meet the minimum requirements.

4. When you do an assignment in the university, you are supposed to read and follow the instructions. This is important, because when you graduate and get your first job, and your employer asks you to perform a task, he or she will want you to do that task, not half of it!

5. Obviously this is a content course. So don't worry about the spelling and grammar. No one in the real world is going to care about that sort of thing.

6. Obviously this is a content course. No one is doubting that. But it is also a course on a degree programme that is supposed to equip you for a professional role in a highly competitive world. Do you really think that a piece of writing like this is going to be acceptable anywhere?

7. I can see that you are very enthusiastic about this course, and I really appreciate that. The only thing is that when we set an assignment, we expect people to follow the instructions. That is a useful real-life skill – and learning to be concise is also an important competence for the future. If you are keen to write more, why not start thinking about the topic for your final project?

ANSWERS: a7, b4, c6, d3, e2.

Writing Rubrics and Checklists

Sometimes evaluating students' work can be exhausting, and so we need to find ways that we can streamline this task. One very useful idea is to use a rubric to define the different criteria used to evaluate the assignment, and to describe the different levels of achievement associated with each criterion. Most international examining boards now use rubrics to grade students' written and spoken production, because they find this method to be highly efficient and reliable.

Some of the advantages of using rubrics are:

- They build a common framework and language for evaluation.

- They help us to be more transparent in our grading criteria.

- They make it easier for us to explain to students what they did well and what they need to improve.

- When several teachers are evaluating similar material, rubrics help them to apply fairer, more homogeneous grading criteria across tasks/classes/courses.

- They are efficient and effective to use.

- When several teachers work together to develop them, they bring their expectations and practices into line with each other, and develop a better understanding of what it would be reasonable to expect.

Rubrics look like matrices or grids. There are basically two kinds of evaluation rubric: analytic and holistic.

- Analytic rubrics set out the different criteria with descriptions of the levels of achievement for each criterion.

- Holistic rubrics provide a description of each level of achievement based on an overall impression of a student's performance.

Analytic rubrics thus provide more detailed feedback for the students, and they have been found to be more reliable (that is, different raters evaluating the same piece of work tend to agree). On the other hand, they tend to be more time-consuming to use. We generally use analytic rubrics when:

- we want to pinpoint the student's strengths and weaknesses

- we want to provide specific, detailed feedback

Holistic rubrics are much faster to use, and help you to put into words that general impression that you get when you look at your student's work. However, the holistic rubric in itself does not help you to give detailed feedback, or to diagnose exactly what is missing/wrong. We often use holistic rubrics when:

- we want to give a speedy impression mark

- we know that students are not looking for detailed feedback

A good rubric can also be used to make it clear to students what evaluation criteria will be used to calculate the grade for each piece of work. In our experience, students' work improves if they are told what they should aim for.

Here is an example for a report writing task like the one described earlier in this chapter, in the form of an analytical assessment rubric (Table 5.6):

Evaluation: The report will be evaluated using the following criteria:

TABLE 5.6 Rubric for Evaluating Written Report

1	2	3	4	5
Inadequate or incomprehensible answer.	Poor control of basic structures and register. No attempt at expansion. Some errors impede comprehension.	Acceptable language and register. No major errors that impede comprehension.	Appropriate academic and specialized language and register. Few errors.	Excellent academic and specialized language and register. No errors.
1	2	3	4	5
Inadequate or irrelevant answer.	Inadequate or poorly organized content.	Acceptable content and organization.	Appropriate content and organization.	Excellent content and organization.

WORKSHEET 5.2: UNDERSTANDING A RUBRIC

Here is a rubric for grading an academic essay (Table 5.7). Read the rubric carefully to understand how it is structured, and how the points in each row are interrelated. Then fill in gaps (a) to (h).

TABLE 5.7 Rubric for evaluating an academic essay

	1	2	3	4	5
Language and style	Responds inadeq-uately, insufficient material for evaluation.	Poor language with frequent (d)........ Style not academic.	Makes acceptable overall (e)....... Language mainly accurate, style mainly academic.	Makes good overall impression. Accurate language and good (f).......... style.	Makes excellent overall impression. Excellent academic language and style.

	1	2	3	4	5
(a)......... and (b)..........	Responds inadeq-uately. Organi-zation not attempted.	Poor organi-zation and content. Some essential parts missing.	Acceptable organi-zation and content. Most paragr-aphs appro-priate.	Good organization and developed content. Effective use of paragraphs.	Excellent (g)..........., effective paragraphs and sophist-icated develop-ment of content.

	1	2	3	4	5
(c).........	No references.	One or two references but not used approp-riately.	Some references used correctly. Bibliography provided.	Good use of references. Bibliography provided.	Effective use of references to support points. Full and correct (h)......... .... provided.

ANSWERS: (a) organization, (b) content, (c) references, (d) errors, (e) impression, (f) academic, (g) organization, (h) bibliography

---

Another approach to grading that some teachers prefer is the checklist. This is a way of stipulating all the formal requirements for a piece of work, and awarding a grade based on the number of points that have been included.

Here is an example of how some science teachers developed a checklist for grading lab reports:

DEVELOPING THE CHECKLIST: Every year, the faculty members responsible for teaching practical laboratory sessions meet to compare the grades they give to their students for their final lab reports. They realize that they are not using exactly the same criteria, and tend to modify their grades according to how well they know the particular student. This means that they then have difficulty explaining to students why they got those particular

grades. Since this is unscientific, they decide that they need to systematize their grading practices. They write a list of the different components required (Title, Abstract, Introduction, Material and Methods, etc.). On the basis of their own professional knowledge, they write a description of what each part should contain. For example, in the case of the Introduction, they write:
The Introduction must:

- explain the scientific background to the study
- present the objectives and purpose of the study
- state the hypothesis, using scientific reasoning

In the case of the Material and Method section, they write:
The Material and Method section must:

- present completely, accurately and precisely an exact description of the process used in the research
- provide enough details of the experimental procedure to allow someone else to replicate the experiment

If they decide to use the checklist for grading purposes, one point could be awarded for each of the elements in the checklist, and for each part of the lab report at least two points are included.

If, on the other hand, they decided to deal with their evaluation issue by developing a rubric, they might go about solving their problem in a different way. First, they could locate some outstanding, good, average and

TABLE 5.8 Analytical Rubric for Evaluating the Introduction to the Lab Report

	o not evaluable	1 inadequate	2 acceptable	3 good	4 outstanding
Introduc-tion	Insufficient material available for evaluation	Little and/or inappropriate background information provided. No references provided. Objectives, purpose and/or hypothesis not stated.	Background and references are provided, but some major points are missing or unclear. Objectives, purpose or hypothesis may be lacking/inadequate.	Adequate background and references are provided, but minor points are omitted. Objectives and purpose are provided. Hypothesis is stated.	Cohesive and well-written background is provided, with full references. Objectives and purpose are fully developed and relevant. Hypothesis expressed appropriately.

weak examples of Lab Reports from the previous year. Then, they could collaborate on a description of the different sections of the Report in each case. Table 5.8 shows a possible checklist for the introduction,

Worksheet 5.3 is based on a checklist for academic essays, but includes a task for you to focus on the different elements to see how they fit together. Once you have completed this task, you will have a checklist for essay writing to give to students.

WORKSHEET 5.3: CHECKLIST FOR ACADEMIC ESSAYS

Here is a checklist for academic essays. Match the self-evaluation statements with the section they should go into.

Checklist for academic essays

Parts of the essay	Items on the checklist
1. Introduction	
2. Main paragraphs	
3. Conclusion	
4. Editing	

a. Do I restate and round off the ideas mentioned in the introduction?

b. Have I used correct tenses in the essay? (e.g. am I using the present tense to mention opinions and ideas from other research)

c. Have I set out my references in an appropriate format (e.g. APA)?

d. Do I have a focused thesis sentence that is relevant to the title of the essay?

e. Does each paragraph have a topic sentence?

f. Do I use examples that are relevant and brief?

g. Have I used appropriate discourse markers to signal my transitions from one point to another?

h. Do I make comments or offer suggestions based on the points discussed in the main text?

i. Do I present a plan for the essay that is clearly linked to the thesis sentence?

j. Have I incorporated ideas and quotations from the prescribed reading into my arguments?

k. Have I checked that all the verbs agree with their subjects and that subject–verb order is followed throughout?

Checklist for academic essays ANSWERS

Parts of the essay	Items on the checklist
1. Introduction	d, i
2. Main paragraphs	e, f, g, j
3. Conclusion	a, h
4. Editing	b, c, k

Benchmarking

Once you have developed a rubric, you may want to compare how you and your colleagues or assistants are actually applying it. This is important if you have a large group with more than one person evaluating the students' work. You may want to undertake some kind of benchmarking procedure: for example, you could ask all the raters to submit a piece of work that is a 4, or a 2, on particular criteria. International examination boards usually have 'sample essays', that is, previously graded pieces of work, which they send to their examiners as a kind of test. This can be part of examiner training in what is known as a 'standardization process' (new examiners learn how to use the rubric and apply the criteria by comparing their own impression marks with those that are awarded by a group of trained examiners). But in many cases, the use of pre-graded writing is also a way of checking that practising examiners are actually all applying the same standards. If the examination board sends out these pre-graded essays to different examiners across the world, they will find out who gives it a grade that is too high or low, and they will see who might need further training.

Alternative Assessment Models

- *Formative Assessment*

If we take seriously the idea that assessment is ultimately all about promoting learning, then we might want to look at the idea of including formative assessment as well as summative assessment. What form could formative assessment take? Probably the most familiar kind is the kind of 'progress test' or 'test yourself' quiz that you might find on a MOOC, or at some intermediate stage during a course. Most universities today have the option of using a Blackboard or Moodle format for creating self-correcting progress tests that students can take to find out how well they are doing on the course. Other options for this would be to write some questions for students using Cahoot or Google Forms. Assessments of this kind allow students to monitor their own progress towards achieving learning objectives, and, if the teacher has access to student results, can also give him or her an important overview of what the students have learned and what they are finding difficult.

In fact, *formative assessment* refers to any kind of evaluation tool or task that enables learners and teachers to monitor student progress and identify learning gaps along the way. The key point is that in formative assessment, the grade or score that the student gets DOES NOT COUNT towards his/her final grade. In other words, it is purely diagnostic, and the goal is to promote learning. Many institutions believe that formative assessment is an effective tool for helping to shape learning: when students understand that the goal is to improve learning, not apply final marks, they often respond positively (Yale Poorvu Centre for Learning and Teaching 2020).

Formative assessment must, of course, be contrasted with *summative assessments*, which are designed to evaluate student learning, knowledge, proficiency or achievement of learning outcomes, at the conclusion of a unit, course or entire programme. Summative assessments are graded, and those grades go onto the students' transcripts, so there will be some extrinsic motivation, in most cases, to ensure that students take these seriously (Table 5.9).

TABLE 5.9 Formative and summative assessment

Formative assessment (not counted towards grade)	Summative assessment (forms part of grade)
Online or in-class quizzes and progress tests	Final exams
'Clicker' tests and surveys	Mid-term exams
Formative writing assignments	Writing assignments (essays, reports, projects)
Practice tests or 'mock exams'	Oral exams or presentations

See also section on 'Assessment Teams' in Chapter 6.

- *Peer Assessment*

Peer assessment is a form of assessment in which students evaluate other students. As we might imagine, it would be unusual for peer assessment to determine the students' entire grades on a subject (for one thing, we have a responsibility as teachers to assess our students' work and provide feedback on it, and we cannot just leave this up to the students!). But we can think of occasions on which peer feedback might fulfil a useful function. For example, in the student writing process, there is often a point at which the student is trying to organize his/her thoughts and write a first draft. This draft may be flawed, but the student really just needs a second pair of eyes to help him/her pull it into shape. At this stage, it might be tedious for you, the teacher, to have to read forty essays and talk to each student about what works, what doesn't, what needs to be improved, what needs to be taken out. So it would be quite practical to dedicate thirty minutes of a class to having the students each read another student's essay and comment on it, either orally or in writing. Here is a peer feedback form that we have used with students writing a long essay. The idea in our case was for the feedback provider to fill the form in, and hand it to the teacher for inspection before discussing it with the student who wrote the essay. In our experience, students are not unhappy at the idea that another student will read their text, particularly since they will get the opportunity to read someone else's writing. Perhaps the curiosity factor is important here! Notice that the questions we ask the students to reflect on are about content and comprehensibility, not about details of language. Students often use the peer feedback session to ask you questions about language ('he has written "criterions" – is that right?' or 'is that how you spell "tranquillity"?'), but this is not the main object of the exercise. You are not trying to turn your students into language teachers! The idea is for students to support each other with something that they really can help with: as educated readers, they are well capable of saying whether the essay makes sense, is clear, is well organized and so on.

CLASS HANDOUT 5.2: PEER FEEDBACK FORM

Name of student who is filling in the form ....

Name of student who wrote the essay ....

Ask your partner how long he/she took to write the essay ....

Then ask your partner to let you read the essay.

Summarize in a few words his/her main conclusions.

What was the most interesting part?

Was there any part which was not clear?

Do you have any additional comments or suggestions for the writer?

5.4 Writing in Exams

Everything we have seen about setting and grading writing assignments over the year should also be applicable to the students' final exams. Strangely,

TABLE 5.10 How to Approach 'Short-Answer Exam Questions' (Adapted from Breeze 2012)

Short-answer questions:
- *require a written response of 4–8 complete sentences
- *often ask you to define or explain a concept and provide an example, or to compare two concepts or examples
- *do not require a large amount of detail
- *contain words and exact instructions that should guide your answer (e.g. define, compare)
- *are usually worth 5–10 points of the overall mark

Your answer should:
- *begin with a general statement or restate the question very briefly
- *show that you have paid attention to the verbs in the question (e.g. define, compare)
- *make a clear assertion
- *strengthen that assertion by use of relevant examples
- *make links between the theory/concept and the examples

---

sometimes we seem to forget everything we know about writing when it comes to this point in the year, and just tell students to 'answer the question' or 'write as much as possible', without thinking about the format or genre that they should be producing. Of course, we have a mental model of what a good exam answer looks like – and this will colour the way we grade those students' exam answers – so in the name of transparency it would be a good idea to try to describe this mental model and tell the students more about what we expect.

If the main genre we require in exams is the essay, then the requirements are not likely to be very different from those of the essays we set during the year (see earlier, this chapter). However, sometimes exams are characterized by an abundance of 'short questions' requiring 'short answers' – something that students have not been faced with during the semester. If this is the case, we could think about making it clear to students what a 'good answer' to one of these short questions would look like. Table 5.10 provides a scheme that one teacher used to make the 'short-answer exam question' easier for students to approach (Breeze 2012. 107).

5.5 Student Presentations

There is one familiar situation in which the students' spoken English is at the centre of attention, and that is when students are giving presentations.

Some teachers believe that presentations are a good task for students to do, in groups, pairs or alone. They are certainly very valuable for the student who actually has to give the presentation, because he/she will be under pressure to acquire presenting skills – organizing information, maintaining audience attention, interacting with listeners, directing a triangular flow of information between him-/herself, the visuals and the listeners/watchers, getting the message across convincingly, pronouncing English clearly with natural intonation, developing skills of persuasion, etc. The list is rather long! Unfortunately, since the speakers are inexperienced, the presentations are also often rather long – in fact, much longer than you or the audience might really wish! So here are some strategies for organizing effective student presentation sessions that benefit the student who presents without losing the attention of the students who don't.

Tips for Organizing Effective Student Presentation Sessions

Keep a strict time limit. In most cases, 5 minutes would be the ideal time, although in some cases ten minutes might be needed. Remind students that at science conferences, it is quite normal just to cut off the speaker after ten minutes. Time's up!!!

To ensure that students really do keep to time, you may use the effective system applied in many conferences, with colour cards for '3 minutes left', '1 minute left' and 'stop!'. You can train the students to do this, so that you can concentrate on what the speaker is saying.

Give students some tips about presenting a couple of weeks before their session. This does not need to be very long. You could look at a video of a good and bad presentation, and ask the students themselves to brainstorm a list of factors that contribute to a good presentation – or to a bad one! Or you could just hand out a checklist of 'dos and don'ts' for class presentations.

Make sure that the other students have something to do while they are listening. Here are some techniques for this:

1. Give out cards with specific tasks on them ('Ask a question', 'Make a positive comment', 'Relate what the speaker is saying to one of the topics in the course', 'Send a tweet about something you liked', etc.). This will encourage the listeners to focus on what is being said. After the speaker has finished, you can select which of the listeners should speak.

2. Ask the speaker to send you some questions based on his/her presentation before the session. Then you can distribute the questions to the listeners, for them to complete during or after the session.

3. Give out a feedback form, so that the listeners can evaluate each session. The best feedback forms are the simplest ones, like the one here:

    ● What did you like most about the talk?

    ● What aspect would you improve?

    ● What question would like to ask the speaker?

You can collect these up and give them to the speaker (filtering them if necessary).

4. If you have a lot of students, divide them into 'shifts' of one hour. In each hour, you can schedule the presentations for, say, six students/groups. All of them will stay for the whole hour – and they will all listen to the six presentations. But they will not have to listen to thirty presentations! You will, of course, but that is part of your job.

Evaluating Student Presentations

A huge number of rubrics are available online for evaluating your students' oral presentations. You can also create your own using platforms like Rubistar (see 'Resources' section at the end of this chapter). These contain a bewildering list of different possible aspects of the oral presentation that you could – supposedly – evaluate. In one of its most straightforward frameworks for assessing presentation Rubistar alone offers eight possible categories for evaluating your students' performance, including pitch, pauses, enthusiasm, attire, time-limit, use of props and maintaining eye contact. There is no shortage of aspects that could be evaluated. However, in reality, if you also want to pay attention to what your student is saying, it is more practical to try to assess just a few salient aspects of his/her performance, such as: the PowerPoint itself, his/her interaction with the PowerPoint, his/her interaction with the audience, overall organization of the talk, content, relevance to topic, time-management, dealing with questions and possibly clarity/comprehensibility/persuasiveness. We can see that if the student has reasonably strong English skills (B2–C1), his/her level of English is only going to have a major impact on a few of these. Table 5.11 displays a rubric for evaluating student presentations.

Finally, we have to mention the point that some EMI teachers feel uneasy about judging students' spoken performance in English because they themselves are not 'perfect' English speakers – while some others, perhaps conditioned by years of English classes, tend to assume the role of an English teacher and take a highly critical stance when a student makes the smallest mistake in grammar or has a strong accent. It is important to

TABLE 5.11 Rubric for Evaluating Student Presentation

	1 inadequate	2 acceptable	3 good	4 excellent
Relevance to topic	It was hard to tell what the topic was.	Stays on topic some (60–79%) of the time.	Stays on topic most (80–90%) of the time.	Stays on topic all (100%) of the time.
Content	Inadequate coverage of points. No effective use of examples.	Covers some points, gives at least one relevant example.	Covers most main points with some relevant examples.	Covers all main points lucidly, with relevant examples.
Timing	Presentation is less than 3 minutes long.	Presentation is 3 minutes long or goes over time.	Presentation is 4 minutes long.	Presentation is 5–6 minutes long.
Eye contact and demeanour	Slouches and/or does not look at people present during the presentation.	Sometimes stands up straight and establishes eye contact with some people.	Stands up straight. Establishes eye contact with most people.	Stands up straight, relaxed and confident. Establishes eye contact with everyone.
Clarity of language	Often mumbles or cannot be understood OR mispronounces many key words.	Speaks clearly and distinctly most (80–89%) of the time. Mispronounces some key words.	Speaks clearly and distinctly all (90–95%) the time, but mispronounces several key words.	Speaks clearly and distinctly all (95–100%) the time. All key words pronounced clearly.

set this straight. As we saw in Chapter 2, the non-native EMI teacher is an important role model for non-native English-speaking students. It is that teacher's job to put English in its place: English is the medium of instruction, and probably the instrument that your students will use for much of the time in their professional future. You can feel free to 'judge' their English much as a hypothetical future colleague might – but always remembering that you are one of the people responsible for their training and you need to help them to reach a high standard.

Resources for Assessment

For rubrics, it is useful to look at the resources on:
https://manoa.hawaii.edu/assessment/resources/rubric-bank/

Also, if you are not familiar with *Rubistar* already, you should check it out. Remember, though, that you must not be dazzled by the infinite possibilities that Rubistar offers. It is really important to be clear that the art of developing a good rubric is not to have as many criteria as possible, but to have a few criteria that are highly relevant to your course objectives! http://rubistar.4teachers.org/

5.6 Alternative Assignment Formats

Class Glossaries or Encyclopaedias

The creation of online collaborative glossaries or encyclopaedias designed to complement and enrich students' learning on a particular course offers many possibilities. Online writing projects of this kind provide a stimulus for learners to interact and share their knowledge in an online space, while allowing the teacher to maintain a controlled environment. In general, it is motivating for students to know that they are writing for a real audience of peers, rather than only for the teacher. Students' degree of interest is heightened if peer feedback options are permitted, since other students' comments may help students develop their writing skills and encourage them to improve their language and content knowledge (Breeze 2014b). On the other hand, with this kind of activity it is important for teachers to make it clear to the students how much guidance and correction they intend to provide, and at what point in the task it will be provided. Students often feel insecure about making their work public, and they tend to accept the idea of publication more readily once they are sure that the teacher will provide feedback that guarantees that their work meets a certain standard.

In the context of language courses for specific purposes, the availability of affordances such as wikis or glossaries enables teachers to design learning activities that allow students to interact asynchronously, sharing or jointly constructing their knowledge of relevant content areas. In an EMI context, such collaboration could take the form of compiling joint glossaries, dictionaries or encyclopaedias, to which students contribute entries either individually or in groups. Since gaining familiarity with specialized terminology and achieving the integration of language and content are two key issues in EMI teaching/learning, tasks related to creating a glossary or encyclopaedia seem to offer promise in this field.

In a teaching innovation project carried out over two consecutive years, one teacher designed and implemented two collaborative writing tasks as part of a university legal English course. This model could equally well be applied to EMI courses, particularly in the first year of a degree programme where students need to gain familiarity with a large body of new, specialized vocabulary in English.

In the first year, the project consisted in compiling an online legal English glossary, with definitions of key terms and examples. In a preparatory stage during class time, students worked in small groups during class time to compile some model entries, which were then discussed in terms of contents and language. Various reference works were recommended, and students were encouraged to draw on the course notes in compiling their entries. Each student was then assigned three key concepts, and given the task to contribute entries containing a definition and relevant example (100–150 words per entry) to the Moodle legal English glossary. In their evaluation of the activity, most students stated that the task had been useful in helping them to consolidate their vocabulary and concept knowledge, and that the final product had helped them to study for their exam.

In the second year, the plan was more ambitious: students were each given a country with a common law or mixed legal system, and asked to research a series of topics in order to write an encyclopaedia entry for that country. To round off this project, students were asked to submit three questions about their given country, which the teacher used to make worksheets. These were distributed to all the participants, who had to read each other's entries in order to answer the questions.

Portfolios

The developments in writing instruction at US universities in the 1980s and 1990s led to an interest in promoting alternative forms of assessment, one of which is the 'writing portfolio' (Hamp-Lyons & Condon 2000). The idea of the portfolio, a collection of pieces of work completed in the course of a period of time, comes from the world of the visual arts, where artist have for centuries compiled collections of sketches or paintings to show to future clients. Portfolios of student writing should include at least three pieces of writing produced over the term or year (sometimes many more), and usually also a reflective statement or self-assessment in which the student explains the contents and what he/she feels he/she has learned from these and how they helped him/her to develop as a writer. Usually the portfolios contain a range of texts belonging to different genres, so ideas about register, lexical range and specificity, readership and appropriateness to social context may all provide material for reflection.

On the one hand, then, the writing portfolio makes space for students to experiment with many different kinds of writing. The portfolio – a collection of the student's 'best examples' compiled over the year – provides a way of looking broadly at what students have written in an open and variable context. On the other, the portfolio encourages students to take a more active role in deciding what they want to work on, and what they would like to have evaluated by the teacher. Since the portfolio is a collection of work assembled by the student, the student has more control over what to work on and what to include, and therefore gets more deeply involved in the learning process. One final point is that the portfolio is an interesting way of observing student development. As Hamp-Lyons and Condon say (2000, 26), portfolios 'provide 'footprints' that show students' achievements or competencies at a particular time' and 'act as a trace of a student's progress from one testing situation to the next'.

Promoting Digital Literacies

There is a strong case for arguing that the ways people access information and communicate with each other have changed dramatically over the last twenty years, and that educational institutions have been slow to acknowledge this. As Jones and Hafner (2012) explain, digital technologies have actually affected the way we do most things in our lives (search for information, communicate with friends, book travel, relax, shop) and they probably also have an impact on the way we build and understand our social identities, the way we make and negotiate meanings and even the way we actually think. They argue that teachers should help students to become more competent – but also more critical and reflective – users of these technologies, and that the university classroom can be a place where this happens in a principled, pedagogically structured way. To illustrate what this means, we can look at a paper by Hafner (2014), which explains a student project designed to equip students with traditional (English-language-focused) and 'new' (multimodal media) literacies in the context of a course for science majors at a Hong Kong university. In the project, the students work in groups to carry out a scientific study on a topic that has been assigned. As in traditional project work, students need to do background reading, collect and interpret data and present findings, but unlike the traditional project, this one has to be reported in two ways: (1) through a digital scientific video documentary addressing a non-specialist audience, shared through YouTube and viewed, and (2) through an individual written lab report designed for specialist readers.

The most interesting and original aspect of this project is the way that the teacher structures the different phases to include the material/technical and theoretical/critical aspects of multimedia production. In addition to the reading and research phases, there are tutorials on aspects such as scripting and storyboarding, performing/filming and editing, which create a structured environment in which students can acquire and hone their digital literacies with expert and peer guidance. As the author comments, all along this process the students have to make decisions about how they should present their work multimodally, what rhetorical strategies they could adopt in order to engage their audience, and what identities they themselves should take on in the video. The teacher can interact with the students over the creative process, not just intervening in aspects of content comprehension and organization, or helping with disciplinary or explanatory language, but also supporting and challenging them in their use of multimodal semiotic resources. The author concludes by citing Schetzer and Warschauer (2000, 172), who point out that 'literacy is a shifting target, and we have to prepare our students for their future rather than our past'.

Case Study 1: Structuring a Student Project

Miriam Symon teaches on the business administration degree at the Interdisciplinary Centre, Herzliya, Israel (see Symon 2017). One of her goals is to promote autonomy and cooperation in her business communication course, by asking students to work in groups to write a SWOT analysis of a particular company. To achieve this, she has devised the following twelve-step procedure:

Step 1: Teacher sets out general guidelines and deadlines.

Step 2: Students choose their group members.

Step 3: Teacher shows students how to gather information.

Step 4: Students gather information (reading, summarizing, taking personal notes).

Step 5: Students meet (face-to-face or online) to share and analyse information.

Step 6: Teacher introduces referencing guidelines.

Step 7: Students write first draft of report.

Step 8: Self, peer and teacher evaluation of report.

Step 9: Preparation of oral presentation.

Step 10: Students deliver presentation (self-, peer- and teacher-evaluation).

Step 11: Students submit final written report.

Step 12: Students evaluate the project process.

Symon comments that 'Student feedback and suggestions have enabled the project to evolve. These final stages approach Nunan's (1997) highest level of autonomy implementation, transcendence, in that learners approximate to teachers in their ability to evaluate themselves and their peers, and even link the classroom to the real world' (Symon 2017, 177).

One final work on this from Miriam is that her well-organized methodology became even more important during the 2020 pandemic. She commented that 'I used Zoom's Breakout Rooms, which gave me an opportunity to work with students in smaller groups, and really reach out to them. It allowed me to see who really had been participating and developing their skills in the first half of the semester'.

Case Study 2: Developing Transversal Skills

The elective subject *Aeroingenia* has been team-taught at the School of Aerospace Engineering of the Universidad Politécnica de Madrid since 2017 by five teachers of technical subjects and one lecturer from the Department of Linguistics Applied to Science and Technology. In its origin, it was created as a source of credits for those students who could not access company internships in the second semester of the fourth and last year of the degree. Today any fourth-year student is welcome to enrol and the subject inspires a large number of final degree dissertations.

The beauty of the subject is that it is entirely collaborative, for both students and teachers, enables learners to practise several transversal skills (critical thinking, creativity, digital prowess, entrepreneurship, teamwork, communication in the mother tongue and in a foreign language) and is highly motivating, as it gives a chance to do hands-on engineering. Assignments are authentic and varied multidisciplinary tasks scheduled all along the team project of constructing a drone, which is co-evaluated by technical and communication teachers, staff from a real aircraft construction company (Airbus), fellow fourth-year students not enrolled in the subject and staff from the Technology Transfer Office of the Universidad Politécnica de Madrid (OTT in Spanish: *Oficina de Transferencia Tecnológica*).

Enrolled students are asked to organize in teams of four or five members in order to design and build a drone according to specific technical requirements regarding MTOW (maximum take-off weight), dimensions, payload and budget, and within a deadline for the final fly test. There are supervised workshop sessions where the technical teachers are available to solve queries and help overcome technical challenges. The best-drone award is granted to the team whose device can stay in the air for the longest time. In their respective rubrics for evaluation, technical content teachers take into account parameters such as creativity, reasoning process, efficiency in the resolution of challenges and problems, and optimization of resources.

The role of the applied linguistics teacher is to deliver a seminar on technology commercialization, one of the project tasks, and accompany them along the preparation of a series of communicative interactions. The seminar deals with academic and professional textual genres most often associated with the dissemination and commercialization of technologies and with persuasive language and advertising strategies. The whole of this input is in English. The portfolio of oral and written texts requested is listed and described in the following table.

TECHNOLOGY DISSEMINATION & COMMERCIALIZATION

TEXTUAL GENRE	DESIRABLE REGISTER	AUDIENCE EVALUATING	SPECIFIC REQUIREMENTS
Blog (May be in Spanish but must contain sections in English addressing international audiences)	Overall informal but formality recommended in technical passages	Content & language teachers plus non-enrolled fellow students (by vote)	→ At least one entry documenting each of the ten work stages → A minimum of one constructive feedback comment post in the other teams' blogs, preferably in any of the mid-work stages
Tweet (At least one must be in English)	Informal	Content and language teachers plus non-enrolled fellow students (by vote)	Two tweets: → One encouraging the educational community to read the team's blog. → Another inviting to the oral presentation event.
Abstract (in English)	Formal, academic	Content and language teachers, Airbus and OTT staff	Two abstracts: → One recounting a major technical challenge or difficulty during the design and construction process and its resolution → Another summarizing the oral presentation, which in turn encapsulates the team's project

TEXTUAL GENRE	DESIRABLE REGISTER	AUDIENCE EVALUATING	SPECIFIC REQUIREMENTS
Oral presentation (English or Spanish, depending on audience)	Mix of formal and conversational	Content and language teachers, Airbus and OTT staff	→ Summary of the highlights throughout the drone design and construction process
Promotional triptych brochure (in English)	Mix of formal and conversational. Overtly promotional style	Content and language teachers, Airbus and OTT staff	→ Advertising of novel or original features, advantages and benefits of the constructed technology

Each textual genre is evaluated with a specific rubric, agreed upon by the professionals involved in assessment. An award is also given to the best blog, with the intervention of the educational community in the verdict.

The degree of satisfaction generated by the *Aeroingenia* subject is usually very high, the main reasons being the following (as reported by students at the end of each edition):

• its hands-on nature

• its authenticity

• the variety of inputs and tasks

• the chance to relate knowledge from several engineering areas

• the chance to practice English in real communication for different purposes and shifting registers and tones according to audiences and situations

• the opportunity of receiving feedback from company and institutional experts

• the chance to advertise the technology via the OTT website and disseminate results via the school's webpage

• the chance to leave an imprint in the school's educational community

For all these traits, students often describe the subject as 'a good taste before leaving the school' or 'the best subject of all'. This is the rewarding and motivating fruit of interdisciplinary collaboration between teachers.

POINTS FOR REFLECTION

It would be a good idea to clarify ideas about formative assessment, a central methodological approach in the European Higher Education Area (EHEA).

1. Which of the following could be accepted as formative assessment?

    - Flipped teaching with classes as workshop time, during which the final task is practised, monitored and given feedback

    - Lecturing plus a final task which is resent with feedback at the end of the term

    - An in-class or online test every (other) week with (almost) immediate feedback

    - Lecturing plus a final exam/test at the end of the term

    - Rubric-based peer assessment after each task or task rehearsal (e.g. mock exams)

    - A brief test/quiz in each class session, with feedback in the next

    - Autonomous learning (self-study) with quizzes and keys to them

2. How might formative assessment of the various kinds listed here prepare students for their summative assessments? What other functions does formative assessment have (for the student, and for the teacher)?

3. How has the move to online teaching challenged our approach to assessment? What can we do to ensure that formative and summative assessment are carried out appropriately when our courses are delivered online?

CHAPTER 6

Teamwork, Networks and Resources

Chapter outline

6.1 An Overall Design for Supporting EMI

As we mentioned in the first two chapters of this book, the decision to move to EMI presents a challenge to the whole university community, not just to the individual teachers involved. To use a metaphor from natural sciences, it brings about a fundamental change in the ecosystem, and everyone has to adapt or adjust a little to this situation. The main stakeholders in this situation are the teachers themselves (indeed), but also the students (of course!), as well as the university's non-teaching staff (administrative staff, security staff, librarians, IT technicians etc.). Moreover, introducing EMI also implies a number of major changes in the way the university communicates with students – and with the wider world – through its webpages, both the promotional ones and the informative or transactional ones. There is no point trying to attract international students if none of them can understand the essential information about how to register, how to choose courses, how to find accommodation or obtain an academic transcript. One can imagine a very long 'to do' list facing any university that is considering a move from monolingual to 'L1 plus English'.

Probably at the top of the list of the things to be done we will find the need to locate teachers who are willing to teach their courses in English and, where necessary, provide them with the support they require to do this well. Statistics do not tell us much about the general level of English language competence among university EMI teachers. Although recent European survey data suggest that 95 per cent of EMI programme directors rate the English proficiency of their teaching staff involved in English programmes as good or very good (Wächter & Maiworm 2014), some other reviews of current practices have highlighted the need for a more structured and rigorous approach to teacher training, as far as both language and methodology are concerned (Dearden 2014; Halbach and Lázaro 2015). As EMI is generally not regulated by national authorities, different universities make different rules about who can or must do it (see Chapter 1).

As we saw in Chapter 2, the existence of a minimum level of English in readiness for EMI courses is also not to be taken for granted in all institutions. In some universities, high entry levels in English language (e.g. C1) have been set, whereas in others this is not the case. Universities where students are admitted with lower levels need to consider providing basic language support for students, but even those with higher entrance requirements ought to look into ways in which they can help students to bridge the gap between school English competence and the kind of adult, professional or academic language proficiency that they will need to do well in their degree and what comes after.

Finally, it is quite clear that a massive organizational effort has to be made to ensure that all the necessary information is available in English, including both the essentials on the public website, and the internal web used for internal transactions and for organizing and teaching courses. Essential facilities (IT services, library, etc.) have to provide the necessary guidelines for students in English. Ideally, students should also be able to obtain transcripts and certificates in English when they leave, without having to pay for the services of an official translator. All of this requires a massive exercise in imagination and planning – and enormous energy to put it in place. In the rest of this chapter, we will go through some of these aspects in which teachers may get involved, and share some good practices from around the world.

6.2 Teacher Support and Training

There is a division of opinion concerning the nature of the change to EMI, and how teachers should respond to this change: some people think that EMI teacher training should be centred on ensuring that the people involved are competent enough in English to teach their classes, while others consider that the move to EMI implies a fundamental change in the teaching paradigm, bringing it closer to the kind of 'content and language integrated learning' (CLIL) model used in schools. In this book, we attempt to steer a course between these two approaches that reflects the reality as we have experienced it. Yes, language training is important, but no, language training is not the whole story. At the same time, we reject the notion that EMI should be regarded as CLIL, because most of the practitioners find this impossible to imagine. On the strength of the changes we analysed in Chapter 2, we can say that it is empirically proven that the change to teaching in English implies a further set of changes, like any other change to the ecosystem. But it does not mean that content lecturers become language teachers – nor are they interested in doing so. What it does mean is that they need to develop a greater awareness of language and language-related issues in order to feel confident in their role and help students to benefit from EMI as much as they can.

To obtain a picture of what is really happening regarding teacher training for EMI in Europe, O'Dowd (2018) carried out a survey of seventy universities in twenty-eight different European countries in 2014–15. He found that only 51 per cent of respondents thought that actually training teachers to teach through English was either 'important' or 'very important' in their institutions, and almost 30 per cent reported it as being 'not important' or 'not important at all'. However, around 68 per cent of the universities which participated in the survey reported that their institutions were already providing training programmes for teaching staff who wished to teach their subjects through English – although the nature and scope of this training were extremely varied: for example, the duration of such training courses ranged from one hour to over sixty! While three quarters of the universities that provided training said that their courses included instruction in actual language skills, fewer than half included a specific focus on methodology for bilingual education. Around half did include 'microteaching', that is, sessions in which lecturers delivered part of a course and received feedback on it from language specialists or pedagogy experts. Overall, the picture painted by O'Dowd (2018) suggests that universities in many European countries give some importance to training EMI lecturers, but we should note that this may be subject to considerable variation. Costa (2016) carried out a similar survey on the implementation of EMI among thirty-eight Italian universities, and found that 77 per cent of these universities reported that they provided no lecturer training for EMI, while 15 per cent said they had provided a language course, and only 8 per cent reported providing training in methodology. From empirical studies such as these, we can conclude that the need to train EMI teachers is largely unrecognized, and that when special training is provided, the focus tends to be on language alone. On the other hand, we know from our own study of teachers who make the transition to EMI, and from other research among similar groups elsewhere (see Chapter 2), that these people feel very insecure about teaching in English, and one of the things they feel they need most is training.

So the question can be posed: what kind of training should universities provide in order to facilitate the implementation of EMI? Rather than approaching this from a preconceived notion of what doing EMI means, or how it differs from L1 teaching, we should look first at what EMI teachers actually think they need most, and how universities can provide them with basic support for that. Empirical research with EMI practitioners would seem to suggest that they themselves mostly do not believe in, or see any need for, a methodological shift from the teacher-centred approaches common in university education to more student-centred approaches, or even for major methodological adaptations to factor in the students' need for more help with language (O'Dowd 2018). In an observational study, Dafouz, Núñez, Sancho and Foran reported that classes in their study of Spanish universities were mainly lecture-based with little interactivity and 'group and discussion are given less space' (2007, 94), which would tend to mean – as common sense might tell us anyway – that there is no reason to suppose that the much-vaunted change in methodology comes about naturally with the shift to EMI.

On the other hand, some authors argue convincingly that introducing EMI does require a significant shift in methodology, and warn that non-language lecturers need to learn new teaching skills and approaches to adapt to the EMI environment (Cots 2013). In this view, EMI involves a shift of focus from the transfer of information (traditional lecture format) to greater student participation and support for students who struggle (both linguistically and conceptually) to construct an understanding of the subject in the L2. Along these lines, Ball and Lindsay (2013, 46) describe an extensive EMI programme in Spain, and defend the view that 'the challenges that teaching through another language inevitably suppose have forced staff to consider new methodological approaches'. If methodological change somehow logically accompanies the change to EMI, then content lecturers need to be told about this – and prepared for the demands of this new way of teaching.

Perhaps this division should best be understood as a kind of continuum, running from the extreme pole of 'no change' to the extreme of 'total pedagogical renovation', with most people situated closer to the middle. Our position in this book has been to occupy the middle ground – but keep our minds open to what we can learn from the extremes.

Some Models for EMI Teacher Training

Given the overwhelming move towards EMI, it is hardly surprising that many high-profile international institutions should have launched courses intended to prepare EMI teachers. One of the best known of these is the British Council's Academic Teaching Excellence Course, which is designed to update lecturers' language skills and offer useful techniques for day-to-day teaching. In this course, it is clear that the British Council takes a pragmatic, hands-on approach, centring mainly on lecturers' 'advanced communication skills in English', and on focused practice in the form of 'intensive micro-teaching sessions'. Although the course promises that participants can use this as an opportunity to update their teaching methodology, this is not the primary focus. Another residential course is the EMI Oxford Course for Lecturers and Teachers, an attractively marketed option for would-be EMI teachers, which is described as equipping people with 'the teaching techniques needed to teach an international class', which 'make lectures more comprehensible, interactive and motivating for international and home students'. The many courses of this type are aimed at a multifarious international clientele, and provide general support for EMI lecturers encompassing language and communication techniques, with perhaps some discussion of the special needs of international students and/or EMI students.

Regarding online training, one of the very best resources on offer is the EQUIIP site, which is the product of an Erasmus+ project in which seven major European universities collaborated (EQUIIP Project 2019, and see also Dafouz, Haines & Pagèze 2019). This well-organized site offers five EMI teacher training modules, which combine videos with reading material and some original classroom activities for use on training courses. Two particular strengths of the EQUIIP approach are

- The special module dedicated to 'Internationalising Course Design', which takes participants through the process of transforming 'Intended Learning Outcomes' into 'Intended International Learning Outcomes' aligned with the competences and profile that we want our graduates to have.

- The innovative module on 'Intercultural Group Dynamics', which provides theoretical background and practical activities that can help the trainee EMI teacher to understand intercultural incidents that can happen in the classroom.

Another way of approaching training for EMI is to set up local programmes that are tailored to meet local teachers' needs. The advantage of such programmes is that they are not so costly, do not involved travel, allow for a sharper focus on the realities of the situation in that country and university, and could potentially encourage teachers to build networks within their local context in order to define needs, share strategies, pool resources and generally create a sense of community. Such EMI training can easily be organized in-house, in combination with use of online modules, or based entirely around the kind of activities provided by EQUIIP.

Sánchez-Pérez and Salaberri-Ramiro (2017) analysed the teacher training needs for plurilingual teaching at a state university in Andalusia (Spain), within the framework of the Plurilingualism Promotion Plan implemented there from 2012 to 2015. They describe the teacher training programme on plurilingual teaching methodologies implemented at this university over three academic years, based on training needs established on the basis of a questionnaire administered to thirty content teachers starting out in EMI. Unsurprisingly, perhaps, the thirty prospective EMI teachers in their study prioritized training in the use of the language itself (43 per cent), particularly English-speaking skills, listening skills and classroom language (2017, 147). Their interest in receiving training in pedagogical matters was much less marked, with around 13 per cent expressing interest in specific training techniques relating to the subject they teach, and 9 per cent showing an interest in training that would help them to design teaching materials. Training in use of technology in the EMI context seemed not to represent a priority for these teachers.

The EMI teacher development programme described by Sánchez-Pérez and Salaberri-Ramiro (2017) and implemented at the University of Almería, Spain, contains five modules:

- general approaches
- planning and assessment
- materials and resources
- experiences in plurilingual classrooms
- resources and strategies

One of the most important things to note about this programme is that it incorporates a large amount of input from teachers already involved in EMI, who report on their experiences and act as effective role models to inspire colleagues who are new to EMI. On the negative side, these authors note that the EMI lecturers who signed up for the course 'were mostly interested in oral communicative skills development, rather than specific methodological techniques and strategies' (2017, 151).

The perception that EMI training is basically about language training is thus very frequent among the actual stakeholders. Similar attitudes were reported by Aguilar and Rodríguez (2012) in a study of EMI training for engineering teachers, who generally stated that they were not interested in methodological strategies, and felt that the way to successful EMI was through improving their own language skills. The findings from our own study, reported in Chapter 2, also suggest that although teachers do actually experience changes in their teaching practice when they start EMI, they are often not particularly satisfied with these changes. As Dafouz (2014) points out, institutions and teacher trainers actually need to pay serious attention to this type of finding, since it uncovers the attitude of teachers actually involved in EMI, who are clearly more interested in acquiring greater language proficiency than in honing their pedagogical skills.

Unfortunately it is not possible for us to cover all the myriad types of teacher training initiative that have been implemented over the last few years. We would like just to mention one more broad approach to EMI training that has been gaining popularity recently, namely the use of various kinds of peer mentoring, in which more experienced faculty members give specific kinds of help to their less experienced colleagues. Some variations on the theme of mentoring and peer support also include the use of video, so that EMI teachers can record parts of their own classes and reflect on them, or submit them to a platform for peer review by colleagues or trainers, while others simply rely on the use of traditional mentoring programmes for junior lecturers, whereby they are assigned a senior colleague whom they can consult, and who can help them over the hurdles of the first few months in the EMI classroom. More ideas about peer-support schemes and other innovative training initiatives will be explained in Chapter 7.

We would like to end this section with a brief reality check. Our experience in our own universities (Universidad Politécnica de Madrid and Universidad de Navarra) over the last fifteen years has taught us that any attempts at 'teacher training' for EMI have to be approached with the utmost sensitivity. Subject lecturers know how to teach their subject! They are the greatest experts on what works and what does not work in their own context, they know their subject and they know their students. They do not need English experts to tell them how to teach. But of course, we know that they will face challenges when they start EMI, and that there will be things that do not go as planned. Many of them overestimate their students' level of English, or underestimate the difficulty of lecturing (or understanding lectures) in a foreign language. One of the most important aspects of an EMI teacher training course is that it should provide a venue for the inexperienced EMI teachers to talk to the more experienced ones. If those people are not from their immediate department/area, this is sometimes better, because the deep rivalries that sometimes exist between close colleagues can hinder productive professional exchange. At the same time, it also needs to open up some discussion about *why* the institution has decided to do EMI. Especially in cases where the individual teacher has not actively chosen to do this, we have often met with incomprehension, and a failure to grasp the universality of the trend to EMI, or the possible advantages for the individual lecturer. Finally, it is also our belief that the various changes that happen (to planning, timing, style, content, relations with students) when a lecturer starts to teach in English should be presented, as they are in this book, as the findings of empirical research. These phenomena are real, and we need to develop strategies for dealing with them. This does not mean some major change in teaching paradigm – for example, towards student-centred learning – because that would be a whole new story. But it could mean creating a culture of openness to change, in which lecturers are invited to think more about the difficulties that students might have (both with the course contents and with the language), about how they formulate and pursue the learning outcomes for their course, or about how they communicate in the classroom. In all these aspects, the change to EMI is an invitation for lecturers to revisit their teaching activity and renew their approach, within the limit of what they themselves regard as productive and legitimate.

6.3 Team Teaching

In the last few years, the values of teamwork have been celebrated in many different contexts. When our students apply for jobs, we often advise them to emphasize that they are 'team players', and that they find it constructive to work with other people. In education, one of the reasons why group work has been promoted throughout the system from primary school to in-house professional training is that people are thought to learn better when they have to collaborate with others. Surprisingly, however, in many higher education contexts it is still not so usual for teachers to work closely together as a team. Particularly in university contexts, the concept of 'team teaching' is not widely understood – a phenomenon that has variously been attributed to the compartmentalization of academic disciplines, rivalry between individuals or departments, absence of traditions of knowledge-sharing, lack of interest in teaching practices and inability to conceptualize the importance of aspects (such as language) that do not fall strictly into a particular teacher's remit (see Li & Cargill 2019 for some discussion of the situation in the Chinese context).

This is a pity, because precisely in higher education, where students need to be exposed to different viewpoints, different styles and different cultures, team teaching has a huge amount to offer. According to some experts, team teaching:

- improves teaching quality, because different experts approach the same topic from different perspectives, potentially giving students both deeper insights and a broader overview

- offers a way to capitalize on our strengths: someone with a strong background in theory could team-teach with someone who is good at teaching practical cases, for example

- helps us to overcome our weaknesses: if we know we are not good at explaining a particular aspect of our course, we could ask a colleague to do that part, and then learn from his/her contribution

- is usually formative for younger teachers or teaching assistants, because they will learn a lot from collaborating with more experienced professors

- promotes equality: by ensuring a balance of teachers from different backgrounds, we will be sending the message to our students that

men and women, old and young, local and international teachers all
have something to offer

- encourages solidarity and knowledge-sharing among teachers:
  instead of competing with each other, teachers learn to pool their
  expertise – and when there is criticism, they learn to handle this
  together, rather than pointing the finger or indulging in negative
  introspection

In short, working in teams encourages teachers to take greater interest in
their own teaching activity, helps to build community and helps to lighten
the load by creating a sense of shared responsibility.

So what is team teaching? Team teaching is a way of describing what
happens when any group of instructors/professors/teachers work together
purposefully to help a group of students learn. In team teaching, the teachers
should:

- set the goals for the course together

- decide how the different aspects of the course should be divided
  between the different members of the team

- compile the course contents (together, or in coordination with each
  other)

- arrange the pacing for the course, with individual lesson plans if
  appropriate

- plan the activities that are to be evaluated, and set the evaluation
  criteria

- ensure that regular communication takes place during the course

- work together to evaluate students' work

- hold a final meeting in which they examine student feedback and
  discuss ways of improving the course the next time round

Teams of this kind could be single-discipline, that is, they could consist of
three English teachers, or four professors of microbiology. But importantly,
in the context of EMI, they could also include a local teacher and an
international teacher, or a subject expert and a language expert. Regarding
the delivery of the course, they could both be present in the classroom at
the same time, offering different perspectives on a subject or interacting
with different students. For example, Lasagabaster (2018) explains contexts
in which the content teacher assumes the leading teacher role, while the
language lecturer sits in the class assuming a secondary role (see examples
herein). However, in our view it is not necessary for both professionals to be
in the classroom all the time. The term 'team teaching', in our opinion, can

be used to cover a variety of different ways in which two or more teachers collaborate on a course.

Here are two examples of how this could work:

- *Local Teacher – International Teacher*

Li Zhang is responsible for a third-year course in public health on the degree in medicine at the University of Singapore, while Judy Hillborne works for the WHO and visits Singapore once a year to teach some sessions on the course.

They set up a session in Google Meet to look at the Course Programme, and to decide on the calendar and contents for Judy's sessions. This means that Li Zhang can ensure that the students have the background knowledge (overview of principles and practices in public health) that the students will need in order to make the most of Judy's sessions (case studies in dealing with public health issues: one urgent, one long term). They also discuss the evaluation criteria. Since, in this case, Li Zhang's part of the course is going to be tested by a multiple-choice exam held at the end of the semester, they need to debate whether Judy should contribute some questions to the exam, or whether students' performance on her part of the course will be evaluated separately. They opt for the latter, and Judy suggests that the students could be given a public health case (similar to one of the ones discussed in class), and that they should produce a written analysis of this case under exam conditions. Li Zhang is interested in this methodology, which was not used during her undergraduate training in Beijing, and she is concerned about how the students' responses can be evaluated objectively. Not surprisingly, she is also worried, because the students' grades for this part of the course will be published after Judy has gone, and she (Li Zhang) will have to explain Judy's grades to the students. Judy, in turn, is surprised at this reaction, since this type of evaluation seems quite normal to her. Such tasks were often used during her own time studying medicine at Melbourne University. But Judy understands Li Zhang's concern, and promises to provide a set of qualitative descriptors to be used for grading the students' answers. In the end, Judy gives the exam and grades the students' answers, which she scans to Li Zhang with some written feedback. Li Zhang finds that the grading criteria devised by Judy are quite transparent, and has no difficulty answering the students' questions about their grades, or providing useful feedback. However, it turns out that the students' performance on this task was not as good as Judy had hoped. In their final meeting on Google Meet to appraise how the course had gone, the two teachers discuss this point, and Li Zhang is able to point out to Judy that the students are quite unfamiliar with what is required in an analysis of this kind, and that they need more support on how to tackle this task. For the next year, they decide that students need a model of how such tasks should be done. They conclude that next time round, Judy will present one case study in the classroom with a view to showing the students how they should actually present a written answer (rather than just discussing it in groups), and that Li Zhang will attend this session in order to mediate between the Singaporean students and the Australian teacher. Both teachers feel that they have learnt from this team teaching experience, and that their students have benefited from it – but will benefit more in the future.

- *Subject Expert – Language Expert*

Fernando González is responsible for teaching a course on the history of journalism in a Spanish university. His expertise in history, and his experience as a journalist, make him the ideal candidate for this position. He studied in the UK many years ago, and is a confident English speaker. However, perhaps because his knowledge of English was acquired in an immersion situation, he feels quite alarmed at the thought of having to deal with the students' written work. He considers that it is important for the students on this course to write essays – just as he did when he was at university in London – but he knows that they will need support with this. He is also particularly worried about grading the students' essays and providing feedback, because he thinks (perhaps irrationally) that since he is neither an English teacher nor a native speaker, the students will not pay any attention to him.

Fernando consults the Institute of Modern Languages, and Matthew, one of the English teachers specializing in academic writing, is asked to set up some practical form of collaboration that will solve Fernando's problem and satisfy the students. The solution they reach has two stages:

Stage 1: Once Fernando has taught the first part of the course, in collaboration with Matthew he decides on a suitable essay title for the group in question. It is important for the writing teacher to be involved at the stage when the task is devised, because writing teachers are usually more sensitive to the rhetorical demands of a particular writing task – and are more experienced at formulating the task description so that students will actually understand it properly. When they have agreed on the task, Matthew then takes over the class for a day. During this time, he runs through the basics of essay structure and academic style, and provides the students with some exercises to practice these, and some resources they can use. He also goes through the system of referencing, and the need to avoid plagiarism. The students take away clear instructions about how to write the essay, and how it will be evaluated (factoring in both content and language).

Stage 2: Once the students have submitted their essays, Fernando and Matthew both evaluate them from their different perspectives (content and language/structure/style). They sit down together to compare their results, and to reach a consensus grade. In a final session with the students, they give the essays back to their writers and provide group feedback, with the possibility of individual consultation where desired.

Some further ideas to foster team teaching are described by Li and Cargill (2019) include creating an atmosphere of openness and collaboration that breaks down the traditional barrier between classrooms/classes. Li and Cargill describe how they invited content teachers to attend a scientific writing course for students given at a first-tier university in China, and asked those who came for their ideas and opinions. This initiative met with only limited success, but the authors considered that such collaborations are worth pursuing, with a view to demystifying and encouraging collaboration between disciplines.

Assessment Teams

For some courses in which two teachers are involved, it makes sense for different teachers to give different grades for the same piece of work, so that content and language are both taken into account. In a course in civil engineering taught at the Cape Peninsula University of Technology, South Africa, team assessments emerged out of a collaborative teaching experience. The content teacher and the language teacher worked together to design the assignment, and then they participated at different stages during the writing process to give feedback and ultimately to award a grade. One of the discoveries made during this experience was that 'the language lecturer did not know enough about Civil Engineering to respond meaningfully to the content, and the Civil Engineering lecturer's feedback was not helping the students to revise and improve the written assignment' (Jacobs 2006, 149). In an endeavour to learn from this experience, they collaborated on a framework to guide teachers through a process approach to the assessment of integrated written assignments, with a view to ensuring that such assessments would help students to develop concepts as well as to acquire relevant academic writing skills. This framework also incorporates a phase in which peer assessment can be carried out (see Chapter Five).

In the framework for team assessment described by Jacobs (2006), four different stages in the assessment process are outlined:

Stage 1: Formative assessment. Content lecturer checks the first draft to make sure that the student has interpreted and analysed the task correctly, understands the key concepts and is aware of the audience he/she is writing for. Feedback at this stage consists mainly of questions to make the writer reflect on what has been misinterpreted and what needs to be improved.

Stage 2: Peer assessment. Students give their draft to another student, who will use a checklist or editing sheet prepared by the teachers to check that the text has all the necessary elements, and that it is generally well organized and easy to understand. Peer assessment takes place during class time in the presence of the teacher, who can clear up any difficulties.

Stage 3: Formative assessment. Language lecturer reads the text and provides feedback on language forms (grammar, vocabulary, spelling, punctuation) with correction where necessary.

Stage 4. Summative assessment. Final grade given by content lecturer only, focusing on the following points:

- Has the task been well analysed and understood?
- Is the writing well structured and coherent?
- Is the language appropriate?
- Is the document well presented?
- Are the references appropriate and correctly presented?

However, this is not the only approach to spreading the weight of evaluation between content and language lecturer. It should be noted that although the language lecturer participates in the formative assessment process, he/she does not contribute to the final grade. One of the main reasons for this is probably that the content lecturer feels, justifiably, that he/she is the main person responsible for teaching the course, and should therefore be the person who decides the grade. In other contexts, it is possible to get round this problem in other ways. For example, in one course on scientific writing in which one of the authors regularly participates, part of the grade on the scientific writing course is awarded on the basis on one section of the students' master's thesis that has to be written in English. In effect, this section is graded twice: once for content and general organization, as part of the grade for the master's thesis, and once for English as such, as part of the grade for the scientific writing course. In another course taught on an undergraduate degree in the School of Communication, the English teacher participates in giving the course, and also in grading the assignments (see section on 'team teaching', this chapter).

Language Teachers in the Content Classroom

All of the proposals just discussed probably fit fairly neatly into the existing possibilities in universities where EMI is being adopted. To some extent, teachers from different areas have always shared courses, and collaboration with language departments is also nothing new. However, some proposals for team teaching go further (Lasagabaster 2018), with the suggestion that language specialists should actually be present in the classroom as the content teacher is giving his/her class, playing the role of 'language expert', troubleshooting, and raising students' consciousness as far as language is concerned. The language specialist would, if required, give feedback to the content teacher about his/her use of language, materials and assessment tasks. The language expert could also conduct research into the content teacher's use of language, particularly code-switching practices, assess their impact on students and formulate some guidelines for productive use of code-switching. Although this is an interesting proposal, in our experience it is risky, because many university teachers are unwilling to have a second teacher in the room when they are with their classes, and particularly so when they are teaching in a language in which they lack confidence. Moreover, to implement such a scheme on a large scale would be costly for institutions. Compromise solutions, such as class observations by a language specialist over a short period of time, would probably prove more practical in the long term.

6.4 Support from Language Departments

One of the less positive aspects of the way EMI has been implemented in some universities is the tendency shown by university administrators to assume that if courses are taught in English, then there is no need for universities to provide English-language teaching in the form of English for Specific Purposes or English for Academic Purposes (EAP) courses. This is short-sighted, because when students take EMI courses, they become intensely aware of their strengths and weaknesses as far as English is concerned, but they are left with no means for addressing those weaknesses within the university system. In reality, language departments have a major role to play in the international university. EMI does not reduce the need for language courses. It may actually trigger increased demand for general English courses (support for EMI teachers, support for EMI students, or courses to prepare students for international certification). Language departments generally have great expertise at diagnosing gaps in people's language skills and designing courses that can meet those needs, and their special competence in this area should be celebrated and harnessed for the benefit of staff, faculty and students, rather than sidelined or ignored. At the same time it is widely acknowledged that internationalization of the university probably also raises the opportunities for courses in languages other than English (Wächter and Maiworm 2014), since there will be a greater need for courses in the local language(s) for international students, as well as a certain demand for courses in other world languages for students with good English who want to learn a third language to enhance their mobility and job prospects.

At the same time as all of this, the transition to EMI offers an opportunity to language departments to reconsider the courses they offer in the light of the new context (higher levels of English among students, EMI courses and widespread use of English within the university). We suggest that the renewal of courses offered by the language department should be shaped along the following broad lines: English for Academic Purposes courses, English for Specific Purposes courses and intercultural communication courses. In addition to this, it would be a good moment to consider other kinds of support outside the 'course' system, such as writing centres and online resources (see later sections in this chapter).

English for Academic Purposes Support

EAP support can be conceptualized as general help with academic English – seeking to help students from different disciplines to push their school English further, and acquire general academic language competences that will help them to do the things they need to do in their subject courses effectively (reading and interpreting long academic texts, writing essays and papers, participating in seminars and discussions, taking notes in lectures, etc.). In Anglophone countries, such courses are often conceptualized as 'pre-sessional courses' designed to help students from other countries get their English up to scratch in academic contexts before they start work on their degree course proper. In EMI contexts elsewhere, such courses would be appropriate in the first year or foundation year. However, care should be taken with such courses in two senses. First, a large number of textbooks are available for general EAP courses, but these fall into two categories: books designed for a global audience, which can be adapted for use in almost any EMI situation; and books intended specifically for students going to study in the United Kingdom, the United States or Australia, in which a large proportion of the contents is aimed at international students who have to adapt to the UK or US culture and university system. When choosing a textbook for general EAP, it is very important to look at it in depth to find out if it is really suitable to your local context.

In broad terms, a general EAP textbook for EMI contexts outside Anglophone countries should contain help with the following aspects:

- general academic vocabulary and register
- general university vocabulary
- understanding lectures and taking notes
- asking and answering questions
- participating in discussions and seminars
- writing academic genres

All of these aspects will work better if they are adapted to the local context: there is no sense in teaching students the vocabulary for talking about the courses, buildings and processes in university life in the United Kingdom or the United States if they are known by very different names locally (see also our section on *Academic Dictionary*, in the following).

Academic Writing Courses

One of the particularly useful aspects of EAP courses is that they can be used to open students' eyes to the demands of academic writing. Hardly any students come to EMI at undergraduate level with appropriate writing skills, and even those with a C1 level in English usually struggle when they have to hand in academic papers, largely because their school system has not prepared them for this way of writing. For this reason, courses designed specifically to focus students' attention on writing skills are thought to be particularly useful.

Academic writing courses can be delivered at a variety of levels depending on the educational stage and language competences of the students. Starting at the top of the range, at PhD level, the students are likely already to have basic writing skills, but may still need help with textual organization and academic register, especially in English. At master's level, similar material can be given, although the students' academic socialization is not so advanced, and they may not perceive the relevance of some kinds of activity. If the students are specializing in science, then a focused scientific writing course is the most useful option, preferably with examples and exercises from the students' own subject area.

For undergraduates, academic writing courses are of necessity less focused (we do not actually know what our students are going to do in the future, or what their writing needs will be). For this reason, it is legitimate to open up the scope to wider educational skills, like essay writing and report writing. An emphasis on academic register and style is always useful, paired with a strong focus on textual organization, particularly paragraph writing, and on writing for different audiences (see also section Writing Centres and Support for Graduate Students, herein).

Figure 6.1 provides the structure of an academic writing course taught to mixed groups of undergraduate students from various disciplines at one of our universities.

However, even though EAP and academic writing courses are useful, there is often a perception that they are not the optimum way of providing the help that students need. The kind of help they offer is very general, and all the myriad differences between disciplines cannot be factored into the equation. For this reason, it is probably best in the long run to design tailor-made English for Specific Purposes (ESP) courses that take the nature of disciplinary discourses and disciplinary knowledge into account. These will be described in the next section.

Structure for Academic Writing Course

Unit One: Writing clearly and fluently. Cohesion. Conjunctions and sentence adverbials.

Unit Two: Developing a formal style. Direct and reported questions.

Unit Three: Structuring the essay. Paragraph structure. Writing an essay.

Unit 4: Writing about numbers. Describing dynamic and static data.

Unit 5: Reporting and summarizing. Reporting verbs. Paraphrasing. Writing a report.

Unit 6: Analysing scientific genres. Academic style and register.

Unit 7: Writing a research paper. Methods and results.

Unit 8: Writing a research paper. Literature review and referencing systems.

Unit 9: Writing a research paper. Introductions and abstracts.

Unit 10: Writing a research paper. Discussions. Correspondence with journals.

FIGURE 6.1 *Structure for Academic Writing Course.*

English for Specific Purposes Support

English for Specific Purposes courses have long been given in non-English-medium universities as a way of helping students to learn the kind of English they will need in their chosen profession. As levels of English have risen over the last thirty years, the kind of course given has moved from courses designed to help students learn technical vocabulary and understand professional texts, to courses in which students practise productive skills – speaking and writing – in a professional context. The best way of thinking of English for Specific Purposes courses is as a shortcut to learning all those language skills that someone might need in the early years of his/her profession.

In medicine, for example, an English for Specific Purposes course aimed at intermediate (B1/B2) level students might focus on strategies for reading professional texts, including (of course) subject-specific vocabulary. But since many students want to do summer internships or longer study visits in hospitals where English is spoken, it might also include areas such as doctor–patient communication, focusing particularly on the typical expressions and vocabulary used when doctors and patients communicate, which might include informal anatomical and medical vocabulary, as well as the scientific terms used in textbooks. Such courses can be structured around what medical professionals already know about taking a clinical history – and there are plenty of videos and handbooks available that can help to make this course more authentic. Moreover, if the students have a good grounding in English (B2/C1 level), such a course could also address areas such as the best way to give bad news and how to talk to your patient's relatives – all of which have been studied by health communication experts, giving rise to an extensive bibliography.

The language of law presents a double challenge to many professionals from other backgrounds: not only is the English terminology very difficult, and the texts (laws, contracts, wills, etc.) very technical and hard to understand, but in many cases, the actual concepts are different from those used in one's own legal system. Unlike medicine, where we assume that the human body and its functioning are much the same across all languages and cultures, in law English for Specific Purposes courses come up against the problem that the law is NOT the same in different countries and cultures. The theory of contract is different in common law countries from civil law countries, for example. Even crimes are different: murder is NOT defined the same way in one country as in another. All of this means that the English for Specific (Legal) Purposes teacher has to acquire familiarity not only with the target legal language (English) but also with the system that it embodies – and also, in the best case, with the legal system that students are familiar with. This does not mean, of course, that the teacher has to teach the students English law – but it does mean that he/she has to have some awareness of the difficulties that students face. Given the difficulty of English for Specific Purposes in Law, it makes sense to prioritize certain areas in which students are likely to encounter legal English. This could mean reading comprehension: learning to understand documents, legislation, etc. But it might also mean learning how to communicate with clients from other countries in speech and in writing (interviews with clients, correspondence, etc.). In all this, it is important to keep in focus the main idea: students do not necessarily need to learn about English (or US) law – they need to learn legal English in order to be able to communicate with any client or legal professional from outside their own culture/language.

Another way of focusing such English for Specific Purposes courses is to offer modules centring on concrete skills that students might want to improve. These modules could include specific short courses on 'Presenting in public' or 'Customer communications' (described herein by way of example). But our universities have also developed a range of specialized courses such as 'Medical consultations in English', 'Nursing presentations' and 'Negotiations', all of which receive excellent student feedback.

- *Presenting in Public Courses*

Many degree programmes or master's programmes would be enriched by the inclusion of a course designed to teach students how to present in public effectively. We have taught courses of this kind to undergraduates and master's students across a range of disciplines, as well as to PhD students, university professors and university support staff. One of the keys to designing a good course of this kind is to make sure that it is clearly structured with plenty of input, and that the practice sessions are focused on different subskills. It is excellent to get students to write/design and give presentations, but we also need to give them ideas about how to do this, and how to improve.

Components of a course on presenting in public would vary according to the subject area and purpose of the students. It is obviously not the same to present a conference paper as to pitch a project proposal to a group of evaluators. Moreover, what may seem to be the same genre (e.g. the conference paper) is often radically different across disciplines. In the humanities it is usual for conference papers to last for twenty minutes, followed by five to ten minutes of discussion. In the experimental sciences or medicine, ten minutes is the norm, and papers that run over this time are literally cut off so that the next speaker can start. One of the authors recently took part in a conference from the area of engineering education, in which each speaker had precisely five minutes to give her/his talk. Other facets of the conference paper can also vary greatly – although PowerPoint and Prezi tend to dominate, there are still disciplines, such as history or literature, where the use of visual support is not the rule. Philosophers, on the other hand, tend to prefer handouts containing lists of points that structure their argument. Anyone planning to give a presentations course needs to start by finding out (e.g. from the prospective attendees) what the main characteristics of the presentation are in the context where these people work, and then doing some research into good practices in this type of presentation. For example, some papers have been published on the ten-minute presentation in science which help the (non-specialist) teacher to give sound advice to students on how to make the most of their time, how many minutes to devote to each point and so on.

In essence, however, the presenting course has two aspects: one structural/organizational, and one interpersonal. The first aspect is about ordering information, ensuring a balance with logical progression, making the main points very clear, etc. The second is about how to build a relationship with the audience, how to choose the right words and use your voice and body language effectively, so that you get the message across with maximum effect.

Probably the ideal scenario for a presenting in public course would be to have the collaboration of a subject specialist and a language specialist. In the real world, however, the job of teaching such courses usually falls to the language teacher – so it is helpful for productive contact to be established between the language teacher and experts in the content area, so that the teacher knows what kind of presentation to aim for.

- *Customer Communications Courses*

Sometimes there is no space for a general business communication course in the timetable, either because such courses are taught in (and focus on) the 'other' language of instruction or because the institution has other priorities.

In this case, it would be sensible to offer specialized modules in some of the key areas where students will need to use English in the future. These could include aspects such as:

- principles and models for effective written correspondence
- strategies for effective telephone communication
- presenting products or services
- building relationships with customers
- dealing with complaints

However, in consonance with the principles of ESP, the objective and material used should be tailored as far as possible to the students' needs and the professional targets to which they aspire (see Lockwood (2019) for examples of how to research for such courses). Designing courses of this kind offers an opportunity for the ESP specialist to learn more about communication in a specific professional area. By way of example, we could mention a section of a course on 'Effective Speaking and Writing' for first-year marketing students, in which one of the authors developed the theme of 'handling complaints' in order to push students to develop their communicative competence in English AND their general understanding of how to communicate in the business world. This part of the course used the idea of the 'TripAdvisor' public complaints system, in combination with business literature on 'Principles for responding to customer complaints'. Students in the class were divided into two groups, one of which had had an unsuccessful weekend in London, and the other of which had gone on a disastrous holiday to the Himalayas (these situations can be adapted in an infinite number of ways). The students first worked in pairs to write a complaint for 'TripAdvisor'. In the next part of the class, they read and discussed the techniques for responding to complaints from an American business journal. They then exchanged their complaints with the other group and took the role of the tour organizer, using the principles they had studied in order to write effective responses. After this, they sent the responses back to the complainants, who evaluated the responses using a standard customer satisfaction scale. This type of mini-simulation is not difficult to set up in the classroom, and a productive course could be built around a set of simulations related to the business world.

6.5 Writing Centres and Support for Graduate Students

When I am teaching students about literacy, I like to get the message across that literacy learning does not stop once students know all the letters:

students go on acquiring literacy skills throughout the course of their formal education. If you don't believe me, compare the way someone with a basic schooling writes with the way a graduate writes. There is likely to be a big difference, not just in grammatical and lexical accuracy, spelling and punctuation but also in the sentence structure, the paragraph structure and the kind of cohesion that underpins the text. So when do we finally achieve literacy, the students ask me. To annoy them a bit, but also to tell them something that they will understand, I usually say, 'When you have finished writing your Final Degree Paper'. In Spanish universities, the composition of the final degree paper is usually the first time that students have to write an extended piece of text, including a review of literature, with full references, and perhaps also including the report of some practical experiment or survey. Until undergraduates reach this point, they usually regard it with awe – unless they have attended an international school or done their schooling in Catalonia, where school leavers also have to write a long essay as part of their 'baccalaureate', nothing in their educational experience will have prepared them for this task. So when I explain to them that they will still go on acquiring new literacy skills up to this point, most of them start to see that there is more to literacy than just forming letters on a piece of paper.

Writing Centres

Within English-speaking countries, there is considerable awareness of the challenges facing international students, particularly at graduate level, where so much depends on their being able to produce clear, well-organized academic texts. For this reason, most English-medium universities offer support to international – and also local – students in the form of writing courses or workshops, or even one-to-one tutorials. These are often organized by university writing centres, which provide a range of resources, as well as teaching and tutorial support for international students.

By contrast, it is rare to find English writing centres in European universities, even though the need for such a resource is equally great, if not greater. In an argument in favour of establishing writing centres in Europe, Breeze (2012, 136–8) points out that European universities would actually be very good places for writing centres to be established – and that writing centres would be able to make an extremely positive contribution to these universities' teaching and research activities. First, since students, teachers and writing centre staff share languages other than English, the guidance provided could be much more tailored to the real needs that exist. Second, as university teachers and researchers are likely to make use of the writing centre, this could become a focal point for dialogue and knowledge sharing between native and non-native English users at different levels within the system. For example, a writing centre teacher working with scientific researchers would be able to plough some of the knowledge she gains in this aspect of her work back into the courses she teaches on scientific writing for undergraduates, or the seminars she gives for master's students. PhD students might also be able to make a positive contribution to writing centre activities by providing coaching for students having difficulties, helping to organize seminars for first-year researchers or building resources for other students to use. On the negative side, the huge pressure on non-native researchers to publish in English sometimes means that when writing centres or the equivalent do exist in European universities, they end up being used as a kind of free proofreading service, which is clearly not appropriate.

Writing Support for Graduate Students

In most universities across the world – not just universities that have prioritized EMI – there is an awareness of the need for researchers to publish their work in English. If this requirement is taken seriously by the institution, then it should consider how it is helping its 'apprentice researchers' – particularly graduate students and postdocs – to become better writers in English. Swales and Feak can be regarded as the leading lights in this area, and their books 'Academic writing for graduate students' and 'English in today's research world' should be required material for all MA/MSc and PhD programmes taught in EMI contexts (see also 'academic writing courses', discussed earlier, for an indication of how academic writing can be taught at undergraduate level).

In many cases, the writing of our MA/MSc and PhD students will improve if they learn to be observant readers and become conscious of the features of their target genre(s). This is particularly important for new graduate students in the early years of their research, who need to learn to write their way into their discipline. We always say that when MSc or PhD students write their first papers, they need to write 'with the bibliography open on the table'. This sometimes raises some eyebrows: 'Isn't that copying?' the students ask. So we point out that everything we learn is in some sense copied, or, to put it differently, all texts are reassembled from previous texts. This is not the same as plagiarism! But when we learn to write as academics, in some sense we are learning to reproduce the professional or scientific 'voice': we are being socialized into a disciplinary way of thinking, talking and writing. For this reason, consciousness-raising exercises designed to make students more aware of the different aspects of the genre they aspire to writing are an essential shortcut to attaining mature writing skills. Worksheet 6.1 can be used with students at many different levels and from many disciplines: the point is that each of them should research their own discipline and target genre. We usually ask the students to fill in the 'genre analysis' form and hang it on the class blog or blackboard site, along with an example of an article that they liked.

WORKSHEET 6.1: GENRE ANALYSIS FOR ACADEMIC WRITING

Go to the electronic journals in the library, and find a journal from your own area of interest.

Call up some of the issues of the journal and look for an article that interests you, or that could be relevant to your research paper.

Before you start writing your research paper, you need to carry out a genre analysis of the type of paper published in your area. Use the article you have found to answer the following questions:

Genre analysis

1. Which journal is the article from?
2. What is the title of the article?
3. Does it have an abstract?
4. If it has an abstract, how long is it? Is it structured (with headings) or how it is organized?
5. How many sections does the article have, and what headings do they have?
6. How much bibliography does the article have?
7. How does the author refer to the bibliography/references in the text?
8. Does it have tables, graphs, or other non-text material? How does the author refer to these in the text?
9. What features of the style do you notice? Look at use of active/ passive verbs, use of personal pronouns (I, we, you), use of contractions (don't), choice of vocabulary, discourse markers (however, moreover), choice of negative forms (there is not any time/ there is no time), phrasing of questions (direct or indirect). If you notice other important characteristics, please note them down too.

(For more detailed language study, see Appendix 3: Language Features.)

Another of the pioneers of writing support for graduate students in Australia is Sue Starfield at the University of New South Wales. She began around twenty years ago by organizing a series of workshops based on what she knew the graduate students needed (see http://www.lc.unsw.edu .au/). In her account of this (Starfield 2016) she points out that although most people think that non-native students are the ones who need most help, in fact the native English speakers also had a lot of difficulties with academic writing – in other words, both the natives and the non-natives had to acquire new academic literacy skills when they started writing a master's thesis or a PhD.

Concerning the focus of the sessions she offers, one of her interesting proposals is to encourage students to locate and use previous PhD theses in their field. These serve as a model, not only of structure (illustrating how the conventional sections of the PhD thesis work, how references should be presented, etc.) but also of the style and language of a particular field. Her aim is to 'develop students' awareness of the structure of texts within their own discipline' (Starfield 2016, 183), an approach used in academic writing support that is sometimes referred to as 'rhetorical consciousness raising' (Swales 1990).

Apart from the general doctoral writing courses, Starfield also describes a specific course with the title 'Developing a research proposal'. In many English-medium universities, students have to submit a research proposal at the end of their first year of graduate studies in order to be accepted into the PhD programme proper as 'candidates'. If their proposal is accepted, the student is formally confirmed as a doctoral student and can go on to carry out their research project and write their thesis – but if it is rejected, they usually do not get a second chance. The writing of the proposal is therefore a high-stakes task – but one for which they receive little formal support. This course focuses on offering students a set of 'conceptual tools' that they might find helpful in the early stages of their graduate studies. There is a big focus on formulating and refining the research question, for example, and students are encouraged to work in groups in order to clarify their thinking and begin to write down concrete proposals. This helps them to clear their mind, face up to criticism and learn to back up their ideas with solid argumentation and reliable references.

One final idea for graduate students is the 'writing boot camp'. In her description of this, Starfield (2016, 193) explains that the boot camp starts on Friday afternoon and runs all day Saturday and Sunday. Her account goes as follows:

> Students are asked to set a writing goal they would like to achieve over the weekend; they bring their laptops, and sit and write. Learning Advisers are available for consultation should students wish to have some advice on their writing. Meals and snacks are provided and students often chat to one another during meal-times. Mostly they sit and write. It is hard to know exactly why the boot camps are so successful with the students. During the first boot camp a student commented: 'there's magic in the room'. Students seem to value both the opportunity to write in a focused environment, the level of care provided to them, as well as the social dimension of the boot camp.

6.6 Collaboration through Professional Bodies

One avenue that offers a lot of promise for EMI practitioners is that of collaboration with colleagues in other universities or even in other countries, who are starting to implement EMI courses in their own subject area. So far this type of collaboration has not been explored – with the result that each individual teacher has to reinvent the wheel.

One case in which there is cooperation between members of a professional group is that of the operations management teachers in Spain, who get together once a year for a conference in which they compare notes about projects and discuss their teaching. Operations management is a subject taught on engineering degrees, but also on degrees in economic and business management, which means that it is present in almost all Spanish universities. The annual conference of operations management teachers consists of five-minute sessions so that each participant is guaranteed a maximum audience, and everyone keeps up-to-date with what is going on.

Teaching methods are a major focus at these events, with sessions on gamification, project work, problem solving, flipped classrooms and, recently, on EMI. Working with one of the association members, some EMI experts were able to gather information about the early days of implementing EMI in operations management, and to make this available to the association members, with a view to providing support and spreading good practices (Alfaro, Roothooft & Breeze 2020). From the information they compiled, it emerged that 80 per cent of the professors questioned felt that operations management was an area with a significant international dimension in which it is natural to teach in English. Among the positive points that they highlighted was the greater availability of teaching material – not just textbooks but also multimedia material, including many useful videos in English. Some of them mentioned the initial investment of time needed to get the course ready in English, but concluded that this was time well spent, because they would reap benefits from this preparation in the years to come. Future projects that could be carried out through the professional network might include the sharing of specific material, such as Spanish–English glossaries, and the joint development of simulations or projects using resources available online. It is our view that professional organizations of this kind, with their ready-made networks of lecturers who are committed to teaching, could provide an extremely useful channel for spreading knowhow about EMI.

6.7 Essential Institutional Resources

The Academic Dictionary

One essential resource for international universities operating in more than one language is the institutional Academic Dictionary. This is not a dictionary that contains all the necessary words for your subject – that would be something that you personally should take responsibility for, and you could provide your students with dictionary resources (e.g. online dictionaries of your area) and a glossary of key terms. The institutional Academic Dictionary is a bilingual or multilingual list of all the key institutions, roles, processes and documents that are needed to ensure that the webpage is properly translated, and that information for international students is not confusing. If your university is working with in-house or external translators, they will be very grateful if you give them access to your Academic Dictionary, and they will probably have useful suggestions about how to improve it and extend it.

By way of example, the University of Navarra, where one of the authors works, has had a publicly available academic dictionary for over twenty-five years. This dictionary is used by the translators working on the university's bilingual webpage, and all the publicity and informative material. It has an important role in ensuring that everyone uses one term to refer to the same thing: without a dictionary, the situation often arises where one translator decides to translate 'Facultad de Medicina' as 'medical faculty', while another calls it 'medical school'. The prospective student who visits the webpage could end up with the impression that these are two separate institutions! Here are some examples of the terms that are included in it:

- Names of schools or faculties: School of Medicine, School of Law.
- Names of degrees: Degree in Humanities, Master's Degree in Pharmaceutical Design and Manufacturing, Doctorate.
- Names of places: Building Laboratory, Reference Library, Office of the Registrar, Institute of Modern Languages, Museum of Natural Sciences.
- Names of university events and activities: Graduation ceremony, tutorial, supervised project, welcome days, admissions process.
- Names of assessment tasks: Final Year Project, re-sit examination, thesis defence.
- Names of documents: Transcript, diploma
- Name of people: Student representative, full professor, president, clinical tutor.

The University of Navarra's Academic Dictionary (English-Spanish) is available on:
https://www.unav.edu/web/instituto-de-idiomas/diccionario-academico

Online Writing Resources

Two good examples of online writing resources that are available on an open-access basis are:

- The Owl at Purdue, the Purdue University writing centre's website with a range of useful resources, including guidelines about how to write a wide range of assignments, and a very handy guide to different kinds of academic style, such as APA. https://owl.purdue .edu/owl/purdue_owl.html

- The Academic Phrasebank at Manchester University, which contains a huge bank of expressions and phrases for use in all the different sections of the academic paper, as well as explanations of how these can be used. http://www.phrasebank.manchester.ac.uk/

Case Study: The Engineering Model

The decision was made to start giving a range of EMI lectures at a small but prestigious Engineering School that is part of a large European university, and a budget was allocated to ensure that the scheme was properly implemented, with quality control, but also with special support for EMI teachers. A budget was allocated for this, and the university's language specialists were called in.

All the lecturers who were willing to teach in English were asked to take an exam consisting of a series of oral tasks (explaining visual information, defining terms, explaining a process, advising a student) relevant to the work of the Engineering School. These exams were graded by language experts, and all the lecturers involved were placed into level A (competent to teach EMI without support), level B (has potential to teach EMI after receiving support) and level C (unlikely to be able to teach EMI).

The scheme was put into practice, and the evaluation process was completed, with a small number of lecturers being assigned to level A, a large number to level B, and some to level C. Those in level B were sometimes surprised that they had not been placed in level A, but agreed that more support would be welcome. Those in level C were often relieved that they were not going to be required to start EMI. The scheme, including exams, was repeated in successive years. Lecturers from level B who had received a year of support often retook the exam, managed to enter level A and went off jubilantly to teach EMI courses. However, because of pressure on the School to provide courses in English, and lack of availability of lecturers, some of the lecturers from level B also ended up teaching EMI, often just as successfully as those in level A.

Although the scheme was assessed as being a successful example of an EMI training programme, as time passed the organizers also became aware that they might have placed too much emphasis on lecturers' language competences at the outset. In particular, the language experts who had graded the lecturers according to level had accorded too much importance to factors such as accent or intonation, or grammatical accuracy, perhaps because of their background in language teaching and examining. As the organizer said, 'Some people are just great teachers, and they can communicate well in any language.' The school has now moved over to a more flexible approach to EMI teacher training, including methodology and academic communication seminars.

On the other hand, it is equally clear from this case study that what the EMI lecturers themselves really appreciated was the interest and support they received from the School. In particular, they singled out the coordinator of the programme for praise, saying that she had inspired them to feel confident in their abilities, and to want to become better EMI lecturers.

POINTS FOR REFLECTION

1. Have you ever thought what type of team teaching you could do with a language expert? Mark the best options for collaboration in your case:

TYPE OF COLLABORATION	YES/NO
Co-design rubrics for oral presentations and written texts (reports, essays, exam questions, final degree or master's dissertations, etc.)	
Co-evaluate student performances, oral and written	
Let the language expert teach the conventions and style of typical professional texts students may submit or present as tasks (news reports, legal case documents and speeches, scientific abstracts, medical histories, technical reports, patents, oral presentations, etc.)	
Let the language teacher lecture parts of the subject which are not too technical (e.g. historical aspects)	
Have your class notes and teaching materials revised and corrected by the language teacher	
Co-design communicative tasks/activities helping students to acquire the discourse of the discipline	

Have your oral and written communicative skills diagnosed
    by the language expert and receive continued personal
    training or coaching from him/her

Have your classes periodically observed by a language expert,
    who might keep a logbook of your communicative progress

Other options?

2.   What are the reasons behind your excluded options?

CHAPTER 7

Achieving Excellence in Global Settings

7.1 Ongoing Teacher Development: Learning from the Experience

In Chapter 2 we started by saying that EMI – like all teaching – is a very personal question for everyone involved. Someone who wants to become a highly competent EMI teacher needs dedication and know-how, and must be willing to accept the specific personal challenge of becoming a good teacher in a different language. As we saw, this means taking on new roles, accepting the need for extra preparation, and moving out of the comfort zone.

For those people who wish to accept the challenge, it really is very important to understand that teacher development is not something that can happen overnight. To develop as an EMI teacher means cultivating a reflective attitude, learning from one's own experiences and developing strategies to do better next time (Sancho Guinda 2013; Farrell 2020). In this chapter we look first at some of the forms this development can take, starting with some ideas about teacher development programmes or shadowing programmes that might be most useful at the beginning of someone's career in EMI. We then move on to look at new initiatives in university teaching and how these could be particularly challenging – but also particularly useful – in EMI. We also address the important issue of culture and cultures, which we have touched on in earlier chapters, in order to round off our reflections on this issue and encourage teachers to take a positive exploratory stance to the ways that culture intersects with our teaching and learning experiences. This chapter then ends with some evidence from elsewhere showing how the initiatives described in this book are very much in line with trends in higher education worldwide.

One way of approaching the wealth of ideas that are available is to look at specific initiatives using particular technological affordances (e.g. video), or particular pedagogical formats or tools (e.g. shadowing, questionnaires). In what follows we describe a few of these, pointing to what we consider to be particularly useful in each one.

Using Video for EMI Teacher Development

Video obviously provides plenty of potential for self-evaluation and supported reflection. In the past, teacher trainers could only sit in the classroom and make notes, hoping that their presence in the room was not creating observer effects to a degree that would invalidate their observations, and then try to explain to the person they were observing what exactly was going well or badly in the session once it had ended. Thanks to easy video recording, the gates have now been opened to unobtrusive self-observation, peer observation, group peer observation, tutor observation and even class replay with the students themselves, in order to diagnose communication problems, reflect on teaching and learning, and analyse every possible aspect of someone's words and actions in the classroom.

One good recent example of this is provided by Llinares and Mendikoetxea (2020), who explain the use of video for in-service EMI teacher training to encourage self- and peer-reflection. They trained teachers to play back the video recordings of their own classes in order to identify different patterns of interaction with their students, see how frequent these different patterns were and consider the effects on the students (degree and type of cognitive, content and language engagement). At the same time, the students' perceptions were analysed through a questionnaire given immediately after the sessions.

The teachers involved in these training sessions seemed to benefit from this triangulation process, in which they were able to see their own teaching from different stakeholder perspectives. Above all, they gained from the reflection that this experience prompted. But no, this is not for everyone. There is also an unwritten rule in this kind of training, which is that the people who are willing to subject themselves to it probably do get something out of it – but the people who may need it most are unlikely ever to sign up to an activity of this kind.

Shadowing Programmes

Shadowing is now becoming known as a powerful tool for learning, because it provides a formalized method through which more experienced professionals can transmit their knowledge, knowhow and professional competences to people with less experience, all within a real-life setting. In this system, the learner or apprentice literally follows or 'shadows' the experienced professional for part or all of his/her working day, observing what he/she is doing and how he/she handles any issues that come up. Ideally, in the course of this process, the learner will have the opportunity to ask questions about what is going on, why a particular decision was made or why a specific issue was handled in a certain way, so that a genuine professional 'apprenticeship' or 'peripheral participation' can take place: the more knowledgeable partner transfers knowledge to the less knowledgeable one, and the latter acquires skills by contact with the real world, enquiry and reflection (Wenger 1998). The technique of shadowing has particular relevance in teacher training and ongoing professional development. In some countries, shadowing an expert teacher is an obligatory part of the practical training for school teachers, and it also holds great potential for teachers in higher education. Among other things, shadowing can:

- help learners to become familiar with the values and practices of a professional community

- enable learners to form ideas about good teaching practices

- provide learners with teaching strategies and resources to deal with future teaching situations

- allow learners to observe and evaluate different classroom management strategies and reflect on their transferability to other contexts

- help learners to understand how to conduct positive, respectful and constructive relationships with students inside and outside the classroom

Sánchez-Pérez and Salaberri-Ramiro (2020) describe how shadowing was used in the context of ongoing EMI teacher enrichment programmes in a Spanish university. In their case, a Spanish lecturer who took part in an exchange scheme used her time in another European university to shadow an EMI teacher and learn from this experience. These authors propose a set of interview questions to use before the shadowing experience, some guidelines so that the shadower makes good use of the observation phase and some questions to discuss with the host lecturer after the experience. Thanks to these, the shadower was able to make good use of her class observation, identifying different kinds of communication going on in the classroom, and also identifying some problems that arose because of students' language problems, or because the lecturer failed to provide enough variety during the sessions. In particular, she noted the need for frequent rephrasing and reformulation in order to support the students with weaker English skills. In general, the experience seems to have been positive, and gave the shadower the opportunity to learn more about how EMI works in practice, what works, and what could be improved. The authors conclude that the shadowing experience probably opened the shadower's eyes to discourse events and communicative strategies in the EMI classroom effectively. Moreover, the fact that she planned her observation and decided to look particularly for the way the host teacher tried to motivate the students to participate in the classes meant that she was able to devote attention to this aspect, which proved more useful than general, unstructured observation.

These authors conclude that all these elements of the shadowing activity are useful, and that this method promotes personal agency and the development of resilience, as well as helping the 'apprentice' to engage with EMI teaching and gain experience in a structured environment, following the principles of legitimate peripheral participation (Wenger 1998). In other professional areas, such as business and law, shadowing has provided the opportunity for young professionals or students to witness the use of work-related skills in the work environment personally, to experience training in context, and to observe the use of occupational skills in their area of interest. The drawback of such schemes is that they might prove time-consuming (and not particularly productive) for the host. But it is likely that shadowing could prove particularly beneficial in a context such as EMI lecturing, where a professional who is already involved in teaching – and comes to the shadowing with plenty of experience of the classroom – can gain insights into a new way of doing things, watch the ups and downs of someone else's classroom, and draw his/her own conclusions about what could be appropriate in his/her own context.

Learning from Student Feedback

For many of us, the moment at which we are forced to think about the way we taught a particular course or group is when we are actually given feedback from the students. Many institutions now implement formal systems of teaching evaluation, such as online evaluation forms for students to complete. In some countries, informal rating websites like 'Rate My Professors' are also popular with students and make stimulating reading.

Since most universities handle the feedback at an institutional level, there is not so much that individual lecturers (like us) can do about it, and we should simply try to learn something positive from the outcomes. However, on occasion it is possible for lecturers to design their own feedback instruments – and this might be particularly relevant when we attempt something new, like EMI. In our experience, some of the most useful feedback comes when we give our students (on paper, online, by mail) a simple form to fill in, that prompts them to tell us what was good, what was bad and what they would definitely change:

- What did you like about the course?

- What did you not like about the course?

- How would you change the course?

But of course, there are many more complex ways of getting student feedback (not all of which are more useful in practice). Questionnaires are inevitable (institutions like them), but often the (very general) questions seem to be off-target for what we actually want to know. Some teachers also use focus groups – getting a group of students together one day to talk about the course, their progress, and what they feel about the way things are going – which could be a good way of getting to know about student problems. But many more options exist. One teacher even uses an 'anonymous form' left in the classroom after the lecture, in which he lets students write messages to him about the course without having to take personal responsibility!

But whatever the instrument you use, we can imagine that some of the feedback will be positive – which is very gratifying – but some other aspects of the feedback may be challenging or even hurtful. So it is very important to approach student feedback with a sound philosophy, which could be based on the desire to learn from experience, and the knowledge that not all feedback is fair. Worksheets 7.1 and 7.2 suggest some pointers for handling student feedback.

WORKSHEET 7.1: HANDLING FEEDBACK ON YOUR EMI TEACHING

We get feedback from our students in different ways:

Informal feedback during or after the class

Official feedback questionnaires (evaluation forms)

Unofficial feedback forms

Complaints

Discuss the following questions with a partner. Do your answers coincide? Report your answers back to the rest of the class.

1. What kinds of feedback do you get from your students? In what format, and when?

2. What use does your institution make of this feedback?

3. Do you look forward to getting this feedback?

4. Do you think the feedback is fair? If not, what factors condition the feedback that particular teachers get?

5. In an ideal world, what kinds of feedback would you prefer to get?

WORKSHEET 7.2: MANAGING YOUR REACTIONS TO NEGATIVE FEEDBACK

Some people have very negative emotional responses to feedback.
People often react to negative feedback by:

- trying to defend themselves

- choosing not to hear what is said – selective reception

- doubting the motives of the person giving feedback

- denying the validity of the feedback

- rationalizing why they behaved the way they did

- making excuses for their behaviour.

What is the problem with reacting to negative feedback in this way?
Here is some advice for managing your reactions to negative feedback. Discuss with a partner which of these statements you agree with.

- Focus only on the negative feedback. If you look at the positive feedback too much, you will become proud and vain. T / F

- Ignore all negative feedback. Paying attention to it will only damage your self-esteem. T / F

- When you find negative comments, look for some positive comments that contradict them. This will help you to get it in perspective. T / F

- Read your feedback with a friend. Then you can laugh about it and try to see the positive side of things. T / F

- Try to get the general picture before you pay attention to the outliers. If thirty people have evaluated your class with 4 out of 5, then one person who has given you 1 is not so significant. T / F

- Look for themes that could be important. For example, if a lot of negative evaluations or comments are related to the way you evaluate students, then you could think of how to improve the evaluation system – or maybe just how to improve the way you explain the evaluation system to your students. T / F

- If you can trace the feedback back to individual students, try to identify why you think they may have evaluated you negatively. This will help you to see if their criticism is fair or not. T / F

- After you have looked at the feedback, write down your evaluation of the class (attendance, behaviour, attention, attitude, effort). Send this evaluation to your course coordinator in order to get revenge on the students. T / F

7.2 Changing the Learning Paradigm

The previous section deals with teacher development, and ways in which individuals or course organizers can learn and improve. None of the ideas suggested implies a fundamental change in the way teaching and learning is conceptualized within the university. However, in some institutions there are more ambitious plans afoot. In this section we provide an overview of some approaches that are currently modifying the way learning takes place within the university, and look at the implications of EMI in those contexts.

Flipped Learning

One new learning paradigm that has attracted a lot of attention is 'flipped learning', in which certain procedures and roles familiar from mainstream education are reversed or, at least, reorganized. The main idea is that students should put in some time and effort mastering some aspect of the course before the class (by watching video lectures, or by doing some prescribed reading). Since this groundwork can be taken for granted, the class time is then used for various activities designed to make students use their knowledge and go deeper – so, for example, the class time might be spent discussing different aspects of the material, or doing exercises based on what the students have already read, or undertaking collaborative group activities.

Choi et al. (2015) describe how they use the flipped classroom to teach an EMI nursing course on 'human health' at a university in Korea. The course included a large number of pre-recorded lectures, as well as other materials uploaded onto the course e-learning site. They found that almost all the students did the course work punctually and participated in the sessions. Given the EMI setting, it was perhaps not surprising that many students reported watching the lectures several times, and made full use of the options for self-pacing (stopping and starting the videos, rewinding, looking up words in an online dictionary, etc.).

On the other hand, these authors also mention some of the key organizational points that have to be borne in mind when designing a flipped course. They stress the need for a well-planned course with structured monitoring systems and motivational environments. Monitoring systems in their case included weekly quizzes and the use of a class discussion board for posting questions and problems and sharing knowledge. Students also felt that it was very important for students to be able to consult their teacher when problems came up. Regarding motivational environments, students felt that it was important for the discussion topics to be accessible and not require too much background knowledge. They also commented that students needed to feel that the class time was being used profitably, with structured activities. Although their overall results were positive and they conclude that 'students were satisfied with the fact that they could choose the time and place for optimal learning' (Choi et al. 2015, 946), they also point out that students required explanations and support at the beginning of the course, since this system was very unfamiliar to them. At the start, some students failed to grasp the point of the course, felt that they were not getting enough support, or needed reassurance that they were doing the right thing. It was only towards the end of the course that these students felt more comfortable and appreciated the freedom, flexibility and intellectual challenge of the flipped course.

On the down side, it is clear that a flipped course of this kind, with most of the material that would normally be taught in the lecture hall made available online beforehand, is more time-consuming for both students and teachers, and requires considerable organizational skills. However, in EMI situations, it is clear that the option of working through material (particularly video lectures) at one's own pace is an added plus for students with weaker language competences, and the more active approach adopted in the classes, with group discussions and problem-solving activities, is also beneficial in that it requires students to apply and improve their speaking skills rather than simply listening and taking notes.

Blended Learning

Blended learning – that is, combining face-to-face instruction with other modes of course delivery, such as online learning – has been around for a long time. Some universities use blended learning systematically, as an integral part of the way some programmes are organized, while others have preferred to stress the importance of the 'traditional' classroom and the face-to-face exchange between teachers and students. However, the events of 2020 brought many people into closer contact with blended learning than they might have wished and triggered a number of interesting reactions. For more about recent experiences in blended learning and useful ideas about how to set up such a course, see Pisoni (2019).

From the EMI perspective, blended learning poses no particular challenge beyond that of preparing lectures and tasks (see Chapters 3 and 5) in English rather than in another vehicular language. Indeed, the opportunities in this sense are rather wide: given the huge amount of online material (videos, courses, reference sites, etc.) available in English, it is easy to imagine how these could be woven into a blended course design using hyperlinks. The question of contact with students is, again, not intrinsically different from what happens in face-to-face contexts (see Chapter 4), but might be more swayed towards written contact through blogs, forums and discussion boards, rather than actual spoken discussions (although these are also very straightforward to set up online, with the advantage that they can also easily be recorded).

Other Models

What both of these innovations have in common is the way that they shift more responsibility for learning to the student and subtly reposition the 'class' or 'lecture' as just one part of a more complex suite of learning opportunities. In this context we could also include fully online courses, as well as forms of group work and project-based learning where the onus is on students to complete a task, and the support provided by teachers is subordinated to the requirements of the task and the individual participants. Again, all of these have their own pedagogical underpinning which would require extensive discussion, but they offer few challenges related specifically to EMI.

7.3 Solidarity and Social Responsibility

The role of the university as part of the society in which it is situated has long been a source of concern for theorists, and recently there have been some moves to promote activities that serve to consolidate bonds with society and develop social awareness among students. In the awareness that university education is often perceived as distant from the social environment where students will eventually work and participate as citizens, many universities have adopted service learning programmes (see Kenny & Gallagher 2002). Service learning is an educational approach in which students carry out some aspect of community service while also pursuing educational aims. The term itself was coined in 1967, in the context of an internship programme in which university students gained credit for work on community projects, but since then the notion of service learning has gathered considerable momentum, particularly in the United States, as it fits with aspirations to make higher education more meaningful and socially relevant and to foster a sense of civic responsibility among students. The core idea is that by taking part in activities designed to tackle real-life problems and benefit the community, students also acquire knowledge and skills that will enhance their education. For maximum benefit to be achieved, students should not only take part in a social project and learn from it but also reflect on their own learning and receive feedback from their social partners, peers and teachers.

The ground plan for a service learning project is shown in Table 7.1.

TABLE 7.1 Plan for a Service Learning Project

Plan for a Service Learning Unit

Stage 1. Research and Reflection

Identify an area where your service learning programme could take place, and do some research into it (reading around the topic, looking at publicly available information or media reports, talking to people involved). Conduct a preliminary assessment of the situation itself, and what you could contribute to it. Decide on the team of people that are going to be involved, and identify the people or institutions that will be able to provide help and support along the way.

Stage 2. Planning

In collaboration with the social institutions involved, the university representatives or, still better, the students themselves, need to plan the activities that they will do. At this stage, all the research that was done in the previous phase will come in useful, but it is also absolutely essential for the planners to listen to the people who are closer to the situation itself. The planning should include materials to be used, a timeline and, of course, one or more ways of evaluating the activity after it has been concluded. If reports need to be written, you need to think about information that you should gather in the course of the different activities. You may also want to think about media dissemination to give publicity to your project.

Stage 3. Putting It into Practice

If the planning has been done properly, the activity should run smoothly most of the time. But there are always going to be a few unexpected incidents. Record keeping and information gathering are usually difficult in practice, because the participants have so many things to do. It is important to keep a good channel of communication open with representatives of the social institutions involved in order to solve problems when they arise. Towards the end of the project you will also need to get some form of feedback from the different parties involved.

Stage 4. Reflection

Once the practical part of the project has been completed, it is important to encourage the students to reflect on what they have learnt about the situation and topic, about project organization and execution, and what they have learnt about themselves. Many experts believe that it is only through structured and critical reflection that learning really occurs.

For EMI programmes there are certain specific challenges involved in setting up a meaningful service learning project. On the one hand, the use of English opens the door to many forms of international exchange or international volunteering (see Crabtree (2013) for discussion of factors to take into consideration when organizing international service learning programmes). However, these are scarcely practicable in the context of a semester-long credit-bearing course. In what follows, we describe two different service learning projects with an explicit EMI focus, conducted over a few weeks in our local university: one was part of a credit-bearing course for undergraduate students of education, while the other was conducted within the framework of the master's thesis.

Project 1: What's Up in the Cloisters?

The local government's Heritage Department had been involved in a lengthy project to renovate the Cathedral cloisters. The funding for the project included a budget for educational activities with local schools. The University's Education Department agreed to collaborate, and established several projects that would bring pupils from primary schools in disadvantaged areas into the cloisters and teach them about art, history and restoration.

This was a wonderful opportunity for the education students, and the lecturers who were teaching cultural heritage education and creative projects immediately set about creating groups to think out a plan for various projects involving music, art and restoration techniques. The EMI group also wanted to join in, but as you can imagine, it was not so easy to think of a project related to the cathedral cloisters that would make sense in English. Then one of the students hit on the brilliant idea of taking the theme of the Pilgrim Road to Santiago de Compostela, the 'Way of St. James', which every year brings thousands of pilgrims from all over the world to our cathedral on their way across Spain. Since most local primary schools teach some English from the earliest years, it seemed practical to work on the subject of the pilgrim road, and to do this in English as the most 'international' language used by the pilgrims. In the end, the education students dressed up as modern and medieval pilgrims, telling the story of the pilgrimage and the reasons why they had decided to take part. After working on the stories themselves, the primary school pupils designed and wrote postcards in English addressed to the pilgrims who pass through the city, which we displayed on a noticeboard with a notebook for the pilgrims to write their answers to the children. The activity was very popular with the children, and quite a few pilgrims answered the messages!

At the end of the project, the material used for all the different activities was made available to other schools in Spanish, Basque and English, along with guidelines about how to put the different projects into practice, and the students who did the project actually presented their work at an international congress on heritage education.

Project 2: *Learning across Generations*

The degree project or master's thesis may be another area in which service learning offers considerable promise. On our master's degree that qualifies graduates to teach in secondary school, one student wanted to do a service learning project, but came up against a mismatch between her own aims and the school's objectives, because she was doing her practicum in an international school that functioned mainly in English. She wanted to get her older pupils (aged sixteen to seventeen) out into the community, to talk to elderly people in the residence across the road from the school. But the school insisted that she was there to teach in English, and all the activities she did with the pupils had to take place in that language. At first, she found it difficult to see how she could meet both objectives: contribute something useful to the local community, and get the pupils to carry out a project in English.

After discussion with her tutor and the school, she finally came up with the solution. The teenagers would visit the elderly people in their residence and interview them about what it was like to grow up in the city sixty years ago, and in particular, about what the local 'fiesta' was like in those days. This would require several visits, since the people were very happy to talk about this. The pupils would record their interviews and also take photographs (with permission, of course).

In the second stage of the project, the teenagers would write articles in English based on the interview material for an exhibition that would be displayed in the entrance to the school for the parents and visitors to see. This gave them hands-on experience with translation, and with complicated questions such as how much could be translated, what could be left in the original or when information ought to be accompanied by an explanation. The pupils also consulted local archives and history books, in order to find more information and obtain photographs of the different places, and of the 'fiesta' in times gone by. This again meant extra work, because the historical background and the captions to the photographs also had to be translated into English.

Regarding the goals of service learning, in their reflections after the project, the students commented on how much they had benefited – not just from finding out more about the city and about the lives of an earlier generation but from communicating with older people and listening to them. The staff of the home said that the residents had been very happy with the experience. In the past, they had considered the international school to be something for elites, disassociated from the city and the local people, but they had now built up a closer relationship and hoped to collaborate more in future.

Importantly for their English-language skills, the pupils themselves also commented on how challenging it had been to reflect what their interviewees had told them using English, because so many concepts were culturally embedded. However, they also expressed satisfaction that their project and exhibition had helped to build a bridge with the local community.

WORKSHEET 7.3: PLANNING A SERVICE LEARNING ACTIVITY

Think about the courses that you teach (or work that you supervise, such as degree or master's projects). In ideal circumstances, which of these might be compatible with a service learning activity? What kind of activity? What would your main objective be, and how would this fit with the objectives of your course?

Once you have chosen a course and an activity type, discuss the following aspects with a classmate:

How could you and your students prepare for the activity (what research needs to be done, what contacts would you need, how would you get permission or ethics clearance, etc.)?

Thinking particularly of the collaboration needed for a successful service learning project, what other people or institutions would you need to involve?

Regarding the students' different abilities and capacities, how would you allot roles within the project, and how would you involve any students with special needs?

Thinking of the logistics, how could you carry out this activity efficiently?

Thinking of the students' learning experience, how could you help the students record their experiences and reflect on them during and after the project?

To what extent would your university, the academic community and the local community be interested in your project? Would you involve the local media or university communications department?

What kind of follow-up would there be? How could you encourage all the participants to give constructive feedback? How would you decide whether it might be viable to repeat the same project next year?

7.4 Promoting Creativity in EMI

In school education, creativity is widely valued. But at university level, where teachers are often less interested in what happens in the classroom, creative teaching is rarely mentioned. Instead, academic discussions tend to be about regulation, standards and reliability. As Maley says, if you asked higher education teachers, they would probably divide into two broad sectors: those who consider that education is a form of personal growth that can be guided but not controlled, and those who believe that education is an institutionalized process which can – and must – have predetermined outcomes. The first of these views could be more typical in liberal arts education, for example, while the second underlies much of the 'competence-based approach' promoted by international agreements such as the Bologna Agreement, and the 'intended learning outcomes' approach described in Chapter 4 on higher education teaching. Nonetheless, although creativity is not foregrounded in much contemporary thinking on higher education teaching, we believe that it does have a role, and that people who are concerned to give good lectures, classes or seminars are usually creative in the broad sense of the word; that is, they devise imaginative ways of communicating key concepts or information, and seek innovative solutions to the problems that come up.

So how can we define creativity? According to Maley (2017), the word itself has acquired a large number of different meanings, and yet we are generally able to recognize creativity when we see it, through a kind of 'family resemblance' (Wittgenstein 1953, 31–2) in which 'any given instance of a complex phenomenon may share some, but not necessarily all, of a cluster of characteristics' (Maley 2017, 86). Some of the features of creativity identified by Maley are:

- Newness or originality: using what we have already learned to create something new.

- Immediacy or spontaneity: sudden inspiration, the 'eureka' moment.

- Respect or recognition by others: when other people exclaim 'why didn't I think of that?'

- Experiment or exploration: well-informed, well-grounded curiosity based on multiple past experiences that have been internalized.

- Genius or magic: the 'divine spark'.

- Seeing new connections: finding new relationships between different aspects.

- Coincidence or randomness: being able to take advantage of chance discoveries or coincidences.

- Ability to work within formal constraints: creativity is not about 'anything goes', it is about working within the given limits of a discipline or genre.

- Appropriacy to context: an idea might be striking or new, but it also has to be relevant in a particular context.

- Flow: states of total absorption that happen when we are intensely engaged in a timeless present.

All of these aspects may be present in major new creative breakthroughs – but we should not feel discouraged if we feel that we have not made any major discoveries so far. These aspects may all be present in some instances of what could be called 'big C Creativity' or 'historical creativity' (Boden 1990). But they also occur, perhaps one or two, or several, in our own personal experiences of what we can call 'small c creativity', or 'personal creativity'. For our own satisfaction and well-being, personal creativity is extremely important.

So how could we foster creativity in our EMI teaching? Maley (2017) proposes various ideas that could be adapted to many different EMI subjects and contexts – but obviously, not to all. It is up to the individual EMI lecturer, with his/her hard-won knowledge and experience, to determine which could be appropriate, and in what aspect of a given course. Here are some of Maley's ideas:

- Do the opposite/reverse the order: for example, instead of explaining the experiment first, and then the results, tell the students the results, and ask them to think how the experiment was done.

- Remove one important piece of information: explain the historical overview omitting one important point and ask the students to find out what it was.

- Change the genre: instead of asking students to write yet another essay, get them to write a letter, a newspaper article or even a parody, involving the facts and texts that they need to study.

- Reformulate: ask your students to rewrite a text in a different genre or from a different point of view.

- Change mode: make more use of visual modes (paintings, images, maps, architecture) or music and sound recordings. For example, listen to a famous poet of the past reading his/her own poems, or analyse paintings representing historical scenes.

- Promote an atmosphere in the classroom that give time and space to imagination.

- Relate: encourage students to build relationships between the texts and ideas they are studying, and real-life problems and issues in the world today.

- Group dynamics: find new ways of organizing the classroom and promoting collaboration among students in which they can learn from each other more.

Before we finish this brief excursion into creativity, we would like to go back to Maley (2017, 95–6), and mention two important points that emerge in the context of creativity in the classroom: one positive, the other negative:

- The positive point is that creativity can permeate everything we do. Creativity is not about 'wacky new ideas'; it is about developing our professional practice, being open to innovation and using our imagination to enrich our teaching.

- The negative point is that creativity has many enemies! Among these we encounter: fear of change; institutional inertia; love of the comfort zone; tiredness.

Creativity can be part of our approach to teaching in the university – and the change to EMI, itself an innovation that will make us revisit our approach to teaching, could provide a good opportunity to find new solutions that make our classes more effective and more inspiring.

CLASSROOM IDEA 7.1: EXPLOITING VISUAL IMPACT

We have seen that EMI somehow pushes teachers – and students – to make greater use of channels of communication other than words. The *visual diagnosis* task is useful as a warm-up activity to review the contents of previous class sessions, to introduce new topics testing the students' knowledge, or to close the session with the elicitation of a quick summary.

A) Through images

Materials: One or more slides showing an entity (organism, object, material, calculation, text, etc.) under a certain state or condition. Optionally, a table with the basic questions to be answered by the students.

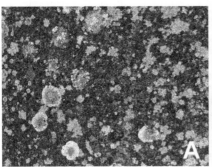

Example of slide showing two instances of *lichen growth* colonizing tombs in a graveyard. In A there is *a parasymbiotic growth of crustose and foliose lichens* on rock, whereas B clearly shows *long-lived foliose lichens* (at least several decades old) growing outwards and dying at the centre (Photographs by Carmen Sancho Guinda).

UNKNOWNS in visual diagnosis			
What?			
Name of phenomenon	Entity/material/part or element involved	Main symptoms or features	Names of similar or related phenomena
Why?			
Causes		Reasons for discarding similar or related phenomena	
How?			
Detection methods	Methods for prevention, mitigation, elimination, or production	Methods of analysis	

Mechanics and variants: Several images may be shown simultaneously for a contrastive diagnosis. Answers may be given spontaneously by individuals or derive from team work. They may be communicated orally or in writing, in which case they may also receive written peer feedback to be subsequently discussed by the whole class.

Simultaneous display of some types of lichen growth and substrate in the 'LICHEN GROWTH WHEEL' for contrastive diagnose in Botany or Forestry Engineering: (1) *Squamulose (crustose + foliose) lichen* on tree bark, (2) *Crustose lichen* on tree bark, (3) *Crustose follicular lichen*, (4) *Parasitic growth* of a *foliose rock lichen* on moss, (5) *Parasymbiotic growth of squamulous and crustose lichens* on a tree trunk, (6) *Foliose lichen with apothecia (disc-like reproductive structures)* on a tree branch, (7) *Fruticose lichen* on tree bark (Photographs by Carmen Sancho Guinda).

Application: This activity involves any phenomenon lending itself to visual identification or detection. It can be a useful resource for formative assessment when the successive performances of stable groups are evaluated (e.g. one point per right answer in every table).

B) *Through visual data (graphs, tables and diagrams)*

Materials: A graph, table or diagram showing the behaviour or the properties of specific materials, substances, agents or organisms, according to certain parameters.

Mechanics: Students must guess what the material, substance, agent or organism is being described. An alternative task is to guess and reason out their possible function and applications (before or after identifying the entity). Examples of questions are:

- *What material(s) is/are this/these? How do you know?*

- *What material would you use to build the following elements and why? What material do you think is never used to build . . .? Can you argue why not?*

Tables may be provided instead:

AIRCRAFT ELEMENT	OPTIMAL MATERIAL	REASONS
Nuts and bolts	steel	
Airframe	aluminium	
Engine components	titanium	
Wings	aluminium	
Heating systems	titanium	
(...)	...	

Elicitation table on the materials for the construction of aircraft items

Variants: The teacher may prompt guesses by giving the names of the entities and students are to match them with their corresponding visual data and possible function/application. Also, multiple-choice and True/False tests on the properties, functions and applications of the entities depicted may serve as review and formative assessment tools at the end of a lesson or a didactic unit.

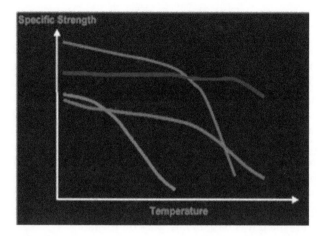

Graph sample showing the behaviour of steel (line that starts lowest)
and alloys of titanium (line that starts highest), nickel (second highest line) and
aluminium (third line from the top).

Application: This activity involves the interpretation of visual data and their
extrapolation to other contexts, the prediction of situations, the argumentation of
hypotheses and predictions, and the interrelation of concepts (different properties,
behaviours and functions) and of disciplines.

7.5 Encouraging Critical Thinking in EMI

One of the comments that often confuse international students when they
start graduate studies in the English-speaking world is the requirement that
they should 'be more critical'. English-speaking students are often taught
from their schooldays onwards that they need to 'think for themselves' and
'take a critical stance towards received ideas'. In some other educational
systems, however, undergraduate studies are conceptualized as a process of
familiarization with the basic knowledge and skills used within a discipline.
However, they are NOT understood as implying any need to stand back from
that knowledge or those skills and imagine what might be incomplete or
contradictory, or where the knowledge gaps in the compendium of received
knowledge lie. Attempts to point to inconsistencies or propose alternative
views are considered risky, because they might be regarded as disrespectful
to the professor (or worse). Among students who are unfamiliar with the
notion of 'being critical', the invitation to take a critical stance tends to meet
with reactions such as 'How can I criticize these authors? They are experts
and I am not', or 'I can't say what is right or wrong about that idea, because
the teacher has not told me the answer to that'. (See "Culture and Cultures

in EMI" (7.6) for more discussion of cultural expectations and the way they shape students' and teachers' attitudes and behaviour.)

This problem seems to be fairly widespread, and has been a matter of discussion among experts and practitioners in international education for some decades now. In response to the evident need to provide conceptual support in this area, many institutions in the English-speaking world provide advice for international students on their websites, or in the guidelines they give to new students, about the need to 'be critical'. Thus, for example, Imperial College's *Success Guide for Master's Students* places 'critical thinking and critical ability' at the top of the list of what students need to be successful, straight after 'what your tutors expect from you'. By way of explanation, this website states that 'A "critical thinker" does not blindly accept a theory, argument or opinion until they have verified the data or hypothesis on which it is based', and goes on to state:

> You should not be mesmerised by star professors, writers, publications and organisations. A postgraduate academic needs to be able to assess information and opinion thoroughly and analytically to determine whether it is accurate and believable. This skill can be mastered with effort and practice.

Building on this, the webpage goes on to make the following three points:

- Focus on evidence: Do not take claims at face value, but rather examine their validity on the basis of the evidence.

- Challenge bias and ideology: Try to see issues from different viewpoints.

- Focus on alternatives: Consider other possibilities before deciding on a course of action.

This advice is useful as a rule of thumb for helping students with the meaning of the notion 'critical', offering them a conceptual entry point to developing a critical approach in their chosen field.

However, we should also remember that this is far from straightforward. The ways of 'being critical' in each discipline are very different: in order to be critical in a productive or useful way, students need to understand the contents they are studying, the shared underlying epistemological assumptions within the discipline (how we know what we know, and what counts as valid knowledge) and the values accepted by consensus within the discourse community. In the words of Moore (2017), critical thinking skills are subject to a good deal of variation concerning the things people are supposed to know and the criteria they are supposed to use: 'the term "critical thinking" appears to defy reduction to some unitary definition, but instead appears to take in a variety of practices, associated strongly with the methods and worldviews of particular disciplines' (2017, 29).

So is it possible to talk about teaching critical thinking in EMI? The answer is that, of course, it is, but with the proviso that this elusive quality

TABLE 7.2 Stages in Developing a Critical Approach (Adapted from Rear 2017: 57)

Step 1: Identify and clarify the issue (formulate/understand the question).
Step 2: Gather information and organize it (understanding sources).
Step 3. Evaluate the information (is it credible? Reliable? Valid?).
Step 4. Analyse the information to address your question.
Step 5. Draw conclusions in which you answer the question.
Step 6. Appraise your own analytical process, conclusions and performance.

of 'criticality' in one discipline will be different from what is described as 'critical' in another. Is there any common ground? At the risk of oversimplifying, some authors propose that we could at least think of a shared method for going about a 'critical' inquiry of a particular issue that is important in our discipline. Rear (2017, 57) offers a very useful scheme covering six components within a 'critical' approach (see Table 7.2).

Since this approach is very broad, it would work as a heuristic for designing or approaching many types of student assignment requiring reading, use of social science data or experimental work. Such an approach could be applied to questions as varied as 'Do students living away from home have a worse diet?', 'To what extent was Charles Dickens a comic novelist', or 'How important were ideas and beliefs in pressure for change in Great Britain during the nineteenth century?' But we can easily imagine that this one-method-fits-all approach also has some severe limitations.

CLASSROOM IDEA 7.2: CRITICAL THINKING IN ENGINEERING

Hierarchies of Ideas

In the following task sample, which introduces engineering students to the *patenting process* of a simple invention, features and functions must be ranked in order to write effective *patent claims*. Students need to think critically and out of the box to understand the patenting process and the implications of each stage along the route to patenting.

Materials: A photograph, drawing, diagram or realia, imaginary or authentic, of a potentially patentable or already patented invention must be accompanied by a list of its features and functions. This list, however, must be jumbled up, so that students must differentiate major features and functions from those which are less central or derive from them. A sample task sheet could be this:

1. **Indicate the key features that label this invention by providing a one-sentence or phrasal definition.**

    - It is made of Brazilian hardwood for durability

    - It has a touch-on/off light

    - It is a walking cane

    - It is fitted with a Tesla-battery

    - It is for gentlemen

    - It is made of etched brass

    - It illuminates dimmer evening strolls

    - It does not have to recharge as two revolving sections keep the static charge flowing into the battery

    - Its design is elegant and simple

2. **Build a hierarchy tree of claims. Which are independent? Where would you place those claims that you consider dependent?**

Mechanics: Before tackling the activity, students must be informed that patent claims are the essence of the patent document, because they specify its legal scope – that is, the right that the inventor will hold to delimit the ownership of his/ her intellectual property and thus exclude others from making, using and selling the invention. A correct hierarchy of features and functions prevents unclear wording and, ultimately, prosecution in the Patent Office and litigation at Court.

They must also know that claims may be *independent* (i.e. covering all the significant characteristics of the invention and reflecting its whole picture) and *dependent* (i.e. hanging on one or several claims) (see Barreiro Elorza & Sancho Guinda 2015).

Variants: The teacher may prompt the task to a larger or lesser degree. For example, (s)he may provide several one-sentence or phrasal definitions or/and several tree-diagrams (either blank or filled out) for students to choose:

1. **Choose the best definition for this invention. Discuss whether or not major features are missed out in any of them or whether they include non-defining or redundant features:**

    - An electric walking cane for gentlemen

    - An illuminating walking cane

    - An illuminating walking cane of wood and etched brass

    - A battery-powered Tesla-light walking cane

    - An illuminating Tesla-light wooden strolling cane for gentlemen

    - A touch-on/-off Tesla-light walking cane

    - A Tesla-light wooden-and-brass walking cane

    - A non-rechargeable Tesla-battery-powered walking cane

    - A non-rechargeable Tesla-light walking cane

    - A battery-powered walking cane

    - (…)

2. **Choose the best claim hierarchy-tree for this invention:**

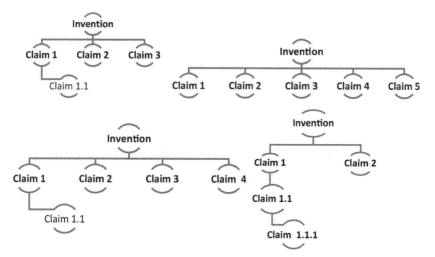

Applications: The ranking of ideas and features is key in every professional practice, from the differentiation of prominent symptoms in medical and technical diagnoses or the ranking of arguments in a legal case, to the evaluation of consequences in predictions with a view to decision-making processes, or the promotion of products and services.

CLASSROOM IDEA 7.3: DECISION-MAKING TASKS

Content-focused decision-making tasks may be aimed to hone identification, identify elements and flaws, make connections, pose questions to delimit problems and explore new contexts, and reflect critically so as to imagine and predict possible situations, evaluate options, especially those involving risk-taking, and make decisions.

- DECISION PATHS

Materials: From two to five sets of cards, depending on how many groups are competing, and preferably of different colours in order to identify groups. The set, of variable length, deals with a case study, a problem, or a method or procedure that must be clearly contextualized in the first card, which offers two possible decisions. Each card must briefly describe the situation resulting from the decision taken in the previous card and offer two new options that lead to another two cards (they might be formerly discarded ones), and so on. At some point, in the middle or towards the end of the process, there may be wrong options that finish the game and eliminate the group.

Mechanics: Each group communicates in the target language: reasons – pros and cons of the two options and their consequences are discussed and finally voted for. A moderator or chair in each group gives the floor, summarizes views and counts votes. Then, (s)he informs the teacher of their decision and the teacher will facilitate the card chosen. If the group arrives at a wrong decision that ends the game, they must display their 'decision path' on the floor or a table, and metacognitively reflect on their progression, spotting their errors and commenting on the alternative strategies they should have followed, to finally report their decision trajectory, the motivations behind it and its effects to the whole class. This report may be presented by a spokesperson, either the moderator/chair or any other member of the group specifically appointed.

Variants: They concern duration, timing, reporting in written form, role-taking, and research. The decision-making process may take up part of one class, the whole of it, or span several class sessions. It may be timed: a time limit may be set for the decision over the options in each card, for the accomplishment of stages involving several cards, or for the entire process. The activity may also be enriched with a final group report submitted by each group, evaluating their performance and analysing their successive decisions. The teacher may facilitate a report template based on authentic documents of the discipline (in-company and laboratory reports, clinical histories, legal procedures, abstracts, etc.). Additionally, the teacher may assign student roles other than those of moderator/chair and spokesperson to smooth out the decision process (e.g. factual contributor, questioner, conciliator) and allow research into similar situations or problems on the internet and/or at the library.

Applications: Medical and technical diagnoses, legal procedures of defence and prosecution, resolution of mathematical problems, research and patenting procedures, financial and investment policies, implementation of pedagogies and didactic approaches, consultancy verdicts on project feasibility, etc.

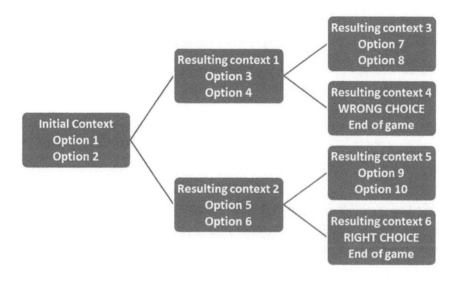

Critical Thinking and Language Awareness

The intersection of specialized discourse (i.e. terminology, register, tone and textual genres; see Bhatia 1993) and disciplinary contents offers a fertile ground for the exercise of critical thinking (henceforth CT). Content EMI teachers may devise customized CT tasks that foster the creation of a 'mental map' of real disciplinary practices and turn the classroom into a Socratic space of conjecture based on permanent dialogue and interdependent interaction. Such a 'map' will require that learners build a 'triarchic mind' (Sternberg 1988) which, among multiple CT skills, basically consists of analysis, synthesis and the practical processing of diverse professional situations.

Recourse to student team work may help this 'mind' become an ability shared by both learners and teachers, a sort of group or cooperative intelligence, termed 'possibility thinking' (Craft 2010), and characteristic of the learning community. Regular collaboration between language and content teachers and among content teachers of different technical and scientific backgrounds may, in addition, favour the application of CT across disciplines, which is known as 'cross fertilisation' (Sternberg 2010, 409–10) and 'transdisciplinary pedagogy' (Moore 2011, 2017).

Although language will hardly ever be the target of content teachers, some tasks raise more awareness of *LREs* (*language-related episodes*, Swain & Lapkin 1998) than others. LREs consist in an awareness of the language being used, which may be gained by means of tasks involving *identification, contrast, analysis* and *production* (including linguistic correction). They are especially frequent when dealing with professional genres, subject to more or less strict rhetorical and lexicogrammatical conventions agreed on by communities of practice and a reflection of their professional routines.

Language-focused tasks are especially valuable in STEM education, since its students are numerically oriented individuals who do not have as much chance to reflect upon communication strategies as students from other disciplines (marketing, political science, the humanities, art, etc.).

CLASSROOM IDEA 7.4: CRITICAL LANGUAGE AWARENESS TASKS

Critical language awareness in professional education revolves around three chief communicative foci: *concision, adjustment* and *promotion*. In what follows, each of these is explained with examples intended for the engineering classroom.

A. Concision-oriented tasks

These tasks involve *summarising* specialized information. Some proposals may be:

- Writing an **abstract** (e.g. of a class project, of a hands-on lab session, or one's own final degree dissertation).

- Condensing a conventional abstract (100–350 words) into a 50-word (**'conference programme abstract'**) version.

- Selecting the **key words** for a conventional abstract.

- Writing **research highlights** for a research article.

- Synthesizing a **technology description** (of 250 words maximum) into one **swooping line** (approximately 20 words). This is a frequent requisite in the submission of technologies and business ideas in entrepreneurial contests, such as *Actúa – UPM* (see its submission form herein).

	Documento de trabajo **Formulario en pruebas XIV** *actúaupm* **Competición de Creación de Empresas**	

TU PROYECTO EN UNA LÍNEA *(Se recomiendan unas 20 palabras)*

```
                                                                          
```

BREVE DESCRIPCIÓN DE LA IDEA
Esta información puede ser utilizada con fines promocionales. Describe bien tu idea, evitando incluir información de carácter confidencial en este apartado. Sé claro y conciso, lo importante es que cualquier persona no involucrada en el proyecto, ni experta en la materia, pueda entender de una forma fácil cuál es la necesidad o el problema a resolver que habéis detectado. También brevemente, en qué se basa vuestra solución. Se recomiendan unas 250 palabras.

B. Adjustment-oriented tasks

The need for communicative adjustment to a particular audience may be caused by the **knowledge asymmetries** between lay people and experts, to the **medium**, or to the **disciplinary culture.** Students may become aware of these factors by means of task of *textual compilation* and *ethnographic research* (observation, interviews to experts, questionnaires, etc.) into the practices of their future professional communities.

B.1 adjustment to expertise level (knowledge asymmetry)

- Genre choices for different audiences (tasks of identification, comparison and production) depending on their knowledge background: blog entries, tweets and video clips to popularize scientific and technical contents in outreach publications and circuits, in contrast with the same genres used for dissemination in expert networks, or with traditional expert genres such as the patent or the research article. What are the most common devices for content *easification* * and *simplification* of specialized knowledge in popular lay genres?

Simplification and *easification* (Bhatia 1983, 1993) are two ways of adapting specialized knowledge to non-expert audiences. Whereas simplification reduces the complexity of expert content by means of lexicogrammatical substitutions or content abridgement, easification makes expert texts more accessible through reader-guiding devices such as glosses, illustration and reduction of the informative load at some points. The purpose of simplification is the construction of simple knowledge, while that of easification is helping to build complex knowledge.

B.2 adjustment to the medium

- Comparison of verbal and graphical and video-abstracts. What resources are used in digital genres? Do they change the register and the tone of more traditional written genres? If so, how?
- Comparison of the academic dissemination of scientific-technical content in conventional written genres and a conference presentation. Does the audio-oral channel make the register more informal? If so, how?

B.3 adjustment to the disciplinary culture

- Compilation of samples of the same academic genre (e.g. research article, abstract) or professional genre (e.g. technical report, patent) in different neighbouring disciplines. How does it vary?
- Identification of one or more *tones* (e.g. personal or impersonal, tentative or emphatic, didactic/explicit or tacit, subtly or overtly promotional) in genres from the same discipline using a formal *register* (i.e. the specific use of the language). Discuss the differences and their reasons.
- Compilation and comparison of texts to find out how a certain genre has changed over time within one same disciplinary community (e.g. abstracts, patents, research articles).
- Adaptation of the same specialized content to different audiences (expert or lay) by means of genres, media and language.

  - ○ A fruitful activity in this regard is the visual and verbal contrast of a research article and a patent dealing with the same achievement as, respectively, a discovery or an invention. In addition, students are introduced into the disciplinary practice of technological surveillance and provided with new a tool (concordance freeware) for critical analysis.

Materials: A research article and a patent document dealing with the same achievement and written by the same authors. Recent samples may be found in engineering high-impact journals (e.g. in Elsevier) and the US Patent and Trademark Office website. An accessible and user-friendly concordance tool is the freeware AntConc.w3.5.8 (Anthony 2018), downloadable from the AntConc homepage. The texts files to be searched with AntConc must be first converted into a txt format.

Mechanics: Students may analyse the roles of visuals in each document. As illustrations, patent drawings are detailed guides 'simultaneous' to the verbal description of the invention, which refers to its numbered parts as they are being described. In research articles, visuals support the line of reasoning developed. As content-anticipating devices, patent drawings give an overview of the invention after the abstract, whereas the tables, graphs and diagrams in research articles offer a panorama of the results, trends and outcomes.

The teacher may assign the electronic search of specific language items to different groups in both documents. After the students have exposed their findings, (s)he may give them some 'food for thought':

1. Why are there expressions in the patent that divide the readers into lay or expert, but not in the article?
2. How does each genre use vagueness?
3. Which genre is more deferential to the lay reader?
4. Where and why are there features or functions emphasized or overtly promoted?
5. Are there any expressions disclosing the author(s')'s attitude?
6. Why are the adjectives 'new', 'useful' and 'feasible' rarely found in patents?

Variants: Students may analyse and contrast any other disciplinary 'twin' genres of their future community of practice, such as patent, research article and grant application abstracts. Also, students may track the section of the document where the searched items tend to appear (there is an application in AntConc), and thus deduce their rhetorical function. Finally, more questions may be added to the whole class discussion of the findings.

With the aid of the concordance tool software, search for the following items in the research article and the patent document.

METADISCOURSE ITEMS	Hits (section)	
• Community pointers	**Patent**	**Research Article**
○ We		
○ Inventor(s)		
○ Skill(ed) in the art		
○ Obvious(ly)		

- ○ Clear(ly)
- ○ Understood
- ○ Known
- ○ Seen
- ○ Shown

- **HEDGES (VAGUE LANGUAGE)**

Modal Verbs

- ○ May
- ○ Can
- ○ Could

Numeral determiners

- ○ Various
- ○ Many
- ○ Most
- ○ Several
- ○ One or more
- ○ At least
- ○ Diverse
- ○ Small
- ○ Large

Approximators/mitigators

- ○ Has been found
- ○ Typical(ly)
- ○ Common(ly)
- ○ Frequent(ly)
- ○ Often
- ○ Nearly always
- ○ Approximate(ly)

○ Suggest

○ Potential(ly)

- **BOOSTERS (EMPHASIZERS)**

○ Far

○ Much

○ Very

○ Of course

○ Indeed

○ Substantial(ly)

○ Considerable(ly)

○ Significant(ly)

○ Important

○ Readily

○ Will

○ Is/are

- **INFORMATIVE GUIDES**

Inferentials

○ Thus

○ Therefore

○ Hence

○ Consequently

○ Since

○ Because

Glosses

○ This/which means

○ That is

○ e.g.

-   i.e.
-   For example/for instance

- **ATTITUDINALS**

  -   Surprisingly
  -   (Un)expected(ly)

- **LOADED ITEMS**

  -   Advantageously
  -   Straightforward
  -   Good/better/best
  -   Sufficient
  -   Effective
  -   Facilitate
  -   Desirable
  -   Helpful
  -   Preferred/preferable
  -   Sufficient
  -   Conveniently
  -   Improved
  -   Easier
  -   Reliable
  -   Problematic
  -   Damaged
  -   Incomplete(ly)

A. Promotion-Oriented Tasks

These tasks help students to perceive the difference between different kinds of promotional language in the genres that they encounter. They could be used, for example, if you provide examples of academic/scientific papers, press releases, media reports, etc., about a particular topic, and set up a task in which the students need to identify the promotional strategies used and explain why these are appropriate for a particular audience. Here are some of the questions that could structure this activity:

- What mitigation devices of intellectual claims are most frequent in conventional expert-written genres?
- What genres allow more overt promotion of scientific-technical work?
- How are empirical data (tables, graphs, etc.) dealt with in research articles and conference presentations? What are the differences?

7.6 Culture and Cultures in EMI

One leitmotiv of this book has been the question of cultural differences. This theme was introduced in Chapters 1 and 2 and has been woven into our discussions and explanations through the different chapters. But we have not addressed it head-on, because we know that university teachers all operate within an ambient culture – the educational culture that has evolved over the centuries in the universities within their own countries, which also reflects the broader educational culture of that country and area, with all its rich heritage and intellectual tradition. It is not our intention in this book to promote one educational culture over another, and certainly not to disparage the cultures of learning in countries different from those where we have lived, studied and taught. Our references to various European frameworks, most notably the Bologna Agreement which contributed to an ongoing reform process across most European countries, are motivated by the fact that these are very well-known frameworks that can scarcely be omitted from any discussion of teaching and learning in higher education. However, while respecting the philosophy and aims of the Bologna Agreement, we consider that other approaches to university teaching may be equally valid, and that what is appropriate in one cultural setting may be inappropriate – or simply impractical – in another.

In Wächter and Maiworm's (2014) update on EMI in Europe, they report that European universities now generally express satisfaction with the level of English-language proficiency among their teaching staff, and are increasingly opening up positions to international applicants with a view to accessing global talent and internationalising their institution. However, the same universities also reported problems that occurred precisely because of this new internationalization policy, and in particular, they pinpointed misunderstandings arising out of cultural differences:

It was noted, however, that the strong English proficiency of the teaching staff does not imply that they can readily handle the heterogeneous command of English, academic and cultural differences of the students in the classroom. As a result, the need to train the teachers, including native English-speakers, to handle linguistic and cultural diversity was mentioned by quite a few of the respondents.

Other researchers, such as Turner (2009), have amply documented the kind of difficulties that can occur in the international university classroom, and the way that stereotypes are activated and perpetuated. She found, for example, that international students in the UK perceived the local students as dominant, intolerant, individualistic and difficult to get close to, while UK students thought that their international classmates spoke poor English, were slow, quiet, incapable of working independently, and generally 'not like us'. Elsewhere, too, there is often a permanent divide between the 'Erasmus' or 'international' contingent in the classroom, who may be both envied and pitied by local students. Moreover, differences in academic culture (expectations, types of assignment, behaviour in the classroom, etc.) also constitute a considerable hurdle for international students the world over (Safipour et al. 2017). For all these reasons, we would like to devote a small amount of space in this book to the issue of cultural differences, particularly those affecting people's attitudes in education, and the way culture might impact on our teaching and assessment practices. We set out on this (risky) adventure with the understanding that culture is dynamic and constantly changing, and that we have to take great care with any statements we make about national or broad area cultures, since these can be misinterpreted and lead to the creation or furtherance of stereotypes. However, we feel that this book would be incomplete without at least opening up discussion on this important topic.

To do this, we will use the classic framework provided by Geert Hofstede (1986, 2020), which is still used and still proves insightful today when we look at the differences beneath the surface in our classrooms. Hofstede's framework is based on empirical, questionnaire-based research in the business world into what he describes as 'collective programming of the mind' – in other words, that mysterious thing called culture that affects the way we think and behave. Two of Hofstede's dimensions are particularly important in this context, and those are the collectivist-individualist dimension and the power distance dimension. Collectivist-individualist dimension covers the way we think, feel and act as individuals and as social groups. Collectivism reflects a preference for a closely bonded society in which 'individuals expect their relatives or members of a particular in-group to look after them in exchange for unquestioning loyalty' (Hofstede 2020). Individualism can be defined as a preference for a loosely knit social framework in which individuals are expected to take care of only themselves and their immediate families. A quick way to pick up the prevailing on this dimension in a particular society is by looking at whether people's self-image is defined in terms of 'we' or 'I'. Many parts of Asia and the Latin world are characterized by a collectivist way of thinking, whereas English-speaking countries (particularly the United States) tend to be dominated by an individualist culture. Power distance, on the other hand, is concerned with 'the degree to which the less powerful members of a society accept and expect that power is distributed unequally . . . People in societies exhibiting a large degree of power distance accept a hierarchical order in which everybody has a place and which needs no further justification' (Hofstede 2020). On the other hand, in societies with low power distance, people conceptualize the distribution of power as being more equal and demand justification for any inequalities that appear. In these cultures, people may have a more egalitarian spirit, show less respect to those in positions of authority and demand greater transparency from them. Countries with high power distance include Japan, whereas low power distance might be epitomized by Scandinavia, for example.

Much of what happens in our classrooms is somehow influenced by our expectations in these two important areas of culture. Hofstede himself gave some consideration to how this might work out in practice, and his ideas provide some material for reflection when we are diagnosing the different currents that operate under the surface in our increasingly international classrooms. Table 7.3 illustrates some of the differences that can exist between collectivist and individualist cultures.

The other dimension we will consider here, because of its obvious implications for the university classroom, is that of power distance (see Table 7.4).

TABLE 7.3 Differences in Teacher–Student and Student–Student Interaction Influenced by Collectivist-Individualist Dimension (Adapted from Hofstede 1986)

Collectivist cultures	Individualist cultures
The young should learn	One is 'never too old to learn'
Students expect to be taught	Students expect to learn how to learn
Individual students tend to speak in class only when the teacher asks them to, or in small groups	Individual students are eager to speak up in class
Large classes divide into rather stable smaller subgroups depending on ethnicity or other affiliation	Different subgroups form according to the requirements of the task at hand
Education is considered a way of gaining social prestige	Education is a way of improving one's economic worth and self-respect
Collaboration with peers is important, and students will not 'betray' each other	Students compete with each other, and may sometimes complain about others' behaviour
It is understood that some groups get preferential treatment because of 'who they are'	Teachers are expected to be strictly impartial

TABLE 7.4 Differences in Teacher–Student and Student–Student Interaction Influenced by Power Distance Dimension (Adapted from Hofstede 1986)

Low power distance cultures	High power distance cultures
Stress on 'impersonal truth' which can in principle be obtained from any competent person	Stress on personal 'wisdom' which is transferred in the relationship with a particular teacher ('guru')
A teacher should respect the independence of his/her students	A teacher merits the respect of his/her students
Student-centred education (initiative and growth)	Teacher-centred education (order and authority)
The teacher expects the students to find their own path	The students expect the teacher to tell them what paths to follow
Students may speak up spontaneously in class	Students only speak in class when invited by the teacher
Students may criticize or contradict the teacher	The teacher is never contradicted or publicly criticized
Learning conceptualized as effective two-way communication	Learning conceptualized as effective communication from the teacher to the students
Outside the classroom, teachers are treated as equals	Respect for teachers is also shown outside the classroom
Younger teachers are usually more popular than older teachers	Older teachers enjoy more respect than younger teachers

Without going into further details, we can also say that Hofstede's other dimensions also shed some light on misunderstandings that occur. For example, his dimension 'uncertainty avoidance' draws a distinction between societies in which people like to have things in black and white, and cultures in which people are content to live within the 'grey area' that lies between. In a 'high uncertainty avoidance culture', teachers are expected to have all the answers, students are expected to learn those answers and intellectual disagreement is interpreted as a sign of disloyalty. In the opposite type of culture, 'low uncertainty avoidance', teachers are allowed to say, 'I don't know', students are rewarded for having innovative ideas, and intellectual disagreement is welcomed!

Is there any evidence that any of these generalizations are true? An empirical study by Marambe, Vermunt and Boshuizen (2012) comparing students in the Netherlands, Indonesia and Sri Lanka uncovered various interesting differences, but did not confirm all the stereotypes about Asian students. These authors found that both Asian groups scored lower on critical thinking skills, and tended to adopt a passive model of learning. However, while Indonesian students conceptualized learning strongly in terms of memorising, Sri Lankan students appeared not to cultivate rote learning skills. So some of the generalizations seem to be borne out by reality, and some do not. As these authors conclude:

> Although the way of learning students bring with them when they go studying abroad may conflict with what is demanded of them in the new educational environment, these patterns of learning are not fixed but changeable. Learning conceptions, orientations and strategies do not necessarily develop and change in the same pace, however. We must acknowledge that this change process may be painstaking and involve temporal frictions between what students believe in, want and actually do to learn. Adequate support geared at knowledge of students' learning patterns may help them develop their way of learning and bring their study views, motives and actions in a new balance again, an enriching result in itself of their experience abroad. (Marambe, Vermunt & Boshuizen 2012, 313)

WORKSHEET 7.4: UNDERSTANDING THE CULTURE CLASH

Most of us have spent time living, studying and working in another country, or in part of our country where the culture is very different from our own. Think about a time when you did this, and make some notes to answer the following questions.

What differences did you notice during the first few days of your stay in the new culture?

(You could think about people's appearance and behaviour; the way cities or towns are organized; food and eating/drinking habits; timetables; leisure activities, etc.)

What differences did you start to notice later on in your stay?

(You may have noticed social attitudes, expectations, reactions, ways of interacting with outsiders, prejudices or stereotypes, attitudes to work and study, etc.)

Were there any aspects that you found particularly difficult or irritating even after you had lived there for a long time?

Now think about the international students at your university. What do you think they notice at the start of their stay? And later on, once they have settled in? What aspects are still difficult for them at the end? How could you (or your international department) help these students to settle in better?

CLASSROOM IDEA 7.5: TEACHING CRITICAL INTERCULTURAL AWARENESS

This activity has been used for several years as part of the three-credit Optional Course 'Communication skills for journalists' at a Spanish university with a large proportion of international students and exchange students.

The activity is designed to raise students' awareness of cultural differences, and at the same time to extend and enhance their written communication skills.

This activity involves three stages.

Stage 1:

Instructions: Imagine you are a reporter for a magazine or newspaper with a highly international readership. You are going to write a piece of news about an event or situation in your home country. You need to include all the conventional components of the news article (headline, story, image, caption, etc.). Please remember that you are writing for an international audience, and therefore you may need to provide more explanations than you would when writing for a home audience, or even focus the article in a different way.

Your article should be uploaded to the Class Blog for everyone to read.

Stage 2:

You need to read at least three of the articles on the Class Blog. Try to read them from your position as a normal reader from your country. In each case, ask yourself the following questions:

Is the headline easy to understand? If not, how would you change it?
Is the image interesting, attractive and relevant?
Is the article easy to understand? Why/why not?
What aspects of the article do you like?
What aspects of the article need some improvement?
Then, write some feedback for the writer in the Comments box.

Stage 3:

Go back to your own article, and read the comments that your classmates have written. You should edit/rewrite your article, and post the second version on the Class Blog.

An example of the Class Blog is shown in Figure 7.1, with examples of the students' responses to blog articles in Figure 7.2 and Figure 7.3.

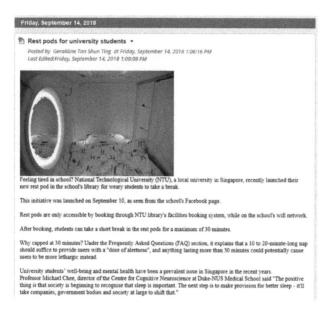

FIGURE 7.1 *Blog article: Rest pods for university students.*

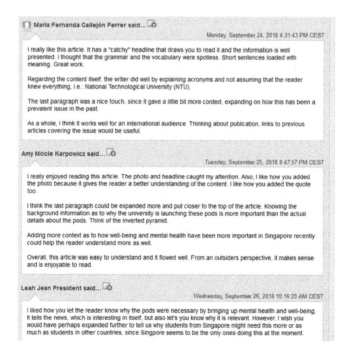

FIGURE 7.2 *Responses to blog article: Rest pods for university students.*

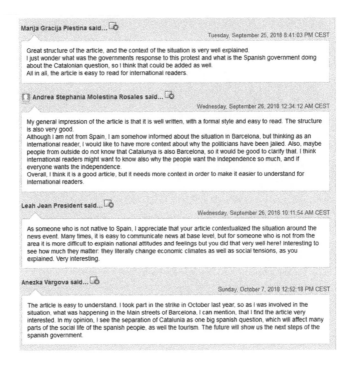

Marija Gracija Piestina said...

Tuesday, September 25, 2018 8:41:03 PM CEST

Great structure of the article, and the context of the situation is very well explained.
I just wonder what was the governments response to this protest and what is the Spanish government doing about the Catalonian question, so I think that could be added as well.
All in all, the article is easy to read for international readers.

Andrea Stephania Molestina Rosales said...

Wednesday, September 26, 2018 12:34:12 AM CEST

My general impression of the article is that it is well written, with a formal style and easy to read. The structure is also very good.
Although I am not from Spain, I am somehow informed about the situation in Barcelona, but thinking as an international reader, I would like to have more context about why the politicians have been jailed. Also, maybe people from outside do not know that Catalunya is also Barcelona, so it would be good to clarify that. I think international readers might want to know also why the people want the independence so much, and if everyone wants the independence.
Overall, I think it is a good article, but it needs more context in order to make it easier to understand for international readers.

Leah Jean President said...

Wednesday, September 26, 2018 10:11:54 AM CEST

As someone who is not native to Spain, I appreciate that your article contextualized the situation around the news event. Many times, it is easy to communicate news at base level, but for someone who is not from the area it is more difficult to explain national attitudes and feelings but you did that very well here! Interesting to see how much they matter: they literally change economic climates as well as social tensions, as you explained. Very interesting.

Anezka Vargova said...

Sunday, October 7, 2018 12:52:18 PM CEST

The article is easy to understand. I took part in the strike in October last year, so as I was involved in the situation, what was happening in the Main streets of Barcelona, I can mention, that I find the article very interested. In my opinion, I see the separation of Catalunia as one big spanish question, which will affect many parts of the social life of the spanish people, as well the tourism. The future will show us the next steps of the spanish government.

FIGURE 7.3 *Responses to blog article: Political crisis remains in Catalonia.*

7.7 Recent Trends in Higher Education Worldwide

In the final section of this chapter, we would like to return to the idea of EMI within the wider landscape of ongoing changes in higher education across the world. It is important to get a broad perspective on this, because it will help us all to understand better where we are going – and what role our own teaching (in EMI or in a local language) might have in all of this.

A report published by the European University Association in 2018 (Gaebel & Zhang 2018) identified a number of ways in which university teaching and learning are changing. They carried out a survey of 303 universities in forty-eight European countries, and were able to identify the following trends:

- Learning and teaching have become an institutional priority: universities are developing strategies and structures for this, by setting up learning and teaching centres, or by conducting research into university teaching. Clearly, change in learning and teaching depends on 'the right combination of top-down guidance and structural support and bottom-up dynamism'. To this end, institutional strategies are being put in place, and individual teachers are being encouraged to collaborate with each other, and to coordinate their activities.

- More universities are implementing the 'learning outcomes' model (see Chapter 5), and most are devoting more time and attention to ensuring that student learning is appropriate, efficient and effective.

- Seventy-seven per cent of institutions are already providing optional teaching enhancement courses, and 37 per cent had made them compulsory in some cases. In addition, two thirds of these institutions also encouraged and supported good teaching through other means, such as use of portfolios, self-evaluations, peer feedback, team-teaching and research on learning and teaching.

- There is increased demand for more flexible provision of degree and non-degree education. A process of gradual change seems to be taking place, moving towards more flexible education and digitally supported learning. Digitally enhanced learning is often seen as a strategic element in innovating the university's repertoire of courses and degrees.

It is clear that the world is changing, and that universities are constantly updating what they teach and the way they teach it. EMI is firmly bound up with this process of adaptation. But it is important to ensure that innovations are accompanied by principled reflection. The move to EMI provides an opportunity for many university lecturers to take a fresh look at the way they have been doing things over the years, and to seek new ways of communicating their expertise in an increasingly globalized environment. Fortunately, in the age of globalization, we have almost infinite opportunities for exchanging ideas, material and expertise, and for building learning communities that will support our development as world-class professionals. We should be optimistic that greater openness and internationalization will bring new opportunities for personal and professional growth.

Case Study 1: Adapting to a New Academic Culture

Sarah obtained her bachelor's and master's degrees in Arabic philology from a Russian university, and later took a PhD while teaching Arabic full time at a university in St Petersburg. In Russia at that time, philology degrees were very systematic and thorough, with a demanding fixed syllabus, tough exams and very few optional courses. When she went to the United States she got a job teaching cultural anthropology at a university in Texas, where the situation was quite a contrast. The students who enrolled in her cultural anthropology course were majoring in psychology, teaching, journalism, forensics, etc., so very little background knowledge could be taken for granted. Moreover, the university provided her with practically no guidance about how to teach the course, offering almost total freedom about what to teach and how: 'It's up to you!'

Wisely, she decided to ask her colleagues for help, and one of them provided her with examples of the kind of thing they did in their courses. This enabled her to put together a list of topics, some obligatory and optional reading material, and some discussion tasks for use in the classroom and in the online forum. One particular difficulty was that the course had to be taught in three-hour sessions, and her previous experience had not prepared her for lecturing for such a long stretch, so she decided to vary the activities (discussions, group work etc.) in order to make the classes more motivating for the students. She also devised the idea of asking the students to write a diary about aspects of their own lives (e.g. food), and then reflect on what they had written in theoretical terms, referring to some of the required reading for the course.

In general, her classes received positive feedback, and she regards her experiences there as a success. Language was not a problem for her, because even though she had not taught in English before, the students had no difficulties understanding her, and many of the students themselves came from multilingual backgrounds with parents who were not native English speakers.

However, there were some cultural issues that caused difficulties for her, especially at the beginning of her time in the United States: plagiarism, grading and, more generally, social attitudes. Regarding plagiarism, all the work that students submitted for the courses had to be uploaded to the university platform, which detected any degree of similarity between this document and any published work or other students' papers stored in the same platform. Despite the fact that the plagiarism detector revealed considerable overlap with other students' work (up to 95 per cent in one case), some students regularly refused to admit that they had plagiarized and protested to the dean. Regarding grading, Sarah had to change her expectations based on the Russian system, because in Texas it was understood that most students would get A or B in all their courses, and a grade below this was considered exceptionally poor and almost insulting. Finally, some social attitudes and behavioural issues surprised her. These ranged from the trivial (students who brought out large snacks to eat during the class) to the potentially damaging (students who were given low grades made accusations of racism). All in all, she was satisfied with her 'American experience', but has no particular desire to return there.

Case Study 2: Academic Writing on the Engineering PhD Programme

The academic writing seminars taught in the doctoral degree programme of the School of Aerospace Engineering at the Universidad Politécnica de Madrid include science dissemination through digital genres. The objective is to raise awareness that nowadays, within the dialogic democratic model of science dissemination every society strives to attain, scientists and technology makers need to undertake communication with a wide variety of publics, thus performing the function formerly fulfilled by science journalists. This recent mission involves awareness of intercultural issues, at both national and disciplinary levels. Graphical and video-abstracts are two genres (or genre variants) very recently demanded by high-impact scientific journals and quite often pointed at by science bloggers as sources of misunderstanding and conflict, even among expert scholars.

In one of the seminar sessions, doctoral candidates are confronted with eight graphical abstract samples criticized in such blogs and in scientific network forums. Their website addresses are the following:

1. https://pubs.acs.org/doi/10.1021/co500146u
2. https://www.mdpi.com/2072-6643/5/5/1622/htm#
3. https://pubs.rsc.org/en/content/articlelanding/2013/cc/c3cc44118k#!divAbstract
4. https://pubs.rsc.org/en/content/articlelanding/2015/cs/c5cs00057b#!divAbstract
5. https://pubs.acs.org/doi/10.1021/acs.joc.7b00540
6. https://pubs.acs.org/doi/10.1021/jz2012534
7. https://pubs.acs.org/doi/10.1021/ja300236k
8. https://pubs.rsc.org/en/content/articlelanding/2016/cp/c5cp04498g#!divAbstract

In a first round of reflection, the majority of students feel that 'something is not right' with the eight samples. By contrast, a minority finds them 'original', 'fresh' and 'amusing', and think that science should popularize achievements and capture the attention of varied audiences.

In a second round of reflection, those students critical of the samples get together in teams to work out what they feel it is wrong or should be improved. Examination of both details and the large picture shown by each sample allows students to conclude, after some time, that there are main causes of concern: *trivialization, confusion/ambiguity* and *offence*, all of them due to intercultural issues.

Trivialization of the scientific content is caused by *prettification* and *discoursal and/or situational appropriation*. Prettification consists in the cartoonish embellishment, usually anthropomorphic, of inert items such as molecules and objects, or by the use of expressive visual devices typical of comic books/strips and cartoons, such as speech and thought balloons, narrative captions and runes. Samples 1 and 2 are obviously 'prettified'.

Discoursal and/or situational appropriation is the use of discourses from other disciplines or social spheres or activities. Sample 3 looks and sounds like a printed or billboard advertisement as it employs a photograph close-up and a direct rhetorical question without any informative clue to build suspense. It is an appropriation of the visual and verbal discourse of advertising. Sometimes, a whole scenario may be employed (with or without discourse) to embody a scientific phenomenon in a literary or filmic plot to make it more comprehensible and sprinkle some humour. Sample 4 compares molecular behaviour with the mood instability of a classic literary character, Robert Louis Stevenson's Dr. Jekyll/Mr. Hyde. Sample 5 does the same with sorcerer Gandalf's silhouette and famous quote ('You shall not pass'), from Tolkien's *Lord of the Rings*, to illustrate the inhibiting action of a certain catalyser. In Sample 6, the reference to Tolkien's ring is less explicit and demands much more shared knowledge on behalf of the viewer. Sample 7 resorts to a widespread item of popular wisdom: Aesop's fable *The Tortoise and the Hare*, which is widely recurrent in chemical physics and physical chemistry to emplot improvements in catalysing speed. These four samples (4, 5, 6 and 7), with their appropriation of scenarios or/and discourses, question the supposed 'universality' of scenarios depicted by western literature and folklore in other world cultures. Locality (of literature, idioms and wise-sayings, folklore) and inexplicitness (an excessive amount of presumed shared knowledge without any glosses or clues, as in Sample 6) may lead to ambiguity and eventually to confusion.

Lastly and more importantly, the cultures based on strong religious values or with social taboos may find certain renderings offensive if cultural differences are disregarded in the metaphorical scenarios chosen to encode the scientific information. Sample 8, for one, metaphorizes the behaviour of chemical elements as human beings dancing in a disco scene. There is a female role, that of the element Zn, depicted as a seductress in tempting attire and with potentially provocative body stances. This conceptualization of women is rejected by Islamic cultures.

All in all, students reflect on:

- what degree of deviation from a 'sanitized style' is admissible in general
- how much trivialization can be tolerated in their particular discipline (aerospace engineering)

- how do the verbal and graphical versions of one same abstract differ

- what type of guidelines to authors should be provided to scholars dealing with multimodal resources and by whom.

By engaging in this sort of discussion, learners gain awareness of the importance of intercultural issues in digital science dissemination. They tend to place responsibility on specialized journals and educational institutions and to conclude that aerospace engineering shows very little tolerance of 'intercultural transgression' in each of the features detected (trivialization through prettification and/or discourse appropriation, emplotment into works of literature and art or popular wisdom and references to metaphorical scenarios or social values).

POINTS FOR REFLECTION

Subsection 7.4 tackles creative teaching for EMI, which is more attractive and motivating for students (and in the end for teachers, despite the effort) than conventional lectures. The question is, is it always 'teaching for creativity'? In other words, does it make students more creative? Do you get a creative response from students to your creative teaching innovations? Does every stimulation of students' creativity need to be creative itself?
Reflection on Classroom Practices:

1. How open is your class to questioning and challenging?
2. How open is your class to collaboration? (It normally spurs creativity.)
3. Do you invite students to share their different insights and interpretations and their approaches to a given problem and later discuss them?
4. To what extent do you welcome error?
5. Do you pose open questions and challenges?
6. Do you encourage exploration and risk-taking?
7. Do you encourage connecting and seeing relationships between apparently unrelated items, concepts or fields?
8. Do you encourage envisaging what might be?
9. What is considered 'creative' in your discipline?
10. How do you foster creativity in your class?

CHAPTER 8

The Way Ahead

Chapter outline

8.1 What We Have Seen

In this book we have tried to situate English-medium instruction in the panorama of what is happening in universities across the world today. We have examined some of the reasons why EMI is expanding so rapidly, and we have looked in detail at what this means to many of the people – non-native users of English – who have already started teaching their courses in English. We have separated out the most salient areas of a university teacher's activities – lecturing, seminars, tutorials, assessment – and examined what it means to do these things in a different language. We have also touched on difficult areas such as culture and educational culture, which inevitably impinge on the way that we interact with international students and the way they perceive our classes. Moreover, because EMI is being implemented at a moment when other broad educational changes are under way in university systems in many parts of the world, we have examined various examples of how teachers could incorporate new methodological approaches in their EMI classes, and we have considered how the change in language both conditions what we can do in our local contexts and opens up new opportunities.

The book has also provided a wealth of worksheets that could be used for self-study, discussion groups, tutorials with language departments or formal in-house training sessions. It has suggested classroom ideas that could be adapted in many different ways to different subject areas. And it has assembled a set of very varied case studies, all based on real examples, which could provide further food for thought (and maybe also some consolation when things do not turn out exactly as we had expected). Finally, the appendixes contain additional material, including a quick 'EMI Toolkit' that could form the basis for a crash course in EMI methodology, and some worksheets on aspects such as pronunciation, which we know are a matter for concern for many non-native speakers who have to use English in public and some guidelines for visiting speakers.

In all of this, our aim has been to put our years of experience training teachers for EMI (and researching on their perceptions and progress) at the disposal of a wider audience. We very much hope that this book will be useful.

8.2 Further Pathways

The basic brushstrokes provided here on the communicative instances and texts that may be encountered by content teachers along the EMI process, and the methodological approaches suggested, need to be expanded and further delved into. There are three major foci that deserve attention and raise a series of questions:

1. *The types of communicative interaction shaped by multimodal affordances and face-to-face teaching and the didactic, rhetorical and linguistic repertoires that may arise from this.*

    a. Is online teaching homogeneous across disciplines/subjects? If not, what online media are preferred to teach in certain subjects and fields and how are they conventionally used? What about face-to-face classes? What lecture structure and textual genres are most often chosen and why?

    b. What expressions are consequently useful to mark transitions between class sections, activities, topic shifts and ideas? What expressions or devices are optimal for face-to-face and digital feedback? Is feedback exclusively verbal or visual? Is it multimodal? Who gives it and on what occasions?

    c. If there are strong disciplinary and medium-based differences in teaching, what are the most effective ways of organizing the information to be transmitted? What activities or tasks should be inserted and when?

d. Is it possible to associate fixed, but open, repertoires of expressions with ritualistic class sections? How much digression and anecdotal insertions are recommendable to avoid monotony, sustain interest. change pace, provide relief and relax? How efficiently do teachers cope with those spaces? Is humour effective and desirable? If so, how can it be introduced without altering the overall academic register?

e. Are differences regarding talk time due to disciplines and media or do they depend solely on the teachers' preferences?

f. Do content teachers foster a balance of learning styles (verbal, operational, visual-spatial, logical-mathematical, interpersonal, etc.)? Are there any specially successful combinations in a given discipline/subject?

2. *The hybridity of academic and professional discourses and textual genres and their bearing on classroom interaction.*

a. How does computer-mediated communication affect the register and tone of a standard classroom in a given discipline?

b. How many textual genres are usually embedded in a conventional face-to-face class session in a given discipline? And in an online one? Do they keep their conventions intact or present some 'bending' for private interests/convenience? Is there a blend of genres? Does this reflect on register and tone? On the rhetorical organization of the information?

3. *The models of interdisciplinary collaboration between content and language teachers and the educational reconceptualizations that they might lead to.*

a. Would content teachers mind being observed by other colleagues or language teachers during class? And be given periodic feedback by students in a class blog?

b. How can content teachers collaborate with language teachers? What ways prove more effective across disciplines/subjects?

   i. Co-lecturing by content and language teacher, with the content teacher(s) in charge of evaluation

   ii. Co-lecturing and co-evaluation

   iii. Co-lecturing with language teacher(s) in charge of class discussions only

   iv. Language teacher(s) in charge of the linguistic and communicative English language supervision only

   v. Language teacher(s) co-lecturing bilingually, with the language teacher(s) 'echoing' the content teacher's speech in the local language

  vi. Language teacher(s) in charge of the training of content teachers and the supervision and correction of class materials

c. How should we label and advertise the previous teaching modes? Bilingual teaching? English-medium teaching with various degrees of English use?

d. What type of 'language-based episodes' are tackled across disciplines? How deeply and with what strategies? What weight do these episodes have in the global evaluation?

8.3 Over to You

What remains is for you to think about how all of this is relevant to you. Not everything fits in every context. If you are teaching in English in China, and 100 per cent of your students are proficient in your own native languages, Mandarin or Cantonese, then you may sometimes wonder what the point of EMI is. But here in Europe we have seen that the introduction of EMI has enabled many universities – and many students and teachers – to become part of a wider international academic circuit. By offering EMI, we are not only helping to prepare our own students for international mobility, we are preparing ourselves for more active participation on the international academic stage, and we are giving our university the opportunity to welcome international students from far afield, with all of the implications this has for the university's reputation and position on the rankings.

So you need to take EMI seriously, and, above all, you have to search for that 'perfect fit' in which your own interests, those of your students and institution, all coincide, and in which you develop your career further as an international expert in your field. Appendix 1: The EMI Toolkit provides some points for you to work on. In terms of teaching methodology, you have to develop an active, reflective approach in which you build your EMI capacity (classroom skills, interpersonal communication skills, intercultural skills) and learn from any disappointments that might come up. In this, we should perhaps try to learn something from the world of sport. Leading athletes or team players push themselves to be better – they practise every day, they are open to learn new ideas and techniques, and they challenge themselves at every opportunity. And if they make a mistake, or lose a match, they know how to convert that disappointment into positive energy to do better next time. We wish you every success in your EMI teaching, and hope that you will find it a truly satisfying experience.

APPENDICES

Appendix 1. The EMI Toolkit

The EMI toolkit puts together the main ideas we have seen in this book, so that you can reflect on your own situation, draw up plans, or use it as a discussion document with your colleagues.

Understanding the Context

(see Chapters 1 and 2)
Why is EMI being introduced in my country?
Why is EMI being introduced in my institution?
How do the stakeholders feel about it?

- Teachers

- Students

- University authorities

- University administrative and other staff

What is my own role in this transition?

Setting a Personal Plan

(see Chapter 2)
Where do I stand now?

- Language skills

- Teaching skills

- International experience

What preparations do I need to make in order to become an EMI professional?
What support or resources are available for me?

- In-house language training
- Specialized EMI courses
- Professional collaboration
- Exchange schemes

What should I prioritize?

- Planning courses and classes
- Preparing powerpoints and handouts
- Practising English

Preparing for the Lectures

(see Chapter 3)
Course contents:

- Mapping the overview of the course
- Drafting a course outline
- Finding material and resources in English (videos, books, articles, etc.)
- Devising tasks and assignments

Communicative competences:

- Designing visually effective powerpoints and checking the language
- Checking the pronunciation of key terms
- Practising explanations or classes with a colleague
- Interacting with the powerpoints
- Predicting questions and practising answers

Preparing to Meet Students

(see Chapter 4)
Understanding roles:
What different roles do I have?

- Lecturer
- Organizer

- Tutor/advisor

- Thesis supervisor

Which of these roles do I need to prepare for?
  How can I prepare for meeting international students?

Dealing with Assignments

(see Chapter 5)
What assignments will I set?
How will I grade them?
How will I provide feedback?

Teamwork and Networking

(see Chapter 6)
What forms of teamwork exist / could exist in my context?

- Colleagues

- Support departments (languages, teaching innovation, etc.)

- Professional organizations or networks

- Exchange schemes with other universities

How can I establish new forms of teamwork?

Reflecting on Experience and Developing as a Teacher

(see Chapters 7 and 8)
If I look back at my experiences of EMI teaching:

- What went really well?

- What would I repeat?

- What would I change?

- What would I discard?

What kinds of innovation could I try out next time?
Where would I still benefit from training, practice or professional support?
Where can I get this?

Appendix 2. Pronunciation Worksheets

These worksheets were originally designed for engineers and scientists, but you can easily adapt them to your own area of knowledge by opening a textbook (or your own class notes) and identifying words that you find difficult. Check the pronunciation using an online pronouncing dictionary, like the one at https://www.howjsay.com and practise the words with a partner.

Task One: Word Stress

Highlight the part of the word which has the strongest stress. The first one has been done for you as an example.

1. presen<u>ta</u>tion	2. collaboration	3. organizational
4. decision	5. provisional	6. technician
7. internationalization	8. technicalities	9. expansion
10. analytical	11. systematic	12. strategic
13. efficiency	14. interesting	15. deficiency

Task Two: Noun-Noun Combinations

Highlight the word which is stressed in each of these typical combinations.

1. <u>production</u> team	2. speech technology
3. consumer choices	4. cost control
5. voice recognition	6. telecommunications engineer
7. research budget	8. wave velocity
9. aerospace engineering	10. health warning
11. speed check	12. quantum mechanics

Task Three: Adjective-Noun Combinations

Highlight the word which is stressed in each of these partnerships.

1. multinational <u>company</u>	2. annual report
3. electronic display	4. digital screen
5. public transport	6. wireless technology
7. global warming	8. managerial skills

Task Four: Abbreviated Forms and Acronyms

How do we usually say these?

UN   NASA   EU   NATO   R&D   CO2

Task Five: Scientific Words

Mark the stress in the following words, and check the pronunciation of any combinations of letters that look difficult using an online pronouncing dictionary:

epithelial	enzymatic	peripheral	dyskinesia	stimuli
cytochrome	macrophage	fluctuation	hepatitis	phagocytic
overdose	regulatory	microorganism	extracellular	pathological

Now read them out, taking care with the 'difficult' sounds ('th', 'g') as well as the stress.

Appendix 3. Fluency Worksheets

These worksheets were originally used with engineers and scientists to help them to loosen up their English when they are speaking, but you could easily adapt them to your discipline – see Task Three.

Task One: Written or Spoken?

Discuss with your partner whether you think the extracts below are from written or spoken sources. Identify the features of the language used that help you to reach a decision.

A. The goal of the present study was to employ the source imaging methods such as cortical current density estimation for the classification of left- and right-hand motor imagery tasks, which may be used for brain-computer interface (BCI) applications.

B. The relative entropy of the covariance matrix of the trial to the left and right patterns are obtained and compared to each other. These relative entropies can be regarded as the distance of the trial to left and right patterns.

C. Liquid crystal display technology is cheap and can brilliantly display text and graphics. It means that you can show films on aeroplane seat backs, play video games on the train, and see photos on the back of your camera.

D. Numerous field observations have demonstrated that the quality factor Q appears to be a constant over a large frequency range in the seismic signal bandwidth.

E. The basic facts about public transport have not changed much over the last three hundred years. You wait at a stop for a vehicle to arrive, and when it comes, it carries you over a fixed route. It is slow and inconvenient.

Task Two

Formal and Informal English

The following table summarizes the differences between formal scientific and informal spoken English. When you are writing a research paper, you probably use more of the features in the left-hand column. But when you are speaking (even in a lecture or a formal presentation), you should use more of the features from the right-hand column. This will make you a more effective communicator.

Formal	Informal
Long words of Latin or French origin e.g. construct, agriculture, nonagenarian, endorsement, coagulation	Short words of Anglo-Saxon (Germanic) origin e.g. build, farming, ninety-year-old, backing, clotting
Single-word verbs e.g. tolerate, extract, postpone	Phrasal verbs, idioms with 'get' e.g. put up with, get out, put off
Formal connecting words however, therefore	Informal connecting words but, so
Impersonal constructions 'it is said that' 'one should do this' 'the man was arrested'	Active constructions 'they say that' 'you should do this' 'they arrested the man'
Abstract nouns 'Is happiness possible during unemployment?' 'After clarification of some problematic issues'	Concrete language 'Can you be happy when you don't have a job?' 'After we had explained the things that people were getting wrong.'
Sentences do not end with prepositions 'Have you consulted the book to which he is referring?'	Sentences end with prepositions 'Have you consulted the book he is referring to?'
Complex sentences containing several ideas	Simple sentences with one idea in each
Formal negatives (with 'no') 'No data were obtained.'	Informal negatives (with 'not' and 'any') 'We didn't get any results.'
Indirect question forms 'It would be interesting to know why this adverse event occurred.'	Direct question forms 'Why did this happen?'
Use of negative inversion 'Under no circumstances are animals permitted in this building.'	Normal word order 'Animals are not allowed in this building under any circumstances'
No contractions 'Inflation does not necessarily lead to economic depression'	Contractions 'Inflation doesn't necessarily lead to economic depression'
Avoidance of personal pronouns, shades of meaning conveyed using impersonal constructions 'Kamala Harris may well be elected the next president of the USA.'	Shades of meaning conveyed in a more personal manner 'I actually think Kamala Harris is quite likely to be elected the next president of the USA.'

1. Easy version: you are going to speak for five minutes about a topic that you are very familiar with. Spend a few minutes making some notes about the points you want to include. Then, explain the topic. Your partner should listen, and mark any of the features from the right-hand column that you use. You can then look at what he/she wrote, and discuss whether this matters or not.

2. Difficult version: Find a research paper in your discipline (which will be written in a dense, concise style). Choose one of your own if you like! Read it and make notes. Then, practise explaining the ideas in English in simple language using subject – verb – object sentences, as if you were talking to a group of first-year students. Use the table to help you loosen up your language and be easier to understand.

Task Three

Read this abstract and underline the features that tell you it is written in formal academic style.

Public figures today are often the target of adverse publicity and hate speech on social media platforms. Such temporary but potentially devastating storms of aggressive emotional outrage, known as online firestorms, are increasingly frequent. Such firestorms are often targeted at politicians, celebrities, academics and other public figures. It is often stated that the anonymity of social platforms is one of the main contributing factors. This paper investigates online aggression in an online setting, questioning whether online anonymity is one of the principal factors that promotes aggression and hate speech. A major social media platform was analysed over three years, generating a dataset comprising 800,456 comments about 945 targets. Quantitative methods are used to test for associations between degree of aggression/hate and anonymity of sender. The results show that in this dataset anonymous senders are less aggressive than non-anonymous senders. These results are discussed in the light of sociocultural identity theory and social media theory.

Now try to explain what the abstract is about, using an informal conversational style.

When you have done this, take some recent abstracts from a journal in your own field. Go through the process again, and practise explaining them using a fluent conversational style with subject-verb-object sentences, personal pronouns (I, you, they) and reducing long technical phrases to a minimum.

Appendix 4. Guidelines for Visiting Speakers

Welcome to the University of Middle Earth. We are very pleased to have you here with us, and we know that our students are looking forward to your lectures (seminars, classes).

Before you start, we would like to offer you some guidelines based on what we have learned from previous visiting lecturers (professors, speakers), and on what our students have told us.

1. Speak slowly and clearly. Remember that the students are not native speakers of English.

2. If you a presenting a formal lecture, take short breaks (2-5 minutes) every twenty minutes. This will help the students to keep up with their note taking and maintain a high level of concentration. It is also good for you!

3. It helps a lot if you use visuals – and it helps even more if you give the students access to your powerpoint or to an overview of the class before you start. This will help them take effective notes.

4. Students in our country are not used to asking and answering spontaneous questions during the class. If you want them to do this, you can help them by allowing them more time to formulate the questions or answers, or by letting them work with a partner for a couple of minutes to come up with a question or answer.

5. Remember that the students come from a very different culture from yours. If they seem not to understand you, it might not be a language problem. So if you are going to talk about something that is very well known, for instance, in the United States, Russia, or Nigeria, and you think the students might not be familiar with it, take a little time to explain it – or show them some pictures.

6. Take care with jokes and asides. They may be a good way to create rapport with students in your home university, but it may not work so well in a different cultural context. Don't be disappointed if they don't all laugh!

REFERENCES

Aguilar Pérez, M. & Arnó Macià, E. (2002). Metadiscourse in lecture comprehension: Does it really help foreign language learners? *Atlantis, XXIV*(2), 3–21.

Aguilar, M. & Rodríguez, R. (2012). Lecturer and student perceptions on CLIL at a Spanish university. *International Journal of Bilingual Education and Bilingualism, 15*(2), 183–97.

Airey, J. (2011). Talking about teaching in English. Swedish university lecturers' experiences of changing teaching language. *Ibérica, 22*, 35–54.

Airey, J. & Linder, C. (2006). Language and the experience of learning university physics in Sweden. *European Journal of Physics, 27*(3), 553–60.

Alfaro, J. A., Roothooft, H. & Breeze, R. (2020). Transitioning to English Medium Instruction on Operations Management courses taught on Spanish business degrees. *Journal of Industrial Engineering and Management, 13*(3), 529–45.

Anderson, L. W. & Krathwohl, D. R. (2001). *A taxonomy for learning, teaching, and assessing: A revision of Bloom's taxonomy of educational objectives.* New York: Addison Wesley Longman.

Bach, S., Haynes, P. & Lewis Smith, J. (2007). *Online learning and teaching: Higher education.* Berkshire, UK: McGraw Hill & Open University Press.

Ball, P. & Lindsay, D. (2013). Language demands and support for English-medium instruction in tertiary education. Learning from a specific context. In A. Doiz, D. Lasagabaster, & J. M. Sierra (eds), *English-medium instruction at universities* (pp. 28–44). Bristol, UK: Multilingual Matters.

Barreiro Elorza, P. & Sancho Guinda, C. (2015). Understanding the inventor's mind through patent analysis: A CLIL team-teaching experience at the Technical University of Madrid. *Procedia – social and behavioral sciences* 212, 283–91. doi: 10.1016/j.sbspro.2015.11.350. www.sciencedirect.com.

Başıbek, N., M. Dolmacı, Cengiz, B., Bu!rd, B., Dilek, Y. & Kara, B. (2014). Lecturers' perceptions of English medium instruction at Engineering departments of higher education: A study on partial English medium instruction at some state universities in Turkey. *Procedia-Social and Behavioural Sciences*, 1819–1825.

Bhatia, V. K. (1983). Simplification v. easification. The case of legal texts. *Applied Linguistics, 4*(1), 42–54.

Bhatia, V. K. (1993). *Analysing genre. Language use in professional settings.* London: Longman.

Biber, D. (2006). *University language. A corpus-based study of spoken and written registers.* Amsterdam: John Benjamins.

Biggs, J. & Tang, C. (2011). *Teaching for quality learning at university.* Maidenhead: Open University / McGraw Hill.

Boden, M. (1990). *The creative mind.* London: Abacus.

Boettcher, J. V. & Conrad, R. M. (2016). *The online teaching survival guide: Simple and practical pedagogical tips* (2nd edn). San Francisco: Jossey-Bass.

Bolton, K. & Graddol, D. (2012). English in China today. *English Today, 28*(3), 3–9.

Borg, S. (2006). *Teacher cognition and language education*. London: Continuum

Breeze, R. (2012). *Rethinking academic writing pedagogy for the European university*. Amsterdam: Rodopi.

Breeze, R. (2014a). Identifying student needs in English-medium university courses. In R. Breeze, C. Llamas, C. Martínez-Pasamar, & C. Tabernero (eds) *Integration of theory and practice in CLIL* (pp. 143–60). Amsterdam: Rodopi.

Breeze, R. (2014b). Moodle glossary tasks for teaching legal English. In E. Bárcena, T. Read & J. Arús (eds), *Languages for specific purposes in the digital era* (pp. 111–28). Dordrecht: Springer.

Breeze, R & Dafouz, E. (2017). Negotiating complex cognitive discourse functions in L1 and L2: Exam responses in a parallel L1-EMI university course. *System,* 70, 81–91.

Breeze, R. & Miller, P. (2012). Predictive validity of the IELTS listening test as an indicator of undergraduate student coping ability in Spain. In L. Taylor & C. Weir (eds), IELTS Collected Papers 2: *Research in reading and listening assessment* (pp. 487–518). Cambridge: Cambridge University Press. https://www.ielts.org/pdf/vol12_report_5.pdf

Breeze, R. & Roothooft, H. (2018). *Becoming an EMI lecturer: Cambridge English exams in early-career training and lifelong learning*. CEFRP R8 Final Report. Cambridge Assessment English.

British Council. (2020). English levels. https://www.britishcouncil.es/en/english/levels

British Council and British Broadcasting Corporation (BBC) (2021, January 9). Teaching English. Retrieved from: https://www.teachingenglish.org.uk/article/teachingonline

Bruner, J. (1996). *The culture of education*. Cambridge, MA: Harvard University Press.

CEFR. (2018). Common European Framework of Reference for Languages. Companion Volume. Available at https://www.coe.int/en/web/common-european-framework-reference-languages

CEFR Video. Available at http://www.cambridgeenglish.org/exams-and-qualifications/cefr/

Chaudron, C. & Richards, J. (1986). The effect of discourse markers on the comprehension of lectures. *Applied Linguistics*, 7(2), 113–27.

Chen, H., Han, J. & Wright, D. (2020). An investigation of lecturers' teaching through English Medium of Instruction - A case of higher education in China. *Sustainability*, 21(10), 4046. https://doi.org/10.3390/su12104046

Choi, H., Kim, J., Bang, K. S., Park, Y. H., Lee, N. J., & Kim, C. (2015). Applying the flipped learning model to an English-medium nursing course. *Journal of the Korean Academy of Nursing*, 45(6), 939–48.

Conrad, R. M. & Donaldson, A. J. (2004). *Engaging the online learner: Activities and resources for creative instruction*. San Francisco: Jossey-Bass.

Costa, F. (2016). *CLIL (Content and language integrated learning) through English in Italian higher education*. Milan: LED.

Cots, J. M. (2013). Introducing English-medium instruction at the University of Lleida, Spain: Intervention, beliefs and practices. In A. Doiz, D. Lasagabaster, & J. M. Sierra (eds), *English-medium instruction at universities* (pp. 28–44). Bristol: Multilingual Matters.

Crabtree, R. (2013). The intended and unintended consequences of international service-learning. *Journal of Higher Education Outreach and Engagement* 17, 2, 7–30.

Craft, A. (2010). Possibility thinking and wise creativity: Educational futures in England? In R. A. Beghetto & J. C. Kaufman (eds), *Nurturing creativity in the classroom* (pp. 289–312). Cambridge: Cambridge University Press.

Crawford Camiciottoli, B. (2007). *The language of business studies lectures: A Corpus-assisted analysis.* Amsterdam: John Benjamins.

Crystal, D. (1997, 2003). *English as a global language.* Cambridge: Cambridge University Press.

Csomay, E. (2002). Variation in academic lectures. In R. Reppen (ed.), *Using corpora to explore linguistic variation* (pp. 203–24). Philadelphia, PA: John Benjamins.

Dafouz, E. (2014). Integrating content and language in European higher education: An overview of recurrent research concerns and pending issue. In P. Joycey, E. Agathopoulou, & M. Mattheoudakis (eds), *Cross-curricular approaches to language education* (pp. 289–304). Newcastle: Cambridge Scholars Publishing.

Dafouz, E., Haines, K. & Pagèze, J. (2019). Supporting educational developers in the era of internationalised higher education: Insights from a European project. *International Journal of Bilingual Education and Bilingualism, 23*(3), 326–39. DOI: 10.1080/13670050.2019.1651818.

Dafouz, E., & Núñez, B. (2009). CLIL in tertiary education: Devising a new learning landscape. In E. Dafouz & M. Guerrini (eds), *CLIL across educational levels: Experiences from primary, secondary and tertiary contexts.* London: Richmond.

Dafouz, E. & Núñez, B. (2010). Metadiscursive devices in university lectures. In C. Dalton Puffer, T. Nikula, & U. Smit (eds), *Language use and language learning in CLIL classrooms* (pp. 213–32). Amsterdam: John Benjamins.

Dafouz, E., Nuñez, B., Sancho, C. & Foran, D. (2007). Integrating CLIL at the tertiary level: Teachers' and students' reaction. In D. Marsh, & D. Wolff (eds), *Diverse contexts – Converging goals. CLIL in Europe* (pp. 91–101). Frankfurt am Main: Peter Lang.

Dafouz, E. & Smit, U. (2020). *ROAD-MAPPING English medium education in the internationalised university.* Cham: Palgrave Macmillan.

Dawley, L. (2007). *The tools for successful online teaching.* Hershey, PA: Information Science Publishing.

Dearden, J. (2014). *English as a medium of instruction. A growing global phenomenon.* London: British Council.

Deroey, K. L. B. & Taverniers, M. (2011). A corpus-based study of lecture functions. *Moderna Språk, 105*(2), 1–22.

Doiz, A., Lasagabaster, D. & Sierra, J. M. (eds) (2012). *English-medium instruction at universities: Global challenges.* Bristol: Multilingual Matters.

Dudley-Evans, T. & St John, M. J. (1998). *Developments in English for specific purposes: A multi-disciplinary approach.* Cambridge: Cambridge University Press.

English, F. (2011). *Student writing and genre. Reconfiguring academic knowledge.* London: Bloomsbury.

EQUIIP Project. (2019). Educational quality at universities for inclusive international Programmes. https://equiip.eu/.

Farrell, T. (2020). Professional development through reflective practice for English-medium instruction (EMI) teachers. *International Journal of Bilingual Education and Bilingualism*, 23(3), 277–86.

Feez, S. (1998). *Text-based syllabus design*. Sydney: McQuarie University/AMES.

Firth, A. & Martens, E. (2008). Transforming supervisors? A critique of post-liberal approaches to research supervision. *Teaching in Higher Education*, 13, 279–89.

Fortanet-Gómez, I. (2008). *Hablar inglés en la universidad: Docencia e investigación*. Oviedo: Septem Ediciones.

Fortanet-Gómez, I. (2012). Academics' beliefs about language use and proficiency in Spanish multilingual higher education. *AILA Review*, 25, 48–63.

Fortanet-Gómez, I. (2013). *CLIL in higher education: Towards a multilingual language policy*. Bristol: Multilingual Matters

Fortanet-Gómez, I. (2020). The dimensions of Emi in the international classroom: Training teachers for the future university. In M. Sánchez-Pérez (ed.), *Teacher training for English-medium instruction in higher education* (pp. 1–20). Hershey: IGI Global.

Gaebel, M. & Zhang, T. (2018). *Trends 2018. Learning and teaching in the European Higher Education Area*. Brussels: EUA.

Gudea, S. W. (2008). *Expectations and demands in online teaching. Practical experiences*. Hershey, PA and New York: Information Science Publishing.

Hafner, C. (2014). Embedding digital literacies in English language teaching: Students' digital video projects as multimodal ensembles. *TESOL Quarterly*, 48(4), 655–85.

Halbach, A., & Lázaro, A. (2015). La acreditación del nivel de lengua inglesa en las universidades españolas: Actualización 2015. Accessed November 17, 2017. http://www.britishcouncil.es/sites/britishcouncil.es/files/british-council-la-acreditacion-del-nivel-de-lengua-inglesa.pdf.

Hamp-Lyons L, & Condon W. (2000). *Assessing the portfolio principles for practice, theory and research*. Cresskill, NJ: Hampton Press.

Hellekjaer, G. & Westergaard, M. (2002). An exploratory survey of content learning through English at Scandinavian universities. In A. Simensen (ed.), *Acta didactica 3*. Oslo: Unipub.

Hockly, N. & Clandfield, L. (2010). *Teaching online: Tools and techniques, options and opportunities*. Peaslake, UK: Delta Publishing.

Hofstede, G. (1986). Cultural differences in teaching and learning. *International Journal of Intercultural Relations*, 10, 301–20.

Hofstede, G. (2020). *National culture*. https://hi.hofstede-insights.com/national-culture.

Hutchinson, T. & Waters, A. (1987). *English for specific purposes. A learning-centred approach*. Cambridge: Cambridge University Press.

Jacobs, C. (2006). Integrated assessment practices – When language and content lecturers collaborate. In R. Wilkinson, V. Zegers, & C. van Leeuwen (eds), *Bridging the assessment gap in English-medium higher education* (pp. 141–58). Bochum: AKS.

Jenkins, J. (2000). *The phonology of English as an international language: New models, new norms, new goals*. Oxford: Oxford University Press.

Jones, R. & Hafner, C. (2012). *Understanding digital literacies: A practical introduction*. London: Routledge.

Kachru, B. (1992). *The other tongue: English across cultures.* Illinois: University of Illinois Press.

Kenny, M. & Gallagher, L. (2002). Service learning: A history of systems. In M. Kenny, L. Simon, K. Kiley-Brabeck, & R. Lerner (eds), *Learning to serve: Promoting civil society through service learning* (pp. 15–29). Boston, MA: Kluwer Academic.

Ko, S. & Rossen, S. (2004). *Teaching online: A practical guide* (2nd edn). Boston, MA: Houghton Miffin.

Ko, S. & Rossen, S. (2017). *Teaching online. A practical guide* (4th edn). New York and London: Routledge.

Krathwohl, D. (2002). A revision of Bloom's taxonomy. An overview. *Theory into Practice, 41*(4), 212–18.

Kress, G. (2010). *Multimodality: A social semiotic approach to contemporary communication.* New York: Routledge.

Kuteeva, M. & Airey, J. (2014). Disciplinary differences in the use of English in higher education: Reflections on recent language policy developments. *Higher Education, 67,* 533–49.

Lasagabaster, D. (2008). Foreign language competence in content and language integrated learning. *Open Applied Linguistics Journal, 1,* 31–42.

Lasagabaster, D. (2018). Fostering team teaching: Mapping out a research agenda for English-medium instruction at university level. *Language Teaching, 51*(3), 400–416. https://doi.org/10.1017/S0261444818000113.

Lee, J. J. (2009). Size matters: An exploratory comparison of small- and large-class university lecture introductions. *English for Specific Purposes, 28*(1), 42–57.

Lehtonen, T., Lönnfors, P., & Virkkunen-Fullenwider, A. (2003). Teaching through English: A university case study. In C. van Leeuwen, & R. Wilkinson (eds), *Multilingual approaches in university education: Challenges and practices.* Maastricht: University of Maastricht. Available at http://h27.it.helsinki.fi/TTE/search.htm

Lei, J. & Hu, G. W. (2014). Is English-medium instruction effective in improving Chinese undergraduate students' English competence? *International Review of Applied Linguistics in Language Teaching, 52,* 99–126.

Llinares, A. & Mendikoetxea, A. (2020). Enhancing interactional competence in EMI: Teacher reflective practices. In M. M. Sánchez-Pérez (ed.), *Teacher training for English-medium instruction in higher education* (pp. 87–105). Hershey: IGI Global.

Li, Y. & Cargill, M. (2019). Seeking supervisor collaboration in a school of science at a Chinese university. In K. Hyland & L. Wong (eds), *Specialised English. New directions in ESP and EAP research and practice* (pp. 240–52). London: Routledge.

Lockwood, J. (2019). What do we mean by 'workplace English'? In K. Hyland & L. Wong (eds), *Specialised English. New directions in ESP and EAP research and practice* (pp. 22–35). London: Routledge.

Madhavan, D. & McDonald, J. (2014). *Webinar EMI: Philosophies and policies.* Paris: OECD.

Maiworm, F. & Wächter, B. (2002). *English-language-taught programmes in European higher education. Trends and success factors.* Bonn: Lemmens.

Maley, A. (2011). The reality of EIL and the myth of ELF. In C. Gagliardi, & A. Maley (eds), *EIL, ELF, global English: Teaching and learning issues* (pp. 25–44). Bern: Peter Lang.

Maley, A. (2017). In search of creativity. In R. Breeze & C. Sancho Guinda (eds), *Essential competencies for English-medium university teaching* (pp. 85–98). Cham: Springer.

Mancho-Bares, G. & Arnó Macià, E. (2017). EMI lecturer training programmes and academic literacies: A critical insight from ESP. *ESP Today, 5*(2), 266–90.

Marambe, K., Vermunt, J. & Boshuizen, H. (2012). A cross-cultural comparison of student learning patterns in higher education. *Higher Education, 64,* 299–316.

Martinez, R. & Fernandes, K. (2020). Development of a teacher training course for English medium instruction for higher education professors in Brazil. In M. Sánchez-Pérez (ed.), *Teacher training for English-medium instruction in higher education* (pp. 125–52). Hershey: IGI Global. http://doi:10.4018/978-1-7998-2318-6.ch007

McComas, W., & Abraham, L. (2004). Asking more effective questions. http://cet .usc.edu/resources/teaching_learning/material_docs/Asking_Better_Questions .pdf

Moore, T. (2011). *Critical thinking and language. The challenge of generic skills and disciplinary discourse.* London: Continuum.

Moore, T. (2017). On the teaching of critical thinking in English for academic purposes. In R. Breeze & C. Sancho Guinda (eds), *Essential competencies for English-medium university teaching* (pp. 19–36). Cham: Springer.

Nunan, D. (1997). Designing and adapting materials to encourage learner autonomy. In P. Benson & P. Voller (eds), *Autonomy and independence in language learning* (pp. 192–203). London: Longman.

O'Dowd, R. (2018). The training and accreditation of teachers for English medium instruction: An overview of practice in European universities. *International Journal of Bilingualism and Bilingual Education, 21,* 553–63. DOI: 10.1080/13670050.2018.1491945

Palloff, R. M. & Pratt, K. (1999). *Building learning communities in cyberspace: Effective strategies for the online classroom.* San Francisco: Jossey-Bass.

Palloff, R. M. & Pratt, K. (2015). *Lessons from the virtual classroom: The realities of online teaching.* San Francisco: Jossey-Bass.

Paran, A., Hyland, F. & Bentall, C. (2017). Managing and mediating the research element on Master's courses: The roles of course leaders and supervisors. In R. Breeze & C. Sancho Guinda (eds), *Essential competencies for English-medium university teaching* (pp. 267–80). Cham: Springer.

Piaget, J. (1969). *The mechanisms of perception.* London: Routledge & Kegan Paul.

Pisoni, G. (2019). Strategies for Pan-European implementation of blended learning for innovation and entrepreneurship (I&E) education. *Education Sciences, 9,* 124. DOI: 10.3390/educsci9020124

Querol-Julián, M. & Crawford Camiciottoli, B. (2019). The impact of online technologies and English medium instruction on university lectures in international learning contexts: A systematic review. *ESP Today 7,* 1, 2–23.

Räsänen, A. (2008). *Redefining CLIL – Towards multilingual competence.* LANQUA Year One Report. Available at http://www.lanqua.eu/files/ Year1Report_CLIL_For Upload_WithoutAppendices.pdf

Räsänen, A. & Klaassen, R. (2006). From learning outcomes to staff competences in integrated content and language instruction at the higher education level. In

R. Wilkinson, V. Zegers, & C. van Leeuwen (eds), *Bridging the assessment gap in English-medium higher education* (pp. 256–78). Bochum: AKS.

Rear, D. (2017). Critical thinking, language and problem solving: Scaffolding thinking skills through debate. In R. Breeze & C. Sancho Guinda (eds), *Essential competencies for English-medium university teaching* (pp. 51–64). Cham: Springer.

Roothooft, H. (2019). Spanish lecturers' beliefs about English medium instruction: STEM versus Humanities. *International Journal of Bilingual Education and Bilingualism*. Online first.

Safipour, J., Wenneberg, S., & Hadziabdic, E. (2017). Experience of education in the interational classroom – A systematic literature review. *Journal of International Students*, 7, 3.

Sánchez-García, D. & Dafouz, E. (2020). Equipping educational developers for inclusive international programs in higher education. In M. Sánchez-Pérez (ed.), *Teacher training for English-medium instruction in higher education* (pp. 21–40). Hershey: IGI Global.

Sánchez-Pérez, M. M (ed.) (2020). *Teacher training for English-medium instruction in higher education*. Hershey: IGI Global.

Sánchez-Pérez, M. M. & Salaberri Ramiro, M S. (2017). Implementing plurilingualism in higher education: Teacher training needs and plan evaluation (pp. 139–56). *Porta Linguarum* II.

Sánchez-Pérez, M. M. & Salaberri Ramiro, M S. (2020). Job shadowing as a training tool for lecturers in higher education bilingual teaching. In M. M. Sánchez-Pérez (ed.), *Teacher training for English-medium instruction in higher education* (pp. 275–96). Hershey: IGI Global.

Sancho Guinda, C. (2010). The emergent role of mind-mapping in CLIL instruction: Textual cognitive resources in engineering lectures. *RAEI-Revista Alicantina de Estudios Ingleses* 23, 83–105. doi: 10.14198/raei.2010.23.06.

Sancho Guinda, C. (2013). Teacher targets: A model for CLIL and EFL teacher education in polytechnic settings. *Language value 5*(1), 76–106. doi: 10.6035/LanguageV.2013.5.5.

Schetzer, H., & Warschauer, M. (2000). An electronic literacy approach to network-based language teaching. In M. Warschauer & R. Kern (eds), *Network-based language teaching: Concepts and practice* (pp. 171–85). Cambridge: Cambridge University Press.

Secretaría de Educación Pública. (2017). *Estrategia nacional de inglés*. Ciudad de México: Secretaría de Educación Pública.

Snow, A. & Brinton, D. (2017). *The content-based classroom* (2nd edn). Ann Arbor: University of Michigan Press.

Starfield, S. (2016). Supporting doctoral writing at an Australian university. *Writing and Pedagogy*, 8(1), 177–98.

Stavredes, T. (2011). *Online teaching: Foundations and strategies for student success*. San Francisco: Jossey-Bass.

Sternberg, R. J. (1988). *The triarchic mind. A theory of human intelligence*. New York: Viking.

Sternberg, R. J. (2010). Teaching for creativity. In R. A. Beghetto & J. C. Kaufman (eds), *Nurturing creativity in the classroom* (pp. 394–414). Cambridge: Cambridge University Press.

Stocklmayer, S. (2013). Engagement with science: Models of science communication. In J. Gilbert & S. Stocklmeyer (eds), *Communication and engagement with science and technology: Issues and dilemmas. A reader in science communication* (pp. 19–38). New York: Routledge.

Swain, M. & Lapkin, S. (1998). Two adolescent French immersion learners working together. *The Modern Language Journal*, 82(3), 320–37.

Swales, J. M. (1988). *Episodes in ESP. A source and reference book on the development of English for Science and Technology*. London: Prentice Hall.

Swales, J. M. (1990). *Genre analysis. English in academic and research settings*. Cambridge: Cambridge University Press.

Symon, M. (2017). Reevaluating the roles of the stakeholders in language education: How student autonomy is promoted through projects in English for Specific Academic Purposes (ESAP) courses. In R. Breeze and C. Sancho Guinda (eds), *Essential competencies for English-medium university teaching* (pp. 169–81). Cham: Springer.

Tatzl, D. (2011). English-medium masters' programmes at an Austrian University of Applied Sciences: Attitudes, experiences and challenges. *Journal of English for Academic Purposes*, *10*, 252–70.

Tatzl, D. (2015). Support measures for content teaching. In R. Wilkinson, and M. L. Walsh (eds), *Integrating content and language in higher education* (pp. 255–72). Frankfurt am Main: Peter Lang.

Thøgersen, J. & Airey, J. (2011). Lecturing undergraduate science in Danish and in English: A comparison of speaking rate and rhetorical style. *English for Specific Purposes*, *30*, 209–21.

Turner, Y. (2009). "Knowing me, knowing you," is there nothing we can do? pedagogic challenges in using group work to create an intercultural learning space. *Journal of Studies in International Education*, *13*(2), 240–55.

University of Otago Graduate Research School. (2020). Supervision of the Master's thesis. https://www.otago.ac.nz/graduate-research/study/otago466401.html

Uys, M., van der Walt, J., van den Berg, R. & Botha, S. (2007). English medium of instruction: A situation analysis. *South African Journal of Education*, *27*, 69–82.

Vinke, A. A., Snippe, J. & Jochems, W. (1998). English-medium content courses in Non-English higher education: A study of lecturer experiences and teaching behaviours. *Teaching in Higher Education*, *3*, 383–94.

Vygotsky, L. 1981. (1931). The genesis of higher mental functions. In J. V. Werscht (ed.), *The concepts of activity in in Soviet psychology* (pp. 144–88). Armonk, NY: Sharpe.

Wächter, B. & Maiworm, F. (2008). *English-taught programmes in European higher education*. Bonn: Lemmens.

Wächter, B. & Maiworm, F. (2014). *English taught programmes in European higher education. The state of play in 2014*. Bonn: Lemmens.

Wenger, E. (1998). *Communities of practice: Learning, meaning, and identity*. Cambridge: Cambridge University Press.

Westbrook, P., & Henriksen, B. (2011). 'Bridging the linguistic and affective gaps' – The impact of a short, tailor-made language course on a Danish university lecturer's ability to lecture with confidence in English. In R. Cancino, L. Dam, & K. Jæger (eds), *Policies, principles, practices: New directions in foreign language education in the era of educational globalization* (pp. 188–212). Newcastle upon Tyne: Cambridge Scholars.

White, K. W. & Weight, B. H. (1999). *The online teaching guide: A handbook of attitudes, strategies and techniques for the virtual classroom*. Old Tappan, NJ: Allyn & Bacon.

Wilkinson, R. (ed.) (2004). *Integrating content and language. Meeting the challenge of a multilingual higher education.* Maastricht: University of Maastricht.

Wilkinson, R. & Zegers, V. (eds) (2007). *Integrating content and language. Researching content and language integration in higher education.* Maastricht: University of Maastricht.

Wilkinson, R. & Zegers, V. (eds) (2008). *Realizing content and language integration in higher education.* Maastricht: University of Maastricht. Available at http://arno.unimaas.nl/show.cgi?fid=12521

Wittgenstein, L. (1953). *Philosophical investigations.* Oxford: Blackwell.

Yale Poorvu Center for Teaching and Learning. (2020). *Formative and summative assessment.* https://poorvucenter.yale.edu/Formative-Summative-Assessments

Young, L. (1994). University lectures – macro-structure and micro-features. In J. Flowerdew (ed.), *Academic listening: Research perspectives* (pp. 159–76). Cambridge: Cambridge University Press.

INDEX